The Law of the Other

NEW PRACTICES OF INQUIRY

A Series Edited by Donald N. McCloskey and John S. Nelson

MARIANNE CONSTABLE

The Law of the Other

The Mixed Jury and

Changing Conceptions of

Citizenship, Law, and Knowledge

THE UNIVERSITY OF CHICAGO PRESS

Chicago and London

Marianne Constable is assistant professor or rhetoric at the University of California, Berkeley.

The University of Chicago Press, Chicago 60637
The University of Chicago Press, Ltd., London
© 1994 by The University of Chicago
All rights reserved. Published 1994
Printed in the United States of America

03 02 01 00 99 98 97 96 95 94   5 4 3 2 1

ISBN (cloth): 0-226-11496-1
ISBN (paper): 0-226-11498-8

An earlier version of chapter 3 appeared as "What Books about Juries Reveal about Social Science and Law," in the journal *Law and Social Inquiry* 16(2):353–72, © 1991 American Bar Foundation. All rights reserved.

Library of Congress Cataloging-in-Publication Data

Constable, Marianne.
    The law of the other : the mixed jury and changing conceptions of citizenship, law, and knowledge / Marianne Constable.
       p.   cm. — (New practices of inquiry)
    Includes bibliographical references and index.
    ISBN 0-226-11496-1 (cloth). — ISBN 0-226-11498-8 (paper)
    1. Jury—Great Britain—History.   2. Jury—United States—History.
3. Minorities—Legal status, laws, etc.—Great Britain—History.
4. Aliens—Great Britain—History.   5. Law, Medieval.   I. Title.
II. Series
KD7540.C66   1994
347.42′0752′09—dc20
[344.20775209]   93-28838
                                      CIP

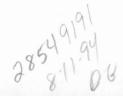

To my teachers,
especially my mother

All I have is a voice
To undo the folded lie,
The romantic lie in the brain
Of the sensual man-in-the-street
And the lie of Authority
Whose buildings grope the sky:
There is no such thing as the State
And no one exists alone;
Hunger allows no choice
To the citizen or the police;
We must love one another or die.
—W. H. Auden[1]

CONTENTS

ACKNOWLEDGMENTS

I have been advised more than once to begin this book with the jury equivalent of torture and a timetable. But the modern jury is not a prison, and if the story of the mixed jury reveals the modern soul on trial, today's jury law nevertheless governs the trials of relatively few modern souls. I therefore begin with thanks.

I owe my greatest intellectual debt to Philippe Nonet, Professor in the Jurisprudence and Social Policy Program (JSP) at Boalt Hall, who not only taught me to read the work of Friedrich Nietzsche, Martin Heidegger, and the great thinkers in jurisprudence but who also introduced me, in part through his own earlier work, to the oxymoronic potential of administrative justice. In seminars and conversations, JSP Professors David Lieberman and Sheldon L. Messinger offered invaluable insights into law and social theory and, in particular, into the work of Max Weber and Michel Foucault.

This work culminates a process that began in JSP, where I was fortunate to transform a seminar paper into a dissertation under the direction of Professors David Cohen, David Lieberman, Sheldon L. Messinger, and Philippe Nonet—with help from Rosann Greenspan, Linda Helyar, Tina Stevens, and especially my grad school buddy, Lucy Salyer. Fellowships from the University of California at Berkeley, a several-week visit to the Huntington Library, and the generous support of the Center for the Study of Law and Society, made the dissertation possible.

In Fall 1990, a semester's leave from Berkeley enabled me, as a National Endowment for the Humanities Independent Fellow in the Scholars' Workshop on the Rhetoric of Political Argument, to take advantage of in-kind support from the University of Iowa's Project on the Rhetoric of Inquiry to revise the dissertation. I am grateful for the participating scholars' valiant attempts to make the manuscript accessible and for the opportunity provided by the Iowa visit to reorganize the chapters.

In Berkeley once more, Jill Frank provided the intellectual companionship of a true friend and Frederick Dolan that of a wonderful colleague. Jennifer Culbert, Alison Edwards, Andrea Hackett, Claudia Myers, and Roger Rabb provided excellent research assistance. Important final revisions are thanks once again to the support of the Center for the Study of Law and Society and thanks especially to the careful readings of Thomas Green of the University of Michigan, Sheldon L. Messinger, and Philippe Nonet.

I take full responsibility for whatever problems remain and I thank the following, as well as those named above, for commenting on various incarnations of one or more chapters of the manuscript, for suggestions that I did and did not take, and/or for their support of the project: John Brigham, Ken Cmiel, Tom Dumm, Felipe Gutteriez, Laurent Mayali, Martha Minow, Katie Neckerman, John Nelson, Phyllis Farley Rippey, Michael Saks, Austin Sarat, Kim Scheppele, Jonathan Simon, Susan Sterett, A. W. B. Simpson, Alex Tanford, John Tryneski, Jack Tweedie, Rod Watanabe, and Margot Young.

Introduction

We have said that law may be taken for every purpose, save that of strictly philosophical inquiry, to be the sum of the rules administered by courts of justice.—Pollock and Maitland[1]

It is fruitful in a certain way to describe that-which-is by making it appear as something that might not be, or that might not be as it is, . . . by following lines of fragility in the present, in managing to grasp why and how that-which-is might no longer be that which is.—Michel Foucault[2]

Many associate the Anglo-American jury with "a jury of one's peers" and consider its emergence, as a democratic institution in which fellow-citizens render judgment, to be a cultural achievement. This work tells the story of the oft neglected half-alien, or mixed, jury. The rise and fall of the half-alien jury highlights the terms—the language and conditions—under which today's jury of citizens emerges as a cultural achievement; those terms reveal the ascendance of positivism.

The story of the mixed jury, from its pre-statutory practice to its statutory abolition in 1870, is, in microcosm, a history of the rise of positive law. It tells of the emergence of a world in which the law of officials assumes exclusive standing as law, in which the territorial jurisdiction of a state replaces the principle of personality of law (that one lives and is judged according to one's own law), in which social science transforms the practices of a people into propositional knowledge of norms, and in which law becomes an instrument of social policy directed toward the management of a population. The story of the mixed jury thus summons a world that brings into relief the positivism through which "we moderns" approach citizenship, law, and knowledge. It raises questions about who we are, what we are to do, and what we know, matters of concern to the disciplines—anthropology, history, law, political science, political theory, psychology, sociology—that today place man at their center.

How can such a remote, seemingly insignificant, and barely noticed practice as the half-alien jury illuminate these matters? It does so insofar as the jury is not simply a procedural device or mechanism for the evaluation of evidence in a lawsuit. Rather, the jury constitutes a practice in which matters of community membership, truth, and law are inextricably intertwined.

1

In declaring the law that is the verdict (literally *ver-dict*), the membership of a community "speaks the truth" or "says truly." Through mixed juries, the membership of the community allows strangers to participate in this verdict or declaration of what ought to be done. On the earliest pre-fourteenth-century mixed juries, these strangers were members of other communities who, with the natives of the vicinage, reached a conciliation of the customs of two communities. Early juries embody a principle of personal law, whereby both non-alien and alien persons are entitled to be judged *secundum legum quam vivit*[3]—by the customs of the community to which the person belongs or, literally, "according to the law by which one lives." With the development of the nation-state, the "alien" members of a jury come to be the alien party's fellow-citizens; later, on juries *de medietate linguae* or "of half tongue," the alien jurors come to be any non-English speakers. Today, in a world defined increasingly by social research, the "other" on a jury is conceived not in terms of citizenship or language but by the statistically identifiable characteristics of race and sex. Today, when parties claim to be governed by different laws, conflict of laws (or private international law as it is now called) bases itself largely on a territorial principle. The laws of the state govern those who reside within the state's geographical boundaries, regardless of the customs of the community to which a person belongs.

The jury verdict of today often is described as the outcome of procedures for applying the law to the facts and is evaluated in terms of procedural regularity for its validity. The verdict of the pre-statutory mixed jury, by contrast, encapsulates a knowledge of the practices of two communities. As a matter of practice, the early jury's verdict is less a matter of following procedure than a claim about what to do. Although pre-fourteenth-century jurors may indeed have distinguished questions of fact from questions of law in their deliberations, the justice or "truth" of the early mixed jury's verdict, a truth that lies in practical reason, is ontologically "prior" to any fact-law distinction. The fact-law distinction accompanies an understanding of law as the propositional knowledge of rules—an understanding that characterizes both the modern law of the jury and the law that is the subject matter of modern sociology, but that is foreign to the early law of the mixed jury which, as custom, embodies communities' practical knowledge of action.

The first three chapters show how contemporary law and sociolegal research share a positivist understanding of the jury and of law as official statements of rules; this understanding differs considerably from the understanding of law of the early mixed jury. Chapter 1 introduces the early mixed juries. Chapters 2 and 3 juxtapose conceptions of membership, law, and knowledge articulated in modern texts about the jury to the conceptions embodied by the earliest mixed juries of chapter 1. Chapter 2 analyses *Batson v. Kentucky*, a 1986 United States Supreme Court case concerned with the jury as a "representative cross-section" of a population, and surrounding legal literature. Chapter 3 focuses on six well-respected jury studies to discuss contemporary social research. Together these chapters point to a change in concerns, from the substantive composition of the early jury to the selection process of the modern jury, from the customary law of the community to the declarations of officials, from the truth of the verdict to the legitimation of social policy.

Chapter 4 asks how the transition from the early to the modern jury, from practical judgment to positive law, came about. It first considers the adequacy of describing this transition in the terms of legal positivism, as the development of a system of positive law. Such an account, like many histories of the common law, finds itself unable to maintain a distinction between the "prelegal" and the "legal," and ultimately treats all law—including the practice of the mixed jury—as a version, of greater or lesser maturity, of positive law. The second section of chapter 4, the heart of the book, next shows how the continually inaccessible moment of origin of positive law is the moment of conquest. In other words, this section shows how positive law grounds itself in the effectiveness of will. The third section of the chapter shows how reliance on a modern understanding of law as a propositional articulation of rules—rather than as the practices that constitute a people—lies behind the positivist need to ground the authority of law in force or will, that is, in sources external to propositional rules themselves. The chapter concludes by turning away from positivist accounts of history, which deny the status of law to practices and customs that are not themselves in need of an external origin.

Chapters 5, 6, and 7 attempt a history of the mixed jury that, unlike positivist accounts, affirms the status of custom or practice as law, while refusing to collapse such practice into a premature version of positive law. Rather than tracing the evolution of the common law, these chapters use transformations in the mixed jury to tell of the decline of law as practice and to consider the implications for membership and language of the absence of an understanding of law as practice.

As a whole, the work challenges in a particular way the truths of the contemporary positivist understandings of the jury, its law, and its history. It recognizes the pervasiveness of positivism and the validity of positivist claims about the existence of legal systems and seeks, not to reject those claims nor to overcome positivism, but to situate positivism. In a now-classic work of legal positivism, *The Concept of Law*, H. L. A. Hart writes that certain state-ments by earlier theorists about the nature of law are "*both* illuminating and puzzling: they are more like great exaggerations of some truths about law unduly neglected, than cool definitions. They throw a light which makes us see much in law that lay hidden; but the light is so bright that it blinds us to the remainder and so leaves us still without a clear view of the whole."[4] Hart's own account of law illumines the entire stage on which earlier theorists had thrown only spotlights; his concept of law clarifies, without emphases or blind spots, the fact that the existence of a modern municipal legal system consists, at minimum, in the unification of the valid rules citizens obey with those rules of validity officials accept.

If Hart's concept exposes head-on the law that exists, the mixed jury sil-houettes the legal system that appears in positivism's steady beam from an-other angle. Introducing dimensions and depths of law inaccessible to or even obliterated by more direct positivist examination, the story of the mixed jury foregrounds matters—such as history and justice—which, in positiv-ism's light alone, lie sequestered or unnoticed.

The story of the mixed jury thus treats, for instance, of the apparent dis-juncture between the pre-1353 references to the mixed jury and the admit-tedly sparse, yet official, history constructed about the mixed jury. Recording official actions from 1353 to 1870, the official history of the mixed jury re-counts the rise of an official common law. Such history disregards earlier traces and attributes the origins of the mixed jury to the 1353 Statute of the Staple. The first *enacted* law to allow suits in England to be judged by juries composed of aliens indeed appeared in 1353, during the twenty-seventh year of the reign of Edward III. The law provided that when a plea or debate be-tween merchants or ministers of the "staple" (or market town) came before the mayor of the staple, to try the truth thereof,

if the one party and the other be a stranger, it shall be tried by strangers, and if the one party and the other be Denizens, it shall be tried by denizens: and if the one party be denizen and the other an alien, the one half of the inquest of the proof shall be of denizens, and the other half of aliens.[5]

One year later, another act extended the privilege of a mixed alien-denizen jury to "all manner of inquests and proofs which be taken or made amongst aliens and denizens." The mixed jury was no longer restricted only to suits between merchants, or only to those before the mayor of the staple:

be they merchants or other, as well before the mayor of the staple as before any other justices or ministers although the king be party, the one half of the inquest or proof shall be denizens, and the other half of aliens, if so many aliens and foreigners be in the town or place where such inquest or proof is to be taken.[6]

As chapter 1 shows, however, historians and legal officials who treat the mixed jury as "instituted by Edward III"[7] and who have taken its history to be a history of official acts neglect earlier practice. Incorporating into the story of the mixed jury the neglect of practice by official histories, rather than rejecting those histories, this work shows how even the history of the history of the mixed jury reveals the rise of a peculiarly modern positivism. Such positivism privileges official law over practice and finds its fulfillment in propositional—sociological or legal positivist—knowledge of "the facts of law," which knowledge ultimately has no use either for law as practice or for history. Limited in its understanding of law to its own declarations of what exists, such positivism threatens to become absolute, an aspect of the completion of nihilism about which Heidegger's work on Nietzsche warns.

The method from chapter 1 onward is to read legal, historical, jurisprudential, and social scientific documents, ranging in origin from the Middle Ages to the present, and to extrapolate from these readings. The accessibility of any given chapter will vary for those in different disciplines. In approaching chapters that may seem either obvious or overly complex and detailed, then, readers are urged to recall that the argument progresses toward a broad understanding of positivism through close attention to the language of works belonging to fields with differing vocabularies and assumptions. Readers unfamiliar with literary criticism will do well to remember that a claim about what a work reveals does not implicate the psychological state of the person who wrote it.

Academic historians and others may find the period covered in this work, 1066 to the present, appallingly broad. Some may declare references to the mixed jury too sparse, or the focus on the doctrine of the mixed jury too particular, to support a work this length. Still others will consider the link between analyses of particular texts and broad issues of positivism and modernity to be without empirical foundation. This work indeed does not focus on information about how often or when particular mixed juries were used, their procedures, or the interests they served—the determination of which remains to scholars of history and to political scientists. Some might call this work a "strictly philosophical inquiry" into law, given that it aims not so much to produce a comprehensive and factual history of some thing as to reach insights into the way we are—into the positivism through which, and in which, we today understand citizenship, law, and knowledge. The resemblance to fact of the story that follows is not coincidental, but the story is not to be taken primarily as a contribution to a storehouse of facts about law.

The reader is also cautioned against taking the distance between the modern jury and the early mixed jury as a gap to be bridged. For this work intends neither to guide current policy nor to lament past practices. Like the sciences of society, it interrogates present practices. Unlike the sciences of society, though, it does so "in an attitude of hostile calm," as Nietzsche put it, that "will allow the strange, the *novel* of every kind to approach one first—one will draw one's hand back from it." It seeks to avoid the "*plunge into* other people and other, things, in short our celebrated modern 'objectivity'"—the objectivity of the outsider whose mastery would transform the world.[8]

In grounding themselves in the texts of positive law, the last three chapters in particular risk being taken as precisely the most positivist of doctrinal legal histories, as presentations of facts whose value lies in their ability to inform social policy. Yet the aim of these chapters, like that of this work as a whole, is paradoxically twofold: on the one hand, indeed, to point to the ascendance of positivism—in which law appears as propositional knowledge of official acts of social policy that are validated by a sociological understanding of facts which, ignoring justice, confirms the coerciveness of the legal system; and, on the other, by showing the extensiveness and the limitations of that positivism, to hold open the possibility of another law.

1   The Early Mixed Jury

Scholars of private international law often assert that, prior to the sixteenth century, the English had no mechanism for dealing with conflict of laws— that is, for deciding which law applies when a party in a lawsuit claims to be governed by the laws of another country.[1] Maitland, for example, claimed that "the fact that there was not in England any race or class of men 'living Roman law,' may have prevented the development of 'personal laws' which is a remarkable feature in the history of the Continent."[2]

Under a principle of "personal law," the law of the community to which a person belongs determines the law applied to the person and his or her transactions; this is distinguished from a principle of "territoriality" in which the laws or customs of a place govern all those who reside there. The basis of law in the Roman Empire was territorial; after the fall of the Empire, a system of personal law developed in which a conquering people lived by its own law, while Roman citizens in the conquered former territories lived by Roman law. Feudalism and the Italian city-state, it is often claimed, reestablished territoriality in Europe.

Scholars besides Maitland also point to English isolation from the rest of Europe and English reliance on a law of domicile rather than of nationality to suggest that in England "the principle of the personality of law never developed."[3] Until the appearance of a system of sovereign states, they claim, England had no need nor opportunity to develop a law of conflict, as she had established a "uniform system of law, powerfully territorial and exclusive, without the slightest demand for that finesse of logic required by jurists in France, Germany, Italy, and the Netherlands in solving the conflicts of statutes and customs."[4]

This chapter suggests that if early England had no need to develop a law of conflict, it was not because she had a uniform and territorial system of law, but because a multiplicity of local communities enforced their laws in such a way as to incorporate a conception of the personality of law. The common law may indeed have been "the negation of the conflict of laws,"[5] but conflicts occurred in England before the common law and its courts came to predominate. With a relatively strong central legislator (and later, legislature), England may have been beset by fewer problems of conflicting statutory law than "the numerous little states of medieval Europe."[6] But she nevertheless encountered conflicts of customs. These conflicts involved disagreement among local customs as well as between English customs and those of persons from "beyond the sea." And while the personality of law was not in England an explicit doctrine, the early jury and its precursors constituted a practice that allowed a person to be judged by the laws or customs of that person's community. In particular, on "mixed" juries, the members of two communities addressed matters involving parties from communities with different laws.

Maitland found "little evidence" that "the Kenting could carry with him his Kentish law into Mercia in the same way that the French or Lombard could preserve his national law in Lombardy."[7] But some "national"—or at least not strictly territorial—law had been recognized in England,[8] even before the references one finds to the mixed jury. The Laws of William, for instance, referring to the customs of Mercian, West Saxon, and Dane Law, distinguish between the fines imposed in the different regions.[9] Edgar (959–75) and his descendants admitted the right of the Danes to their own laws. The laws of King Alfred (871–99), formulated in one of the first attempts to unify the country, note the different laws of the three former great kingdoms of Mercia, Wessex, and Kent. And Offa, King of Mercia (758–94), apparently allowed Charlemagne's merchants—if not the men of Kent—their customs. Charlemagne, in a letter to Offa, says: "You have written to us about your merchants; . . . we would have them enjoy our protection and defence within our realm according to the ancient custom in commerce, and if in any place they are distressed by unjust oppression, let them appeal to us and we will order justice to be done. Show the same favour to our merchants."[10]

This chapter argues that by the thirteenth century, central courts and, earlier, local communities used mixed juries in a variety of cases to settle differences when the members and customs of two communities came into conflict. It suggests that private international law scholars' slighting of the personal law implications of the mixed jury reveals something—beyond a relative paucity of data about mixed juries—about the conceptions of law presented in texts about Anglo-American law. As do attributions of the origin of the mixed jury to fourteenth-century statutes, the views of these legal scholars take for granted a positivist understanding of law and knowledge that, as the following chapters show, forecloses understanding law as anything other than an officially authorized system of rules.

1. Customs and Communities

Twelfth-century England, historians inform us, "was not a homogeneous society. There was considerable variation in patterns of settlement and farming, in the layout of the fields, and in the power lords exercised over their tenants."[11] While it was no longer true that "a journey of a day or two or even less might take a traveller from the heart of one king's dominion to another,"[12] courts, customs, dialects, and even units of measurement varied from place to place.

Many different courts operated throughout the land.[13] Although royal justice established its jurisdiction over administrative and judicial matters in all these courts during the twelfth and thirteenth centuries,[14] local customs flourished even as royal power extended itself into the counties, and the recognition of local differences remained integral to notions of justice. "In the twelfth century," Maitland writes, "customs were many and important."[15] Looking back, the identification of these customs is difficult. The *Domesday Book* (1086) prepared during the reign of William the Conqueror was "the first and last record in which local customs are recorded side by side under one cover. Local custom, even viewed fiscally, never again was made a main issue in governmental inquiry. The customs of shires and hundreds were soon reduced to an almost complete uniformity under the pressure of central government; the boroughs were left in undisturbed possession."[16]

The identification of pre-Domesday customs is problematic only for the modern historian and the foreign conqueror, however. At the time of the *Domesday Book,* or rather before, a community's customs would be known to its own members who, insofar as they knew their customs, would have no need to write them down.[17] Even after the *Domesday Book,* when local customs were "reduced" to the "almost complete uniformity" of the common law (and eventually to the "facts" of legal history and the "norms" of social science), courts passing judgment justified their decisions by appealing to the customs of particular communities.

Communities, like courts and customs, were also many and important in the twelfth century. To us, the boundaries and definitions of medieval communities appear vague and indeterminate. Even at the time, because English country people did not live in "largely identical but mutually antagonistic and bounded territorial groups, segmented 'into units of high similarity and low mutual interaction,'"[18] it might have been hard to isolate independent communities and to identify their members definitely. People from one or more villages, parishes, or manors might come together to act collectively on common interests, such as roads, policing, farming, trade, or churches,[19] and for such purposes they formed a single body. Different meanings of "foreigner" overlapped in the borough (or town), referring at times to the unfree who dwelled within the borough, to those who dwelled outside the borough, to those who did not pay customary dues to the town (or were not in "scot and lot" with it), or to non-English, and so too notions of community overlapped.

Immigrants from other lands sometimes became part of already established communities and sometimes formed their own communities. In 1066, and again in 1085 when the Danes threatened England, William's army had been comprised not only of Normans, but also of Picards, Flemings, Burgundians, and Bretons.[20] Many of these "Francigenae" or "Francus" coming over in the Conqueror's train settled in England, not only as tenants in chief but also as cultivating tenantry, holding small estates of less than a knight's fee.[21] Through the next hundred years, Flemish mercenaries crossed the Channel to fight in English wars. Some "did not escape the fortune of war," but William and his successors retained others "at special points in what we may call military colonies."[22]

By the time of Edward the Confessor (1042–66), who had been reared in the Norman court, a "frequent succession of foreigners . . . took a prominent part in the administration of the realm, both civil and ecclesiastical."[23] Religious settlements, as well as secular ones, were entitled to retain their own customs. William "graciously admitted men of foreign nations to his friendship [and] honored them without bias."[24] In addition to providing different laws for Frenchmen and Englishmen, William ordained that Francigenae who had settled in English towns in the time of the Confessor, had adopted English customs, and had begun to pay "scot and lot" should be treated as English and not as French.[25]

Communities of immigrants with their own customs sometimes adjoined English communities. The *Domesday Book* describes a French town at Norwich, as well as the English one. At Nottingham, a French town adjoining the castle "preserved its separate existence and special customs for centuries." Although French burgesses at Shrewsbury "do not appear to have been separately organized," they were not in scot and lot with the rest of the inhabitants. "Double towns, consisting of two districts inhabited by men with distinct privileges and obligations had had their analogies on French soil long ago." Unfortunately, "in the cases of Norwich and Nottingham the union of their component parts occurred at such an early date that little information about the exact position of the French townsmen has survived."[26]

Aliens also inhabited special quarters, organized as communities, within towns. Members of the London gild of weavers, who lived under the protection of the crown and maintained an independence from city authorities until the fourteenth century, were probably immigrants. The names and special disabilities of weavers and fullers or dyers in Marlborough, Beverley, and Lincoln suggest that these gilds were originally communities of foreigners. In Winchester, weavers paid special fines for the right of preserving their own customs and choosing their own alderman.[27]

Of the French who had settled in England, we are told that by the time of Henry II (1154–89), "the two races had become so blended that the distinction between Norman and English had almost disappeared."[28] Until 1340, however, the hundred was liable to the king for the murder of any man unless it could disprove the presumption (through a "presentment of Englishry") that every man killed was a Frenchman.[29]

Given the permeability of community boundaries, the maintenance of separate customs identified communities and their members. In numerous charters, kings affirmed the "ancient custom" of localities and granted privileges, for instance, to persons and groups "according to the ancient law of the borough which they had in the time of our ancestors."[30] Charters entitled towns to hold their own borough and piepoudre (or fair) courts which, unlike the hundred and shire courts that came to be administered by royal officials, retained their local officials. And although particular practices differed by borough and court, towns modeled their charters on one another, making some generalization possible.[31]

Rural and royal courts, as well as borough and fair courts, attributed some sort of community identity to all persons. Borough charters explicitly recognized "ancient customs," such as the notion that persons should be judged by their own kind and according to their own custom. These ancient customs were, most likely, the customs of the rural courts (as well as of the town or market courts) before the preemption of rural custom by royal law. As Susan Reynolds writes: "Not only in towns but in rural communities grants of privileges quite often included the right of people in the local community to judge themselves or to appoint their own judges. The usual emphasis on the novelty of such a right and its origin in special grants is, however, mistaken. It was normal in the English countryside, where charters of liberties are more or less unknown."[32]

Borough charters protected the town and its members, at least somewhat and for a price, from economic and legal demands made in the name of the king. They also guarded the boroughs' economic and trade interests from the encroachment and claims of outsiders. Custumals of the boroughs and the records of their courts distinguish between burghers (or burgesses) and non-burghers—or "foranei," "forinseci," "extranei," "extrinseci," or "estraunges."[33] Many charters forbade the impleading of burgesses outside their boroughs, and at least one, Yarmouth, also prohibited its burgesses from pleading outside.[34] Burgesses could only be judged by their fellows[35] in borough courts which had to follow specific appeal (or accusation) and arrest procedures—procedures to which foreigners, charged with offenses in the borough, were not entitled.[36]

Although towns jealously guarded their interests from outsiders, they recognized that their well-being was dependent on connections and relations with others. In most towns, an association known as the Gild Merchant developed, composed of almost all who did business in the town: the burghers, tradesmen, craftsmen, and even craftswomen[37] residing in the town; trades and crafts persons dwelling nearby in the same hundred; and burghers from other towns. All these "merchants" were entitled to trade freely in the town and were exempt from toll or the taxes imposed on other traders. In exchange, the gild merchants were in scot and lot with the town, paying some customary dues.[38] Special rules, which did not extend to nonprivileged foreign merchants, governed proceedings regarding the privileged gild merchants, in the distraint, replevy, and pledging of alleged debtors, for instance.[39]

Just how exactly to define a "burgher" or "burgess" is unclear. Distinctions between the free and the unfree, the free and the villein, the burgher and the gildsman, and the townsman and the foreigner are problematic.[40] Certainly by the fourteenth century, these distinctions, if they were ever clear, had begun to run together. "Gradually and silently, by a process of absorption, rather than usurpation," the burgher and the gild merchant became, at least in some cases, indistinguishable. As "an official organ of the municipality, the Gild naturally identified itself from the outset, with the general welfare of the latter."[41] This "solidarity of interests," combined with the fact that many of the men who served as the bailiffs or provosts of the borough served as the aldermen or stewards of the Gild,[42] led to the amalgamation of the two in many locales.

"A person could be an inhabitant of a town without being either a burgess or a gildsman,"[43] though. The fullers (or treaters of woolen cloth) of Lincoln during the reign of John (1199–1216), tenants of privileged sokes situated within the limits of the borough, villeins who sought refuge in the towns, and Jews residing there were neither burgesses nor members of the "brethren."

Yet, like the foreign merchant who did not belong to the gild, members of these groups were regarded not as independent individuals but rather as members of some other community. That is, although they were not "citizens" of the town, towns identified and treated them as subject to their own law or custom, as opposed to the true outsider or "outlaw" who was "without the law."

Identity as a community member involved responsibility under the laws and customs of one's own community, as well as liability for one's fellow community members. Borough members, local residents over whom a borough did not have jurisdiction, and foreigners might each be held liable outside the geographical bounds of their own communities for the deeds of their fellows.

Many boroughs allowed the taking of distress, for example, from the countryman of a man who owed a debt in the borough. Courts held merchants responsible in other cities and in other lands for the debts of their fellow townsmen. The borough, of course, attempted to protect its own men from such distress. Like several other charters, the Bristol Charter, dated 1188, states: "No burgess anywhere within my land or my power shall be distrained for any debt, unless he is himself the principal or his pledge."[44] In 1275, the Statute of Westminster formally ended the system of intermunicipal reprisals against English merchants in England,[45] but for many years such reprisals continued against those who came from overseas.[46] Eventually, the Statute of the Staple extended protection against such reprisals to non-English merchants, "though with a saving clause that may have robbed it of much of its value."[47]

Before their abolition, reprisals were carried out against those of the same "fellowship" as the debtor or, according to *Fleta*, of "'affinity' with the debtor 'as of one society or city.'"[48] Although some charters mention the debtor's "community," others refer to those of the debtor's "county," and one historian suggests that the bond between the debtor and the person against whom reprisals were taken need be "no closer than that both were justiciables of the same court."[49] Even this jurisdictional formulation however, does not show that bond to be independent of community. Indeed some English counties holding their own assemblies and courts, such as Norfolk and Suffolk, may have originated as tribes or nations.[50] Moreover, "it is possible to trace far back a distress by way of reprisal against persons connected with the accused by kinship, or by the bonds which replaced kinship. Just as the whole kin was involved in the feud arising out of an act of violence, and involved in the payment of a composition to bring the feud to an end, so the whole kin was responsible for the debts of a kinsman."[51]

The recognition of the other as member of another community extended also to matters of proof. The Normans had brought trial by battle to England. This method of proof was then used in the king's courts, but London, Winchester, and Lincoln, by the time of Henry I (1100–1135), had received exemptions.[52] Trial by battle appears not to have been used in borough courts in cases involving only English parties, although borough courts made exceptions for cases involving the death of a foreigner[53] or an appeal by a foreign accuser (i.e., an accusation by a convicted criminal, pardoned on condition that he accuse his associates) against a freeman.[54] London's charter stated that its citizens were not to judge in trials by battle, since the citizens did not use it.[55] Other boroughs explicitly required burghers to defend by the law of the borough, that is, by oath,[56] or prohibited them from fighting against foreigners unless they quit the borough.[57]

While foreigners were allowed proof by battle,[58] they were encouraged to use the oath. Records of the fifteenth century show that boroughs still allowed "a man from foreign parts" ("partibus longinquis") to "send to his own country to acquit himself by his countryman if he can" ("ut possit mandare ad partes suas ad acquietandum se per vicinos suos si poterit").[59] Charters guarded burghers' own right to defend by their law or to "wage their law" through 40, 36, 24, 12, or 6 oath-helpers who would swear either to the truth of a claim, or to their belief in it, in the king's courts. In pleas of the crown, Londoners were entitled to purge themselves by thirty-six men, eighteen from the east side of the Walpole, and eighteen from the west.[60]

Although communities were in some ways amorphous, lacking in physical and geographical definition and containing few guidelines as to who their own "citizens" were, the preservation of customs as practices served to separate communities and to distinguish their members from one another. Rural courts and royal courts, as well as borough, fair, and piepoudre courts, attributed community identity to persons who came into contact with them.

How did these courts operate? Before the twelfth century, local courts, and central ones to some extent, operated less like today's tribunals than like modern assemblies, making collective decisions without strongly distinguishing between legislative, judicial, and administrative functions. The first written laws in England, for instance, the "dooms" occasioned by the conversion of the Anglo-Saxons to Christianity in about 600, were made by King Aethelbert of Kent, in consultation with the *witan,* or assembly of the great men of the country (from the verb "witan," to know).[61] Locally, through the twelfth century, "courts and meetings were different in degree rather than in kind: courts dealt with general political and administrative business as well as with law in the narrow sense, while meetings, even of voluntary associations, were apt to make rules and impose penalties on their members. Both made their decisions, or were supposed to make them, either by general consensus or through juries or other panels, which, however chosen, were supposed to represent the whole community."[62]

In disputes in such forums, parties would bring their own witnesses to support their pleas.[63] After hearing the pleadings,[64] the person presiding over the "trial"[65] would declare the judgment of the community, a judgment reached after conferring with others present. The judgment might be definitive, based on an examination of witnesses or charters, or upon simple consideration of the pleadings. Or it could declare which issues were to be proved (or tested),[66] and by what manner of proof—generally, by oath or ordeal.

In these early "cases," distinctions between jury and witness, like those between judge and jury, were less clear than today. Whether judge, juror, or witness, all came from the community; what they did was speak, and what they spoke about was an amalgamation of what we now call "fact" and "law."

Historians disagree about when the distinction between judge and jury, and the now-corresponding distinction between law and fact, emerged and what their sources were.[67] These questions cannot be answered any more clearly now than in 1930, when one author wrote that "none of the writers shed clear light on the supposed transition period, when jurors, as such, ceased to be witnesses and the latter, as such, ceased to be jurors."[68] To whatever origin or whatever period one traces the modern jury, one can always find, in its precursors, a body of persons, representing the community, speaking the truth about the matters at hand without apparent explicit distinction between fact and law.

Early jurors—like witnesses and judges—came from nearby, from the neighborhood or vicinage where the matter they were to try was supposed to have happened.[69] Often they were the "senioribus et legalioribus" of the community,[70] who would know its customs or practices.[71] ("Practice" here serves to emphasize the connection between custom and action. "Custom" is sometimes taken as the social expression of "mere habit," of convergent or repetitive *behavior*. But while custom may be said to stem from habit, it does so in the sense that actors habituate themselves to what will become second nature through practice. This "second nature" is a disposition to act which, unlike "nature," is noncompulsory and involves practical reason.)[72]

Selected for their knowledge of the community—or as members who share in the practical wisdom that consists of the community's customs—and of the parties or of the particular situation, jurors gave evidence to each other in inquests conducted by other community members (and later before the king, or in the assizes of novel disseisin). How and whether jurors took other evidence into consideration is disputed. Those who knew about the matter at hand, irrespective of the later distinction between questions of fact which go to the jury and questions of law which are for the judge, decided early cases. Their task was to speak the truth ("ver-dict")[73] at a time before truth referred to propositions of "fact" and before law was relegated to a question of "values."[74]

Even with the coming of "royal justice," such bodies for a time continued to speak the truth of the community. Although they might not explicitly *decide* what to do, what they said remained in some sense the law, or the truth of the community. Whether at Norman inquests or Angevin ones, for presentment juries or juries as proof, the truth lay without distinction between fact and law. Even after the Norman kings summoned community members to testify before the king's representative at inquests used "both in legal controversy and in administration,"[75] the jurors' task was to speak the truth of a matter.[76] Under the Angevin kings, too, although the community and its representatives did not preside over deliberations of justice, local testimony continued. The 1166 Assize of Clarendon ordained that in every county and in every hundred the twelve most lawful men of each hundred and the four most lawful men of each vill should be sworn to present to the king's justice or the sheriff any man who was suspected of serious crime.[77] And when the 1216 edict of the Fourth Lateran Council at Rome prohibited ordeals, changes in methods of proof led to even greater reliance on the judgment of "the country" or of the early jury.

2. Early Mixed Juries

References to the use of early mixed juries—in local courts and in cases of Jews and merchants in central courts—must be considered against the background of the plurality of communities, customs, and courts just described.

The earliest references to the use of mixed juries occur in records of local customs throughout Britain. When persons from two communities were involved in a dispute, both communities would be represented. Local courts treated as "others" not only members of distant areas but also local residents who belonged to "other" communities. The borough courts again provide records of what were most likely more ancient and widespread practices.

Should a burgess be brought to court "in the foreign," the burgess was entitled to be judged by fellow burgesses. In Hereford and in the Welsh town of Rhuddlan, men who lived in the "liberty of the city or the suburb thereof" were entitled to assizes, juries, and inquests "made only by men of that city, and in that city, unless the matter concerns the lord king, or his heirs, or the community of the city, and in that case we ought to make them according to our ancient customs, which are these: that one half of the inquest or jury shall be of the said community, and the other half of other neighbouring cities or boroughs or vills which are of our condition."[78]

Fourteenth century records of Kilkenny, Ireland, state that "if any of the burgesses of the aforesaid town be impleaded, before whatsoever judge, of trespass, debt, account, covenants, or of any manner of contracts made in the foreign, or be adjudged of felony or of conspiracy in the foreign, and should put himself on the country, half of the jurors of that country shall be burgesses of the aforesaid town and the other half foreigners, of the place where the said deed was supposed to be done."[79]

In London in the twelfth century, a foreigner impleading a citizen had to have two witnesses from the city. Conversely, at least one of the witnesses of a citizen impleading a foreigner who was not of the city and had no land there, had to be "of the county in which the foreigner dwells" (or "de comitatu in quo manet").[80] In Scotland, the *Leges Quatuor Burgorum* of about 1270 declare that in pleas between a burgess and a country-dweller, where oaths were to be made, "the burgess shall purge himself by the sixth hand with burgesses against the other" (that is, with six compurgators), while the countryman ("rure") shall do so "by the same number of men such as he is himself." And "if the case ought to be proved by witnesses one against another, it behoves that part of the number of witnesses be burgesses and part country-dwellers."[81]

The origins of such practices at the local level are unclear. Lambard (1568), seconded by Coke on Littleton (1628), attributed such a practice to the Saxons, for whom "twelve men versed in the law, six English and an equal number of Welsh, dispense justice to the English and Welsh." Coke writes:

This trial of the fact per duodecim liberos et legales homines is very ancient: for heare what the Law was before the Conquest. In singulis Centurijs comitia sunto, atque liberae conditionis viri duodeni aetate superiores una cum praeposito sacra tenentes iurano, &c. Nay the tryall, in some cases, Per medietatem linguae (as we speake) was as ancient. Viri duodeni jure consulte, Angliae sex, Walliae totidem, Anglis & Wallis jus dicunto, and of ancient time it was called, duodecim virale judicium.[82]

At least one assembly of "'a good thousand' representing several counties is said to have sworn its judgement" in the Anglo-Saxon Charters.[83] In 1101, royal writs show that "men of two shires" were brought together to give a verdict.[84] Bracton refers to the 1233 Colchester assize of land by six burgesses and six outsiders,[85] and the Dunwich charter of 1200 mentions amercements assessed by a similar body.[86] In 1308, a king's writ ordered an action of ejectment for lands in Shropshire to be tried by a jury half English and half Welsh.[87]

The references above indicate that mixed juries were used in a variety of local disputes, both in local courts following local custom and in local courts under royal control. Centralized royal courts too, used mixed juries in cases involving distinct communities, as in the case of the Jews.

The Jews, unlike the assimilationist Franks, were expelled from England in 1290. But from the Conquest until their expulsion, the Jews lived in English towns, where they maintained their own customs and communities. Many of the English hated them. But the king held them in special regard for the services they performed as moneylenders and for the riches they brought to the royal treasury. Although the Jews lived in their own communities, they worked as lenders, bankers, and traders and were thus in constant contact with non-Jews. Instances of religious conversion, both to and from Judaism, and of religious intermarriages appear in the records.

The Jewish court, the *Beth Din* or "House of Judgment," exercised jurisdiction over disputes among the Jews. In about 1200, confirming even earlier privileges, King John declared that "excesses which may arise among them except those which belong to our crown and justice, as homicide, mayhem, premeditated assault, burglary, rape, theft, arson, and treasure-trove, shall be brought before them according to their law and remedied, and they shall do justice thereon among themselves."[88] Even in the pleas of the crown named above, "although none of them has become an accuser thereon, we will cause that charge to be investigated by our lawful Jews of England, as the charter of King Henry our father reasonably testifies."[89] In cases involving dietary custom, debt, petty crime, marriage, and inheritance, Jewish law was applied by and among the Jews. English courts recognized marriages of Jews made according to the *lex Judaica,* "even in the case of claims to land by a widow in respect of her dower or a son in respect of his inheritance."[90]

In quarrels between a Christian and a Jew, an 1190 charter from King Richard to "Ysaac, son of Rabbi Joce, and his sons and their men" provided that the plaintiff must have a lawful Christian and a lawful Jew as witnesses. If Jews defend themselves by writ, "the writ shall serve them for testimony; and if a Christian have a quarrel against the aforesaid Jews let it be adjudicated by the peers of the Jews." The charter also confirmed that the Jews could be quit of an appeal (accusation) on their own oath upon their Book, and it provided that if a Christian and a Jew quarreled about the settlement of any money, "the Jew shall prove the capital and the Christian the interest."[91] A general charter in 1201 from John makes similar provisions for "all Jews of England and Normandy." It claims to confirm privileges granted to the Jews not only by Henry II (1154–89), but also by Henry II's grandfather, Henry I (1100–1134).[92]

Clergy, in a state paper addressed to Henry II around 1164, had petitioned for privileges like those of Jews and Londoners:

Behold, London is the chief seat of the kingdom of the English. If its citizens are accused, if they are summoned to the pleas of the crown, they answer in their own city, they are judged by their own laws: they do not purge themselves by the laws of battle, or the ordeal of water or red-hot iron, unless they choose these of their own accord, but there their oath is the end of all controversy. . . . So, too, for the Jews, by the proposed law their oath is the end of all lawsuits, whether civil or criminal. Would it not seem to thee unworthy, my lord the King, unless the clergy were granted a privilege which is indulged to lay citizens or Jews?[93]

Items from the Pipe Rolls (the King's copy of the annual balance sheet of the accounts of the sheriffs of the counties with the Exchequer) also confirm that the Jews did exercise their privileges (since the Rolls record the fines or amercements paid to the king for such exercise).[94] Jews apparently did turn to other courts occasionally, if not in England, at least on the Continent, where they also had the right to their own law. Thus the Council of Avranches in 1172 decreed that ecclesiastical benefits be cut off from those who place Jews "under jurisdiction to be administered by the secular powers."[95] And a Synod of Rabbis "of Troyes, of Dijon, of Auxerres, of Sens, of Orleans, of Chalons, of Rheims, of Paris, of Melun, of Etampes and their neighborhoods; of Normandy, of the Coast of the sea, of Anjou, of Poitou; and of the great men of Lothair" excommunicated "every man or woman, far or near, who summon his neighbour before a Gentile tribunal, or compel him through Gentiles, whether lord or common man, ruler or official, unless the consent of both has been given beforehand in the presence of pure Jewish witnesses." Further, even

if the matter comes round indirectly, and is heard by the Government or Gentiles generally, and thereby one [Jew] can compel the other, we again decree and excommunicate such a man, to redeem his neighbour from their hands and give him peace against the Gentiles on his side, so that he may suffer no damage or be in fear, and thus not lose what he has demanded from him; and he has to do this according as the seven good men and true [elders] of the place decide, and if there are no elders in the place, those of the nearest community. . . . And we, the undersigned, ask all the frequenters of the court to punish, by means of the Gentile courts, all who trespass against our decrees.[96]

In 1194 in England, the king established a registry for Jewish loans and deeds. Loans and payments of loans were made under the supervision of officials, half of whom were Jewish, half Christian. This office later became a special branch of the Exchequer, or the Jewish Exchequer, which was

both a financial bureau and a judicial tribunal. It managed all the king's transactions—and they were many—with the Jew, saw to the exaction of tallages, reliefs, escheats and forfeitures, and also acted judicially, not merely as between king and Jew, but also as between king and Gentile when, as often happened, the king had for some cause or another "seized into his hand" the debts due to one of his Jews by Christian debtors. Also it heard and determined all manner of disputes between Jew and Christian. Such disputes, it is true, generally related to loans of money, but the court seems to have aimed at and acquired a competence, and an exclusive competence, in all causes whether civil or criminal in which a Jew was implicated, unless it was some merely civil cause between two Hebrews which could be left to a purely Jewish tribunal.[97]

Records from the Jewish Exchequer refer to at least four cases during 1278 involving a Christian and a Jew where mixed Christian/Jewish juries were used. The cases involved the unlawful detention of three books, rape, and the killing of a man in the Jewry. Several such records also remain for 1280.[98]

Occasionally, pleas involving Christians and Jews were heard in other courts. The constables of the royal castles heard cases of small debts, the court of the University of Oxford claimed pleas between Jew and scholar, and the civic court of London held plea touching land between Jew and gentile.[99] At least one hundred heard a charge that Bonefand, a Jew, "ementulated" Robert of Sutton's nephew, causing him to die. (An editor suggests that this was a case of conversion and "that the charge was practically that of performing circumcision." The "jury say he is not guilty, and Bonefand is therefore quits, and Robert at the King's mercy for a false appeal.")[100]

The Oblate Rolls, which form a link between the Exchequer and the law courts by listing the offerings made to the King to obtain certain privileges or evade certain penalties,[101] mention Hugo Bard's payment, in about 1200, of a palfrey and a blue sparrow-hawk

to have an inquest of 12 lawful Jews of Lincoln and 12 free and lawful Christian men of the neighbourhood of Lincoln [inquire] if those charters which Manser, son of Leon the Jew, and Solomon of Edon, and other Jews of Lincoln produce about the debt which Alexander de St. Wast owed them, and made fine thereon with Aaron, Jew of Lincoln, for 10 pounds sterling to quit him of the whole debt which he owed to all the Jews of Lincoln [,] are included in that debt which he owed then and whereon he made fine.[102]

Simon de Kyma, too, sometime between 1202 and 1204, paid 20 marks to have "a jury of lawful Christians and Jews" find whether Simon's father had owed a debt to some Jews on the day he died.[103] In the ninth year of Edward I's reign (1280–81), "we read, that Solomon, a Jew had a cause tried before the Sheriff of *Norwich*, by a jury which were *sex probos et legales homines, et sex legales Judaeos de Civitate Norwici, &c.*"[104] Or, to use sixteenth century terminology, a Jew in the time of Edward I "had his trial per Medietatem Linguae, viz Judaeorum, and they were sworn on the 5 books of Moses, held in their arms, *and by the name of God of Israel, who is merciful.*"[105]

To summarize then, in the twelfth and thirteenth centuries, king's officials presided over courts where suits between Jews and non-Jews were brought. Mixed half-Jewish, half-Christian juries heard such suits. Where disputes occurred among Jews, the Jews' own court heard and decided such cases according to their own law.

Special privileges were also extended to non-Jewish foreigners, even those not permanently settled in England. From early times, kings had granted special privileges to particular groups of merchants, allowing them to sell goods at certain terms, under guaranteed conditions, free from new exactions. Alien merchants were granted exclusive rights to engage in trade, to buy and sell retail and wholesale, and to act as financial agents.[106] Richard I (1189–99) allowed the Hanse merchants to hold a "gildhall" in London free from city tolls and customs, and Edward I (1272–1307) permitted the Gascon wine-importers to keep their own cellars and table in disregard of regulations made for the hosting of strangers. Both the Gascons and the Hanse were entitled to mixed juries in noncapital cases.[107]

In exchange for royal protection and favor, foreign merchants lent money to the crown, held jewels in pawn, helped finance wars and expeditions, and were instrumental in securing naval support from abroad.[108] Starting in the fourteenth century, they paid higher customs than did English merchants, and the king could thus raise revenue by placing additional commodities in their hands.

Although nobles and townspeople benefited from the importation of goods and increased business, they complained that the royal grants to aliens encroached on English rights. The control of local trade, for instance, had been granted to the towns, who reserved such rights for their freemen, to the exclusion of both English and alien outsiders. Royal grants to the aliens, to the towns, or to the nobles (that the latter might buy from whom they would), promoted rivalry among the three groups, each of which attempted to assert its rights at the expense of others "conflictingly enfranchised."[109]

Such rivalry sometimes made alien privileges difficult to enforce. Thus although aliens were not to be held liable for debts of which they were not the principal debtors or sureties, after two Lombards fled England without paying for goods, the goods of members of two societies were seized and held for five years until agreement was reached before the king.[110] Conversely, some burdens on aliens, such as the inability to inherit land, or to acquire it save by the favor of the king (to whom the land escheated at the alien's death), served as but slight disabilities. Aliens could obtain land by purchase, lease, or gift and could rent shops and tenements. Their wills could be proved in England, their executors could bring suit for the collection of outstanding debts, and their heirs could inherit personal property. Through the favor of the king, aliens could also attain positions scarcely distinguishable from those of subjects: knight, king's counsellor, purveyor to the wardrobe, king's merchant.[111]

Like the demarcations between townsmen and strangers at the local level, the differences between "alien" or foreigner, king's subject or denizen, and town citizen, were neither stable nor clear cut. Letters patent issued by the king to alien merchants granted them commercial privileges enjoyed by native-born merchants and stated the rate at which to pay customs. These letters, "the forerunners of the letters patent of denization which conferred on aliens a limited kind of naturalization," gave the aliens the right to trade throughout the realm as the king's merchants and as denizens—or natives ("sicut indigene"). In the fourteenth century, though, "the distinction between naturalization by act of parliament and denization by letters patent, and the resulting distinction between a naturalized subject who has been admitted to practically all the rights of the native-born, and a denizen who has been admitted to certain rights only, cannot be drawn." Sometimes the king would declare that the alien should enjoy all the privileges of a citizen of London in the city and throughout the realm. But this privilege would be of little value in the city itself unless supplemented by a grant of "citizenship," which was technically wholly in the control of the towns. While the king, nobles, or influential persons might recommend persons for citizenship, cities could and sometimes did refuse to recognize alien merchants as denizens or accept them as citizens. (One historian thus argues that citizenship was most likely a "prelude to the grant of denization and that an alien was regarded as a denizen in the matter of customs and taxes only as long as he was a citizen or contributed to city taxation as such."[112] This seems compatible with the policy noted earlier that "Frenchmen" in scot and lot with a town would be treated as English.)

The privilege of a jury "made up half of their own countrymen, if enough could be found," had been practiced in London[113] and granted by the king to particular groups,[114] even before a 1303 royal charter made the practice universal.[115] The Carta Mercatoria of 1303 "secured to aliens the benefit of a jury composed wholly or in part of aliens."[116] A charter by Edward III (1328), appearing in an eighteenth-century collection of treaties between England and other powers, recites and confirms what may be the same charter from the thirty-first year of Edward I (1302–3). The latter, providing for the "protection and convenience of foreign merchants sojourning within the realm,"[117] declared that

in all pleas in which merchants are impleaded, *except in capital cases,* whether they be plaintiffs or defendants, half of the inquest shall consist of foreign merchants residing in the city or town, provided a sufficient number of them can be found, and the other half of good and lawful men of the place where the plea is held. But if six foreign merchants cannot be found there, then the number is to be made up of other merchants, and the remaining six are to be other good and sufficient men of the place.[118]

Although the legal provisions of the Carta Mercatoria generally "were concerned only with the treatment of foreigners in the local courts of fairs and towns and did not affect their position in the central courts,"[119] it appears that after the charter the privilege of a mixed jury was enforced in both local and central courts.[120] In 1309, a jury half of Lombard merchants and half of Boston men was summoned before the Barons of Exchequer at Westminster in an action of debt to inquire into a writing made by Richard of Chipping Norton, which Richard claimed he had been forced to sign while in prison.[121] In the same year, "24 as well merchants of the parts of Almain as of other alien merchants nearer" came before the king at Westminster to certify whether the Bishop of Utrecht or the king of Almain had temporal jurisdiction over the town of Groningen.[122] In 1320, according to Parliamentary rolls, Louvain merchants prayed that an action about some cloth be tried by a jury, twelve foreigners and twelve natives.[123] A king's writ in 1337[124] allowed a half German jury in a merchant's trial in 1340, and in an action of trespass against the peace in 1350.[125]

The idea of a special law for merchants or what, by the fifteenth century, was described as "the law of nature, which is called by some 'Law Merchant,' which is law universal throughout the world,"[126] seems to have originated in England, as on the Continent, in the customs of the towns: "Wherever a market or fair was held it had been customary from a very remote period that, when disputes arose as to the terms of a bargain, the questions at issue should be decided by four or five of the merchants present on the spot, who were expected to apply the principles and customs recognized as obtaining generally among the trading classes. This practice is referred to in a charter of Henry III [1216–72] as having prevailed from many years previously."[127]

The records of the fair court of St. Ives (whose rents on the whole went to the Abbott of Ramsey) refer to many mixed juries of merchants and nearby neighbors in cases arising during the fair. These cases range from mercantile matters to cases of assault (including "assault with vile words"), contempt, and trespass.[128] In several instances, no decision was reached because the attendance of merchants was too small.[129] One record mentions "all the merchants of the fair, both natives and foreigners, to whom judgements belong according to the law merchant."[130]

Every commercial European country had its own version of the law merchant, which was everywhere conceived as distinct from the ordinary law of the land.[131] While the law merchant differed in detail from place to place, it shared certain characteristics: it was customary and known to those who used it, its justice was prompt, and it was founded on notions of equity and of good faith among merchants.[132]

By the fifteenth century, "mixed merchant juries" were no longer composed half of natives and half of merchants from the foreign merchant's own country. Yet foreign merchants in England under the king's safe conduct still had their special law; they were "not bound to sue according to the law of the land, nor to abide the trial by twelve men and other solemnities of the law of the land, but shall sue in the Chancery and the matter shall be determined by the law of nature."[133]

Pollock and Maitland claim that this *lex mercatoria* consisted of "what would now be called rules of evidence, rules about the proof to be given of sales and other contracts, rules as to the legal value of the tally and the God's penny." They argue that it is "the law for a class of transactions," rather than the "law for a class of men."[134]

But although it may have become such a law, the early law merchant, the "*ius gentium* known to merchants throughout Christendom,"[135] was not simply a body of rules for commercial transactions. Rather, it was (as Maitland suggested elsewhere, in calling it "the private international law of the Middle Ages") "in its origin a personal law, the law of a special class."[136] It was a law based on the usages of the merchant class, administered by the merchants themselves, and not limited to particular issues.

Even when the merchant jury was not composed half of aliens from the foreign merchant's own country but of any merchants, such "mixed" juries embodied a principle of personal law. Insofar as the law merchant was based on the usages of a merchant class, administered by merchants, and not limited to particular issues, the law merchant was like the law of other communities. It was the custom of a community, known to the members of that community. When disputes or questions about what to do arose, those familiar with the customs of the disputant—if not familiar with the situation and the disputant himself (or herself)—were called upon to determine the matter.

3. Positive Law and Personal Law

What is one to make of the mixed jury? Some may argue for understanding the privilege of a mixed jury as a "political" favor, granted by those with less power to those who in some way have the upper hand. That is no doubt an explanation of *how* the royal privilege comes about, an explanation of its cause or origin. But understanding the mixed jury this way alone denies the significance of a conception of law that at one time "attached" to the person as a member of a community (or class) in England as on the Continent—in the same way as understanding a text solely through an author's intention to make a living impoverishes language.

The mixed jury epitomizes the principle, accompanying the multitude of customs and courts in England in the Middle Ages, of personal law: the judgment of a person must be according to the law or customs of that person's community; such judgment must be by those with knowledge of those customs or—what amounts to the same thing—by those who share in those customs and belong to the same community. In early England, conflicts occurred. When they did so, as anywhere else, a variety of strategies might address, avoid, or resolve such conflicts. Mixed juries in local courts, in cases involving Jews and Christians, and in early merchant cases, addressed conflicts which involved the members of two communities, and the truths they declared were law. In the practice of allowing each community to participate and to speak its truth and hence the law, lay an implicit notion of personal law. Although cases in central courts involving the later law merchant in some sense represent the law of but one community, both that law and the practice of allowing Jews their own law in cases among themselves also point to a respect for the law of the other. Thus, although, in England, Kentish and other law could not be carried into neighboring regions "in the same way" (in Maitland's words) as the laws of the European nations on the Continent, the English, by the eleventh century, and throughout the twelfth and thirteenth, recognized the laws of others in their own way.

That historians and writers concerned with conflict of laws and with the mixed jury have seemingly dismissed the community-based and personal-law implications of the practice of mixed juries raises questions about their understanding of law, an understanding that grounds law in the strength of a unifying territorial power. What has led students of Anglo-American law to neglect the practice of the mixed jury and even to ignore the presence of mixed juries before the fourteenth century?

The chapters that follow suggest that the answers to these questions lie not so much in the history of the mixed jury as in the legal positivism of its modern interpreters. That is, modern texts about juries, as we shall see in chapters 2 and 3, reveal a particular understanding of law as doctrine and as official behavior, which denies to practice or custom the status of law. H. L. A. Hart's *The Concept of Law,* discussed in chapter 4, articulates theoretically the particular understanding of law found in modern legal and social scientific texts about juries. These texts presume, even when they do not make explicit as Hart does, a legal system of a particular sort.

Both those who consider the 1353 Statute of the Staple to be the origin or source of the law of the mixed jury, and those who fail to consider as law the respect for the customs of others embodied in the practice of the mixed jury, assume a positivist outlook on law. For them, law begins, as Hart puts it, with "the mere reduction to writing of hitherto unwritten rules," and the crucial step "from the pre-legal to the legal" is "the acknowledgement of reference to the writing or inscription as *authoritative,* i.e. as the *proper* way of disposing of doubts as to the existence of the rule." For them, the story of English law is the story of the common law, of the rise of the law of the officials, of official doctrine.

But there is another tale to be told, in which more is at stake than simply the matter of properly understanding the mixed jury. Its main point is not that particular views of the mixed jury are historically inaccurate. Nor indeed is it that we should or could strive for a return to the early mixed jury, whose justice was admittedly often brutal and harsh. The point, rather, concerns the way we think about law. Attributing "law" only to the authoritative declarations of officials or perceiving the mixed jury solely as the privilege of politically (or physically or economically) powerful or useful groups, treats law simply as *deriving* from powerful sources. It loses sight of an important aspect of law—namely, the justice that accompanies respect for the other—which, insofar as we are all legal positivists, we are in danger of forgetting.

Hitherto neglected mixed jury references suggest that when two communities met, law emerged from both their practices. In the gathering of the members of two communities jointly to speak the truth of both communities lay the essence of the practice and tradition of the mixed jury.

With communities' encounters with the king and the law of the state, the *history* of the official *doctrine* of the mixed jury, as distinct from the *tradition* of its *practice,* began. Rather than the traditional merging of two laws, the state (like the church before it) gradually declared itself the *source* of law, and, as it did so, the unity of tradition and practice broke apart. (That is, tradition is unified with practice in customary law; the introduction of a "source" of law distinct from law points to the emergence of history, in which the customary unity of tradition and practice ruptures. Both history and law become propositional. And history provides an account or documentation of two things that are conceptually distinct from law: a chronology of authoritative declarations by the sources of law in the past and a story of the transformation of law from practice to proposition.) The history of the mixed jury is thus the story of the disappearance of the traditional practice of the mixed jury.

Indeed, what else could a history of the mixed jury be, given its sources, the records of law, than the story of the rise of official law and the decline of practice? What can legal history be other than the history of its sources? And what can legal sources be other than the declarations of officials? The remainder of this work dwells on the ambiguities contained in the "what else" of these questions—on the seemingly simultaneous insistence that history could not have occurred any other way and that one is about to discover another possibility.

2   The Modern American Jury

Recently, at Cambridge, a statistical laboratory has for the first time been established. Something of this kind is perhaps destined to become the symbol of modern justice in the place of a simple pair of scales.—David Daube (1951)[1]

Although mixed juries no longer exist as such, jury mix remains an issue in the United States' law of jury selection. In judicial opinions and law reviews two concerns organize the discussion about who serves on a jury. Those concerns—for an "impartial" jury and for a jury "of one's peers"—occur within the context of broader considerations of American "pluralism," a pluralism that is very different from the heterogeneity of communities, customs, and courts that characterized early England.

Just as references to the early mixed jury suggested particular conceptions of community, law, and knowledge, so too do contemporary legal texts point to modern conceptions thereof. The "other" who emerges from such texts is not the foreigner or the alien, but the nonwhite, or occasionally non-male, who is identifiable by the statistically reliable indicators of race and sex. The community is a population, of which the jury is a "representative cross-section," and the jury's verdict, based on evidence as to the facts, affirms or nullifies the law—of the judges. The knowledge that informs this understanding of the jury and the accompanying procedural approach to jury mix comes, whether or not explicitly acknowledged by judges and commentators, from the science of the state: statistics. Indeed, even those who today address jury mix as a matter of substantive composition share, with their procedural counterparts, particular presuppositions about the nature of community, law, and knowledge that will be characterized (only preliminarily in this chapter) as "social scientific."

A note on sources and method: this chapter treats judicial opinions and the commentaries on these opinions that appear in law journals and casebooks, as "data" to be analyzed for their presentation of particular matters. Quotation of opinions and conclusions does not imply agreement with or acceptance of particular arguments; neither is it an objection to use of such material that some of the texts presented—especially those calling for sub-

28

stantive composition of juries—do not reflect the attitudes of judges or others in the profession of law. For the concern here is neither to propose policies nor to characterize the attitudes of the legal profession as such. Rather it is to uncover the understanding of community revealed in legal discussion of jury mix. For legal professionals, jury mix is not a meaningful issue; rather, three distinct constitutional doctrines are considered relevant: the "fair cross-section" and the "impartiality" requirements of the Sixth Amendment, and the "equal protection" requirement of the Fourteenth Amendment. What follows, clearly, must deal with such doctrines; it is not organized around them, however, since the purpose is neither to describe the law as judges and lawyers see it nor to suggest the direction that interpretations of doctrines should take. What emerges are the conceptions of law and community that underlie the writings of both mainstream legal writers and their critics.

1. A Representative Cross-Section of the Population

The Sixth Amendment of the Constitution provides for the right to an impartial jury: "In all criminal prosecutions, the accused shall enjoy the right to a speedy and public trial, by an impartial jury of the State and district wherein the crime shall have been committed, which district shall have been previously ascertained by law." When passed in 1791, the Sixth Amendment, like the rest of the Bill of Rights, applied to persons' relations to the federal government. For some time after its passage, individual states governed their own citizens according to state law. Then during the nineteenth century, national citizenship emerged. The Fourteenth Amendment, passed in 1868 to protect the newly won civil rights of blacks, extended citizenship to American-born blacks by defining citizenship as belonging to "persons born or naturalized in the United States," rather than by identifying it, as had previously been the case, with citizenship in a state. The Fourteenth Amendment forbade the states from making or enforcing any law "which shall abridge the privileges or immunities of citizens of the United States," from depriving "any person of life, liberty or property, without due process of law," or from denying "to any person within its jurisdiction the equal protection of the laws."

Eventually *Duncan v. Louisiana* (1968) "incorporated" the Sixth Amendment right to an impartial jury into the Fourteenth Amendment; that is, it made the Sixth Amendment applicable to the states through the Fourteenth Amendment.[2] Since *Duncan,* state and federal courts have increasingly, although not exclusively, interpreted the impartiality clause of the Sixth

Amendment to require the selection of a fair cross-section of the community for criminal juries. The final jurors, but not the venire or panel, must also be "impartial" in the sense of willing to put aside biases and abide by the law. And, in the context of jury selection as well as elsewhere, when the state takes action—whether through a judge, jury commissioner, prosecuting attorney, or other official—it must comply with the Fourteenth Amendment's "Equal Protection Clause" that prohibits discrimination against a disparate minority on account of race, sex, and so forth. This chapter explores the representative cross-section that is the modern jury and considers the conceptions of community and law it implies.

Pluralism seems to make it impossible to require a jury to be composed of a strict cross-section of the population:

> We have never held that the Sixth Amendment requires that "petit juries actually chosen must mirror the community and reflect the various distinctive groups in the population." Indeed, it would be impossible to apply a concept of proportional representation to the petit jury in view of the heterogeneous nature of our society. [Citations omitted][3]

Similarly, the pluralism of American society seems to make it impossible to guarantee the defendant a jury of peers, except in the sense of formal legal equals. Courts have declared that jurors must be the "peer(s) or equal(s) of the person whose rights it (the jury) is selected or summoned to determine; that is, of his neighbors, fellows, associates, persons having the same legal status in society as that which he holds."[4] Yet despite the language of "neighbors, fellows, and associates," one's peers, in court, are ultimately those of "the same legal status."[5]

Thus courts prohibit the *exclusion* of particular groups from certain stages of jury selection, but they have never required anyone's *inclusion*—whether as a peer, or as a representative of all or part of the community—on any particular petit jury. The Supreme Court has declared that "the number of our races and nationalities stands in the way of evolution of . . . a conception of . . . equal protection" that demands the defendant's right to a "petit jury composed in whole or in part of persons of his own race" (or nationality).[6] Or, again: "It is simply not possible to define jury impartiality, for constitutional purposes, by reference to some hypothetical mix of individual viewpoints. Prospective jurors come from many different backgrounds, and have many different attitudes and predispositions."[7]

How then do courts and commentators understand a "fair cross-section of the community"? The discussion that follows suggests that, in the context of criminal juries, "a fair cross-section of the community" refers in large part to a *method* of selecting jurors that is best described as "statistical." Recent developments at all stages of jury selection reveal the pervasiveness of the statistical approach in reasoning about the jury.

Jury selection occurs in several stages. After determining who is eligible for jury duty, officials compile the names onto a master list from which to draw potential jurors' names. Officials then notify and summon potential jurors to come to court, where those whom the judge does not excuse form a *venire*. The venire is usually divided into "panels" of twenty-four or so. Only one panel at a time is sent to a courtroom. Then, at *voir dire,* judges or lawyers ask questions of these potential jurors to select the petit jury. The lawyers may challenge potential jurors either for cause, in which case a reason must be given, or peremptorily, in which case—until *Batson v. Kentucky,* described below—no reason need be stated. In the last twenty years, all stages of jury selection have come under attack, in ways that help reveal the contemporary understanding of the "fair cross-section of the community" that is the jury.

Before 1975, the "cross-section" terminology had been used in a few non-Sixth Amendment cases about juries.[8] In 1940, the Supreme Court of the United States had held that the exclusion of blacks from juries violated the Equal Protection Clause of the Fourteenth Amendment by preventing juries from being "truly representative of the community."[9] In 1941, the same Court, acting in its capacity as supervisor of the federal courts, denied a defendant's claim that because female jurors' names had been gathered only from a League of Women Voters's list, his jury had not been selected from a fair cross-section of the community. Although the Court found that the defendant had not proved his allegations, it reiterated the idea of the jury as a cross-section of the community.[10]

In 1975, in *Taylor v. Louisiana,*[11] the Court first used the "cross-section" terminology in the context of the Sixth Amendment right to an impartial trial. *Taylor* concerned the jury pool and venire. It extended the 1968 *Duncan v. Louisiana* holding that the Sixth Amendment must apply to the states through the Fourteenth Amendment.[12] The Court in *Taylor* held that "the presence of a fair cross-section of the community on venires, panels, or lists from which petit juries are drawn is essential to the fulfillment of the Sixth Amendment's guarantee of an impartial jury trial in criminal prosecutions."[13]

Since *Taylor,* the phrase has blossomed into a full-blown standard. In 1979, the Supreme Court announced what commentators take to be a three-part "test" for establishing the elements of a prima facie violation of the Sixth and Fourteenth Amendments.[14] The *Duren* test, as it is called, ties[15] the Sixth

Amendment requirement of an impartial jury to what law review writers have dubbed "cross-sectionality"[16] or "cross-sectionalism."[17] It ushers Sixth Amendment jurisprudence, like that of discrimination law, into the age of social science, demography, and statistics.

Under *Duren,* an appellant contesting the composition of a jury must show three things: (1) that the group which was excluded from the jury is "distinctive"; (2) that the group is underrepresented on the venire relative to its representation in the community; and (3) that the underrepresentation is the result of systematic exclusion in the jury-selection process.[18] *Duren* does not establish that the venire, much less the petit jury, must represent a cross-section of the community, but rather that the selection of venire members must be random.

Various refinements of and controversies about the *Duren* test for establishing a prima facie case of violations of the Sixth and Fourteenth Amendments have occurred. Questions include: What constitutes a "distinctive" group? What is the appropriate community against which to compare representation on the venire? Is the underrepresentation to be computed comparatively or absolutely?[19] Can systematic exclusion be shown through statistics? And, could the *Duren* test for a prima facie violation apply to the final stage of jury selection, or to the petit jury itself? All of these questions and their proposed answers provide rich material for analyses of modern conceptions of community and law. The analysis below touches on discussions of most of these issues in passing, but focuses on discussion of the last—the extension of the cross-section requirement to the petit jury itself.

Courts have certainly not extended *Duren*'s cross-section requirement or the notion of purely random selection to the jury itself, nor have they required randomness at the stage of voir dire. Indeed, the Court has explicitly stated that the cross-section requirement of the Sixth Amendment cannot be interpreted to prohibit peremptory challenges, which, as discussed below, some consider to be the major obstacle to random selection.[20] Further, there is no indication that courts would ever require the *composition* of any particular jury to reflect the composition of the population. Yet the courts' approach to the jury can still be characterized as "statistical." For, as every statistician knows, a normal distribution, or a perfectly representative sample, is the ideal average of many random samples of a population and is not to be expected in any particular randomly drawn sample—or on any particular petit jury. Accordingly, the cross-section requirement does not mandate a perfectly representative jury in any given case; it requires only a sampling *process,* or a jury selection *procedure,* that is reliable. The judicially constructed *Duren* test for determining constitutional violations at the first stages of jury selection is *compatible with* (although of course it does not require) the extension of statistical cross-sectionality to the final stage of jury selection, the selection of the petit jury, since neither *Duren* nor the statistical method requires that juries be composed in any particular way.

Consider statistical method: it requires one to draw samples in investigations, social scientific or otherwise, where one cannot gather data on every member of a population. Obtaining significant results requires reliable sampling methods and the avoidance of skewed samples.

To be reliable, the pool from which to sample must approximate the population. In recent years, legislatures have increasingly required the expansion of the pool of potential jurors beyond the traditional voter registration lists to driver registration lists, tax rolls, and so forth.[21] The California Court took the lead when it interpreted the second prong of the *Duren* test for establishing a prima facie case of violation of the Sixth and Fourteenth Amendments in *People v. Harris.* It declared that reliance on a voter registration list in Long Beach resulted in underrepresentation of blacks and Hispanics on the venire in comparison to their numbers in Los Angeles County's population.[22]

A sample must also be randomly drawn: every item in the population must have an equal probability of being selected, and each must be selected independently of the selection of any other particular item. In the 1960s and 1970s, blue-ribbon juries, appointed by special commissions, were abolished. The 1970s also brought efforts to restrict judges' discretion to excuse potential jurors before voir dire and to limit possible excuses.[23]

Further, to obtain significant results, the sample must be large enough. In the 1970s considerable debate about jury size followed passage of several state laws allowing juries of fewer than twelve. The Supreme Court, ruling on the constitutionality of these smaller juries, turned to an evaluation of social science research. Finding "no evidence that the reliability of jury verdicts diminished with six-member panels," it held six- member juries to be constitutional.[24] A few years later, it declared five-member juries *un*constitutional, again using "recent empirical data": "The data now raise doubts about the accuracy of the results achieved by smaller and smaller panels. Statistical studies suggest that the risk of convicting an innocent person (Type I error) rises as the size of the jury diminishes. Because the risk of not convicting a guilty person (Type II error) increases with the size of the panel, an optimal jury size can be selected as a function of the interaction between the two risks."[25]

In the face of the concern just described to ensure the reliability of jury selection, the practice of peremptory challenges not surprisingly appears problematic. Critics of challenges claim that peremptory challenges (and sometimes challenges for cause) distort the randomness of the panel. Such critics attack voir dire for the biases that they allege it introduces into the process. They propose limiting or even abolishing one or both parties' peremptory challenges.[26]

A line of cases from the state courts represents the vanguard of an attack on voir dire from the direction of purely random cross-sectionality. First among these cases was California's 1978 *People v. Wheeler.* Drawing on the state constitution, *Wheeler* presents what one commentator calls "an elusive dichotomy" between "group" and "specific" bias. Peremptory challenges are to be permitted against the latter, but "group" bias that arises from something other than personal experience is to be tolerated as essential to the "demographic balance" necessary "to achieve an overall impartiality."[27] (The California decision anticipated a Second Circuit modification of the third prong of the *Duren* test for Sixth Amendment claims, the requirement that underrepresentation result from systematic exclusion. In *McCray v. Abrams,* the Second Circuit used a single instance of abuse of discretion to find "systematic exclusion."[28] Several state courts[29] have also followed California's lead.)

More recently, the Supreme Court too has restricted the use of peremptory challenges along lines compatible with a statistical model. In *Batson v. Kentucky* (1986), it "overturned" a long-time favorite target of the law reviews, *Swain v. Alabama* (1965). The defendant-petitioner in *Swain* had claimed that the prosecutor's use of peremptory challenges against all six blacks on the venire violated the Equal Protection Clause of the Fourteenth Amendment. The Court was unwilling to recognize a prima facie case of discrimination without a showing that the prosecutor "in case after case, whatever the circumstances, whatever the crime and whoever the defendant or the victim may be, is responsible for the removal of Negroes who have been selected as qualified jurors by the jury commissioners and who have survived challenges for cause, with the result that no Negroes ever serve on petit juries."[30]

Lower courts' interpretation of *Swain*'s "systematic exclusion" standard, according to commentators, represented an "insurmountable obstacle" to defendants seeking to challenge prosecutorial exercise of peremptories: "No federal court in the decade following *Swain,* in spite of frequent claims of discrimination, found a violation under the standard. The difficulties which defendants and courts have encountered stem in part from the nature of the peremptory and the proof required. Few jurisdictions maintain comprehensive records of peremptory challenges, and it is difficult if not impossible for defendants to establish evidence of systematic exclusion by the prosecutor."[31]

In *Batson,* however, the Court reversed and remanded the conviction of a black man by a jury from which the prosecutor had peremptorily challenged all blacks. The petitioner sought to establish violations of both Sixth and Fourteenth Amendment rights "to an impartial jury and a jury drawn from a cross-section of the community," apparently to avoid asking directly for reconsideration of *Swain (Batson,* 1732, Burger dissent citing Pet. for Cert. i). The Court "express[ed] no view on the merits of any of petitioner's Sixth Amendment arguments" (1716, n. 4), holding instead that racial discrimination in this case indeed violated the Fourteenth Amendment's Equal Protection Clause and that to the extent that a prima facie case under *Swain* required discrimination over a number of cases it was overruled:

> Although a prosecutor is entitled to exercise permitted peremptory challenges "for any reason at all, as long as that reason is related to his view concerning the outcome" of the case to be tried, the Equal Protection Clause forbids the prosecutor to challenge potential jurors solely on the assumption that black jurors as a group will be unable impartially to consider the State's case against a black defendant. (1718–19, citations omitted)

Although *Swain* had been interpreted as requiring "proof of repeated striking of blacks over a number of cases," the "crippling burden of proof" this placed on defendants led the Court to "reject this evidentiary formulation as inconsistent with standards that have developed since *Swain* for assessing a prima facie case under the Equal Protection Clause" (1721).

The Court turned to the "disparate treatment" cases of Title VII[32] to articulate a new test for establishing a prima facie case that may rely "solely on evidence concerning the prosecutor's exercise of peremptory challenges at the defendant's trial" (1722–23). The defendant must show that "he is a member of a cognizable racial group and that the prosecutor has exercised peremptory challenges to remove from the venire members of the defendant's race." Then, rather than having to show systematic exclusion of the group over time, the defendant may rely on "the fact, as to which there can be no dispute, that peremptory challenges constitute a jury selection practice that permits 'those to discriminate who are of a mind to discriminate'" (1723). The defendant must then show that these and other facts raise an inference that the prosecutor excluded veniremembers from the petit jury on account of their race.[33] The burden then shifts to the prosecutor to "articulate a neutral explanation" for challenging black jurors. The explanation "need not rise to the level justifying exercise of a challenge for cause," but mere denial of discriminatory motive or affirmation of good faith is insufficient (1723).

At first, *Batson v. Kentucky* may appear to move toward a more substantive approach to jury composition (a substantive or nonrandom cross-section as opposed to a statistical cross-section), in that it seems to mandate, in a particular case, the inclusion of particular members of the venire. But this is not so. *Batson* has shifted the focus of analysis from the randomness of the sampling process over time (*Swain*) to the randomness of the sampling process at a particular stage (*Batson*). The randomness of the selection process has been extended somewhat from the first stages (*Duren*) into the final stage of jury selection, but there are still no formulas as to the ultimate composition of the petit jury (whether in relation to the venire, the pool, or the population), and peremptory challenges and challenges for cause are still allowed.

A distinction between two types of "impartiality" helps show how the justification *for* peremptory challenges, like the critique of peremptory challenges, is also framed in terms compatible with the procedural concerns of a statistical model of the jury. "Cross-sectional" or *jury* impartiality concerns the *process* of jury selection. "Individual" or "psychological" *juror* impartiality, or even "juror indifference," as it is sometimes called, concerns the jurors on the ultimate petit jury. It refers to "jurors who will conscientiously apply the law and find the facts,"[34] and it is juror impartiality to which the Court refers when it declares that "the Constitution presupposes that a jury selected from a fair cross section of the community is impartial, regardless of the mix of individual viewpoints actually represented on the jury, so long as the jurors can conscientiously and properly carry out their sworn duty to apply the law to the facts of the particular case."[35]

Juror impartiality ostensibly lends support to an argument in favor of challenges: "Whenever counsel either establishes juror partiality or suspects partiality and exercises a peremptory challenge . . . the ideal of citizen participation in justice yields to the more fundamental ideal of juror indifference, and the goal of systemic impartiality gives way to the notion of individual impartiality."[36] Even as the impartiality of individual juror indifference seems to provide a reason for peremptory challenges, though, such challenges threaten the first kind of impartiality that calls for random selection of the jury.

Both sorts of impartiality thus suggest positions, one against and one for peremptory challenges, compatible with and indeed reflecting current controversy over statistical method. For in statistical studies, aberrations or "outliers" may be thought to skew the results for any given sample. Statisticians sometimes ignore these outliers by taking them out of their samples, a practice that yet other statisticians consider highly questionable. Challenges, whether peremptory or for cause, to continue the statistical analogy, might be thought to allow the removal of "outliers"—independent thinkers or jurors with knowledge independent of what is presented at trial—from the jury. (Challenges for cause may be based on findings of actual or implied bias. Actual bias requires a finding of prejudiced state of mind; implied bias may be presumed from the existence of certain relationships or interests of the prospective jurors. Examples include a relationship to a party or service on a jury that tried another person for the same offense.) Thus although challenges interfere with the randomness of the jury, restricting peremptory challenges or making them more like challenges for cause—as *Batson* and its progeny do—allows, in the language of statistics, the sifting of "outliers" believed to skew results. As *Swain* observed: "The function of the challenge is not only to eliminate extremes of partiality on both sides, but to assure the parties that the jurors before whom they try the case will decide on the basis of the evidence placed before them, and not otherwise."[37] Maintaining "neutrality" or guaranteeing the absence of independent or substantive jury knowledge is thus given as a justification for the apparent nonrandom institution of challenges. In this sense voir dire appears compatible with the concern for selection procedure that characterizes the statistical model of an impartial jury.

The particular justification for voir dire just described requires that jurors *not* have particular knowledge or biases. It does not require jurors to have alternative substantive or affirmative knowledge (as do arguments that address the substantive composition of a jury of peers, discussed in section 2). Both the argument against voir dire (that challenges skew the randomness of the sample) and the argument for voir dire (that challenges remove outliers who would otherwise skew the sample) are procedural and concern the selection of jurors bereft of relevant knowledge. Justice Burger's opinion, favoring the statistical cross-section model in regard to the first two stages of jury selection but objecting to its extension to voir dire, exemplifies the view that jurors are not to bring their own insights or "concerns" to bear on a case. In his dissent in *Batson,* Burger writes, in favor of peremptory challenges: "To suggest that a particular race is unfit to judge in any case necessarily is racially insulting. To suggest that each race may have its own special concerns, or even may tend to favor its own, is not" (1736).

To the extent that *Batson* limited itself to claims by a defendant that members of *that defendant's race* ("his race" to the Court) had been excluded, the majority opinion seemed also to identify "defendant's interests" with the defendant's own race.[38] At the same time, though, the Court's position, again like Burger's dissent, does not follow a substantive "peers" approach. The decisions that follow *Batson* have extended the right to bring equal protection claims for discriminatory use of peremptory challenges not only to prosecutors, who may challenge white criminal defendants' exclusion of black jurors, but also to white criminal defendants who may challenge the exclusion of black jurors by prosecutors.[39] In these cases the "interests" of defendant and prosecutor justify their standing to bring equal protection claims on behalf of the "interests" of excluded jurors. As in these cases, the *Batson* Court does not take a defendant's racial-group members to be the members of the defendant's "community." Rather, the Court's concern is with ensuring the nonexclusion of prospective jurors because of the "harm" such exclusion may cause to the "interests" of jurors, defendant, and even the state.

The types of arguments expressed in the *Batson* opinions render traditional arguments about the jury increasingly tangential to modern formulations of the issue of jury mix. Rather than discussing whether the jurors are the defendant's peers or whether the community as a whole has been represented, the Court, although it does not say it in so many words, treats the matter of jury mix as a problem of statistical selection and ultimately of perceptions of interest representation. Closer examination of Justice Marshall's concurring opinion and Justice Rehnquist's dissent in *Batson* makes this startlingly clear.

Marshall argues that the majority opinion does not go far enough, and that peremptory challenges should be abolished outright so that neither party has the opportunity to discriminate racially. Marshall nowhere makes explicit his conception of the jury, nor does he discuss the interests of either the defendant or the community. Presumably he sees the randomly selected jury as in the "interests" of both; certainly he never presents the peremptory challenge as functioning to eliminate biased individuals. (Some may argue that since *Batson* was decided on Fourteenth rather than Sixth Amendment grounds, there would be no reason to address such points. But simply that the Court need express "no view" of Sixth Amendment issues in a case challenging the impartiality of a jury supports the overall point that traditional ways of framing controversy about the fairness of a jury are becoming obsolete.)

Even the *Batson* dissents are compatible with the statistical model, and can be framed in its terms. Rehnquist, for instance, argues that

there is simply nothing "unequal" about the State using its peremptory challenges to strike blacks from the jury in cases involving black defendants, so long as such challenges are also used to exclude whites in cases involving white defendants, Hispanics in cases involving Hispanic defendants, Asians in cases involving Asian defendants, and so on. . . . As long as [case-specific use of peremptory challenges] are applied across the board to jurors of all races and nationalities, I do not see—and the Court most certainly has not explained—how their use violate the Equal Protection Clause. (1744–45)

Rehnquist maintains, in effect, that when the same (or parallel) error occurs in every sample, the samples are consistent. Rehnquist's view of equal protection has been characterized as "procedural" because it requires one defendant to be treated the same as all other defendants. But if one thinks in terms of the statistical model, the *Batson* majority's view is also procedural. The disagreement between Rehnquist and the *Batson* majority concerns whether law is more concerned with consistency across samples or with the accurate representativeness, that is, procedural fairness in selection, of any given sample.

Relying on *Swain*, Rehnquist accepts the legitimacy of treating the individual as an undifferentiated member of a group: "Hence veniremen are not always judged solely as individuals for the purpose of exercising peremptory challenges. Rather they are challenged in light of the limited knowledge counsel has of them, *which may include their group affiliations,* in the context of the case to be tried" (1743, citing *Swain*). The *Batson* majority and the California *Wheeler* court, on the other hand, affirm the distinctiveness of individuals (and of individual bias) and reject treatment of individuals, at voir dire, that is based on group affiliation. But group affiliation is part of the individual's identity, and, ironically, the Court must first turn to an analysis of the "cognizable" or "distinctive" group to which an individual belongs, before determining whether such affiliation was wrongly considered at voir dire.

One way of understanding the disagreement between the *Batson* majority and Rehnquist, then, is as a disagreement about how to treat difference. The majority takes seriously the claim of the black defendant that he, and his race, have been treated differently, and that that difference cannot be ignored. The Court attempts to compensate for past errors in the system, where it knows those errors were most likely. In doing so, it highlights and furthers difference in the name of equality.

Rehnquist, on the other hand, takes seriously the claim that members of any group should be treated the same as one another, even if this means failing to distinguish—and at times distinguishing in order to make a point of failing to distinguish—among individuals on the basis of group membership. According to his critics, he thus compounds the effect of inequities that have come before.

Both sides thus appear caught in a double bind. Both associate difference, or otherness, with inequality, and sameness with equality, and, despite disagreement about whether peremptory challenges should be allowed, both sides share a concern with promoting equality, as they define it. Rehnquist, as mentioned above, wrote that there was nothing unequal about the State's use of peremptory challenges against blacks in black trials so long as the State also challenged whites in white cases, and so forth. The *Batson* majority, citing *Strauder,* writes: "Discrimination within the judicial system is most pernicious because it is a 'stimulant to that race prejudice which is an impediment to securing to [black citizens] that equal justice which the law aims to secure to all others'" (1718).

Both sides also share a concern for procedural regularity. So far, this concern has been referred to as "statistical." But there is another aspect of this concern that "statistics," unless conceived more broadly as a science of government or of the state, does not capture. That is, for both sides, public confidence in the system accompanies procedural regularity. The majority writes: "The harm from discriminatory jury selection extends beyond that inflicted on the defendant and the excluded juror to touch the entire community. Selection procedures that purposefully exclude black persons from juries undermine public confidence in the fairness of our system of justice" (1718, citations omitted).

Burger's dissenting opinion, in which Rehnquist concurs, declares that, on the contrary, "today's holding will produce juries that the parties do not believe are truly impartial. This will surely do more than 'disconcert' litigants; it will diminish confidence in the jury system" (1740). Public confidence in the system also lies at the heart of Burger's defense of peremptory challenges. He cites one commentator who claims that peremptory challenges "avoid trafficking in the core of truth in most common stereotypes." Yet, the commentator continues:

Common human experience, common sense, psychosociological studies, and public opinion polls tell us that it is likely that certain classes of people statistically have predispositions that would make them inappropriate jurors for particular kinds of cases. But to allow this knowledge to be expressed in the evaluative terms necessary for challenges for cause would undercut our desire for a society in which all people are judged as individuals and in which each is held reasonable and open to compromise. . . .

Although experience reveals that black males as a class can be biased against young alienated blacks who have not tried to join the middle class, to enunciate this in the concrete expression required of a challenge for cause is societally divisive. Instead we have evolved in the peremptory challenge a system that allows the covert expression of what we dare not say but know is true more often than not.[40]

The concern with avoiding "societal division" and promoting "public confidence" recurs in the cases expanding the *Batson* holding.[41] More striking, however, it also appears in the arguments of those who favor a more substantive approach to the issue of jury mix than that expressed on all sides in *Batson*. That substantive approach views the jury as a jury "of peers," transforming the issue of jury mix from the negative procedural question, "Has the process not excluded any part of the population?" to an affirmative one about the composition of the jury. It is to that approach that this chapter now turns.

2. Jurors as "Peers": Nonrandom Identification and Selection

The negative procedural question of jury mix, "Has the process not excluded any part of the population?" that characterizes courts' approaches to jury impartiality, creates something of a quandary, no less real for having been pointed out many times.[42] How is one to identify parts of a population without differentiating between what are formally recognized only as equals? As one writer suggests: "The goal of a jury from which blacks have not been systematically excluded (particularly a petit jury . . .) assumes that either the presence of blacks or their nonintentional exclusion will bring about a 'fair' jury, i.e., one not tainted by racism. But does not the mere statement of the proposition serve to refute it?"[43]

For Sixth Amendment claims, the problem of group identification is raised by the first prong of the *Duren* test, which requires that those excluded from the jury belong to a distinctive group. Although the Court elsewhere defined cognizability in terms of whether a group had been singled out for distinctive treatment in the past, more recent formulations are "less colored by the orientation of equal protection," according to one commentator.[44] Under these formulations, group claims based on race, sex, national origin, religion, and economic status, have been upheld (although not necessarily in the context of jury discrimination).[45]

For Fourteenth Amendment claims, *Batson*'s first requirement for establishing a prima facie violation is now taken to mean that the excluded jurors are members of a "cognizable racial group." *Batson* restricts itself to race, although equal protection principles in non-jury-related cases accord various levels of protection for group membership based on sex, religious or political affiliation, mental capacity, number of children, living arrangements, employment in a particular industry, or profession. At least some courts and commentators have begun to consider the possibility of gender-related *Batson* challenges.[46]

If members of groups for whom it matters (for equal protection or other reasons) that they have been excluded from a jury can be identified, then why not include them? Such a question is seldom raised in court, so accepted is the reasoning mentioned at the beginning of this chapter: the United States' pluralistic nature (and the size of the jury) as well as the statistical approach to jury selection preclude such affirmative inclusion.

A few commentators, however, do address the issue of jury mix as a matter of substantive jury composition. Their proposals, rather than relying on the fairness generated by the random sampling of statistical selection, generally require some affirmative selection of jurors. They support their views by appealing to a conception of the jury as the peers of the defendant. An examination of their proposals reveals that they hold a peculiarly modern conception of peers or of fellow-community members; "peers," for them, refers not only to the formal legal equals of the proceduralists, but also to individuals belonging to the same race.

"The all Black jury" that is "one item of the Black power programme" makes this understanding of community membership or group identity clear. The entire "Black" population serves as the pool for the all-Black jury of peers. As a separatist movement, the Black power program, however, does not concern itself with "mixed" juries.[47]

For other commentators representing the substantive approach to jury mix that is characterized by the desire to include members of particular groups on the jury, race is also the identifier of "community." But even in these proposals for mixed juries, the presence of racial minorities on juries is expressed less in terms of the coexistence and acknowledgment of two communities (the black and the white communities, for instance), than in terms of the appearance or representation on the jury of the various interests or viewpoints that race signifies.[48] Like those who treat jury mix as a procedural issue of nonexclusion, those concerned with the "mandatory inclusion of racial minorities on jury panels" view race as a factor or variable that marks out differences in population. Race (like gender) serves as a demographic identifier; it does not point to the existence of an "other" culture or community, which is, in an important sense, the "same." That is, on the early mixed jury, the shared law of a community linked alien parties and alien jurors; today, the few supporters of mixed juries seldom treat the connection between defendants and jurors as more than a demographic one.

Further, like arguments framed in terms of jury selection, arguments about the substantive composition of juries again express the need to foster public confidence in the trial process. When modern proposals or laws seek to transcend the empirical nature of demographic categories (as in the Court's definition of a legally cognizable group as one that displays distinctive "qualities of human nature and varieties of human experience" or a unique perspective on events),[49] their articulation serves only to identify the group in question as a part of a larger human population whose participation is required to maintain the legitimacy of the system. No one today proposes seriously that mixed juries be comprised of equal numbers of members from two communities, or even from two races.[50]

Two articles proposing a substantive approach to the issue of jury mix illustrate these points. In the first, "Black Innocence and the White Jury," Sheri Lynn Johnson suggests that "a reasonable compromise between expediency and effectiveness is to assure the defendant three racially similar jurors."[51] While she acknowledges that the "historically split" jury of half and half would be preferable, she argues that the difficulty in obtaining six jurors of the defendant's race in some areas, and the incentive this would provide for states to go to smaller juries ("a change generally deemed undesirable"), make such a jury impractical. At the same time, she claims, "jury dynamics research shows that a single dissenting juror virtually never succeeds in hanging a jury, let alone reversing its predisposition." So, since "laboratory and field studies show that without a minority of at least three jurors, group pressure is simply too overwhelming," to Johnson the "findings suggest" that three is a "reasonable compromise" ("Black Innocence," 1698–99).

Johnson raises the issue of mandatory inclusion of racial minorities on jury panels because "a large body of social science research . . . reveals a widespread tendency among whites to convict black defendants in instances in which white defendants would be acquitted" (1611). The purpose of the "mixed" jury is thus to protect minority defendants from racial bias, a justification which the author also attributes to the English and African practice of the mixed jury: "Several African countries, mindful of the realities of racial prejudice, have recognized some variation of this right. For analogous reasons, English law for a time provided alien defendants with juries composed of six aliens and six citizens."[52]

According to Johnson, the "right to racially similar" jurors is to be accorded to blacks and, "although the empirical evidence concerning prejudice against Native Americans and Hispanics is less extensive," to Native Americans and Hispanics. "'White' defendants should be granted a reciprocal right to some 'white' jurors because the mock jury studies show that black jurors treat white defendants much the same way that white jurors treat black defendants," she claims. For Asian-Americans, "the question is a close one," she continues, since prejudice against them tends to be less intense and wide-spread and, among the prejudiced, the stereotypes "less commonly include propensity to commit crime." But because "a rule that accords the same rights to all racial groups is *likely to seem fairer* to the layperson" (1696–97; emphasis added) and because, in a few areas, stereotypes of Asian American criminality may be common, Johnson would extend the right to them.

Johnson bases her arguments in part on "a large body of social science research," on "empirical evidence," on "jury dynamics research," and on "laboratory and field studies." The following chapter will consider similar types of work in detail. Meanwhile it is noteworthy that the justification Johnson articulates for extending the right in question to Asians reveals a concern for legitimacy and for what *seems* to be fair—the appearance of justice—rather than with justice or what *is* fair.

The authors of "Note: The Case for Black Juries,"[53] take a similar stance. For them, the jury in part serves a "legitimation function": "Legitimacy . . . is enhanced when people *feel* they have participated in the promulgation of the laws. . . . Legitimacy is similarly enhanced when people *believe* it within their power to participate, via the jury, in the application of law. . . . [But] the jury is a legitimating device only to those who are a part of the community whose norms the jury expresses" ("Note," 531; emphasis added).

For these authors, the jury also serves an additional function: as "a finder of fact." Fact-finding on the jury "is not a process in which skill in 'scientific' analysis is more important than insight into human behavior," they write. Because society has seemed "to value ability to reason scientifically over ability to tap the pulse of the community or familiarity with similar situations," however, a "middle-class, all-white jury" has emerged. Such a jury, representing only one segment of the community, "sacrifices factfinding ability as well as legitimacy." The authors claim that their proposals will increase the efficiency of what they call fact-finding, and also promote political effectiveness or legitimacy (532–33).

They propose to structure the jury system "to produce a substantial number of blacks on juries trying cases directly affecting the interests of black litigants or of the black community" (537). Because the "purposeful inclusion" of blacks on juries would "leave control of the jury selection process in white hands," they do not call for such a measure. Instead they suggest two alternatives for solving "the problem of both numbers and control." The first entails redrawing jury districts: in Northern urban areas, each black community would constitute a jury district or vicinage, the consequence being all-black juries; in the rural South, where black and white communities are not

so easily separated, "we would do better to require that every jury be propor-
tionately representative of the black *population* in the vicinage. In most cases
this would yield juries that are at least three-quarters black" (534; footnotes
omitted). Their second alternative, which they admit is less feasible, is to establish a formula making the number of black jurors "dependent upon both
the degree to which race is central to the decision and the number of jurors
necessary to bring about an equitable result."

The discussion of racial discrimination by the "Note" authors focuses not
only on the black individual, and on society as a whole, but also on the black
community:

Although most discussions of racial discrimination in jury selection focus on unfair-
ness to defendants, it is important to remember that exclusion of blacks renders the
jury as illegitimate to the black *community* as it does to the black criminal defendant or
civil litigant. The jury lacks legitimacy not only because the black community does
not participate, but also because black people perceive that white institutions of social
order are considerably more concerned with ensuring that white citizens and the
white community are not disturbed by blacks than with order *within* the black community. (534)

In contrast to Johnson, these authors claim that white juries are "lenient towards *black* defendants accused of crimes against black people." But, "this is
not a valid argument against black juries," they argue, affirming "the interests
of the community" in having blacks on juries, because "no defendant has the
right to profit by discrimination against his race" (547). While concerned
with order "within the black community," the authors consider the black
community to be part of a larger social order, whose favorable *perceptions*
of that order are to be gained also through the group's participation. The
authors consider "lay participation" to be "a creative process by which community standards are injected into the legal system to guard against possible harshness, arbitrariness, or inaccuracy in the administration of justice"
(531). In what at first appears a bizarre linguistic move, the authors call
the neglect of these community standards "inefficient" yet "scientific" fact-
finding. This usage allows the authors to claim that their own proposals further both the fact-finding and legitimating functions of the jury. That is, by
characterizing the black community as sharing in "non-scientific" knowledge
necessary to "efficient" fact-finding, they technically avoid the criticism that
they are simply sacrificing scientific ability and fact-finding for "psychological and political functions" (533).

The black community of the "Note" authors is characterized by a particular sort of knowledge that the vicinage proposal would tap since "legal prob-

lems that black people face tend to arise where they live and carry on their daily business" (548). But even as this text presents a richer conception of community than that of many other contemporary legal writers, their first alternative reveals the extent to which, here too, the black jury represents a fair variation, in the case of the oppressed black community, to a jury that is fundamentally a representative sample of a larger population. Because the black community is part of a larger social order in which the legitimacy of the jury is at stake, public confidence in the fairness of the system means—to paraphrase another (substantive cross-section) argument—acceptability to the community as a whole; what is acceptable to the community as a whole must be acceptable to its parts; for the parts to be satisfied they must partici-pate.[54] (As the oft-cited Van Dyke writes: "A jury representing the broad spectrum of society is a jury whose independence and impartiality need not be suspect, and whose legitimacy is protected.")[55] The "Note" authors' second proposal, which follows "the pattern of an ideal modern legislature, . . . requir[ing] that those interests most clearly affected by an issue play the major role in its resolution" (549), reveals how close these authors are to un-derstanding black "community" as racial "interest representation."

In sum, like supporters of procedural cross-sectionality (discussed in sec-tion 1), advocates of affirmative juror selection recognize race as somehow other. But while the early mixed jury (of chapter 1), composed half of "others," or aliens, and half of natives, represented two communities and their law, the "substantive" approach to the composition of the modern jury views the racially mixed jury as a "fair" variation to what it takes to be a sample of a population. Further, again like the procedural approach, the substantive ap-proach to jury mix today exhibits an explicit concern with legitimacy—with public belief in the appearance of justice.

3. Reliability and the Modern Verdict

Modern American law concerned with jury mix treats the jury as a statistical sample of a population, whose task is less to speak the truth or know the law than to produce a verdict that "seems" fair and promotes public confidence in the system. To this end the verdict must be "reliable." Reliability is not the same as justice. It betrays a concern with what *appears* to be just: with the accuracy and consistency of results that legitimate the procedures by which they are reached.

In the jury size cases mentioned in section 1, for instance, the Court treated the question of whether juries of fewer than twelve were constitutional as a question of reliable decision-making, or of the validity and correctness, or accuracy, of outcomes reached by smaller-size juries. It made assumptions about the percentage of guilty and innocent defendants going to trial and addressed the problem of jury size by analyzing rates of Type I and Type II errors—rates of finding innocent defendants guilty and guilty ones innocent—by the juries. The Court agreed with commentators who concluded that "the optimal size, for the purpose of minimizing errors, should vary with the importance attached to the two types of mistakes." And, continued the Court, "after weighting Type I error as 10 times more significant than Type II, perhaps not an unreasonable assumption, they concluded that the optimal jury size was between six and eight. As the size diminished to five and below, the weighted sum of errors increased because of the enlarging risk of the conviction of innocent defendants."[56] The point here concerns neither the ultimate size of the jury nor the Court's ultimate decision. The point is that the verdict in any given instance was treated and evaluated by the Court as correct or in error, as true or false, not as just or unjust. An external or objectively existent guilt or innocence was posited, against which to evaluate the accuracy of jurors' decisions. The jury neither established nor determined, in a deep sense, the guilt or innocence of a defendant; rather, the standard for ascertaining "true" guilt and innocence lay outside the jury.

Recent debate about the majority versus the unanimous verdict also illustrates the distance that lies between modern and early understandings of the jury. Many states allow majority verdicts in civil trials before both twelve- and six-member juries. Some states permit majority verdicts in minor criminal or misdemeanor trials, and two even allow such verdicts in felony trials for noncapital offenses.[57] Here too, the notion of "verdict" used by state legislatures, some courts, and the social scientists on whose work they rely differs from the earlier notion of the verdict as the voice of the community declaring the law. The possibility that a verdict consists in a jury of twelve peers speaking as one is absent when the verdict is presented probabilistically and evaluated in terms of propositional truth values or correspondence with an external measure.

At the same time as the language of the Court suggests that the judgments of juries can be measured for their correctness or rates of accuracy, the studies on which courts rely are more cautious. In the jury size case above, the Court described the assumption that Type I error was ten times more significant than Type II error as "perhaps not an unreasonable one." The researcher on whose study the Court relied, however, later explained that he based his weighting of errors this way on Blackstone's saying that it is ten times worse to convict an innocent man than to let a guilty one go free. Indeed, as will be discussed further in the next chapter, the inaccessibility of an ostensibly external standard by which to measure jury verdicts has led social researchers to evaluate such judgments not in terms of accuracy but for their consistency—with the verdicts of other juries, with what judges would do, or with public opinion.

The tension between characterizing the verdict as potentially accurate "fact" and presenting it as a consistent or coherent reflection of public "values" reveals a dilemma whose manifestations pervade much modern thought. In philosophy of social science the dilemma manifests itself as the debate between behaviorism and interpretivism; in philosophy of language, as the debate between correspondence and coherence theories; in political theory, as the need for a single right answer or for effective action in the face of a multiplicity of opinions about what ought to be done. Like the general thrust of argument about the desirability of the jury—it makes mistakes, hence is inefficient, versus, it represents the public, hence is legitimate—the two sides of these issues are flip sides of the same coin. That coin today indicates a situation in which truth and justice are neither universal nor the shared knowledge of community members about what to do.

3   Sociological Society

The increasing intellectualization and rationalization do *not*, therefore, indicate an increased and general knowledge of the conditions under which one lives.

It means something else, namely, the knowledge or belief that if one but wished one *could* learn it at any time. Hence, it means that principally there are no mysterious incalculable forces that come into play, but rather that one can, in principle, master all things by calculation. This means that the world is disenchanted. One need no longer have recourse to magical means in order to master or implore the spirits, as did the savage, for whom such mysterious powers existed. Technical means and calculations perform the service. This above all is what intellectualization means.—Max Weber[1]

Even as legal texts reveal ways of thinking about jury mix that are compatible with statistical approaches to gathering data, courts do not admit using social science. Further, social scientists often accuse the legal profession of neglecting social research and criticize the profession for its "use/abuse/misuse"[2] of such research.

While judges ostensibly ignore social research and resist social scientific approaches, there is no doubt that, since 1970, relations between law and social science have grown. Legal opinions do, at times, refer to social scientific research. Social scientists testify as expert witnesses in court. Lawyers rely on social science consultants in jury selection. Law students take courses on quantitative methods. Law journals publish articles on econometrics in the courtroom. And social scientists and lawyers, deploring the misuse and abuse of social science research in the courtroom, explain how to improve legal use of social science.

This chapter examines the conceptions of law revealed in six generally well-respected, social scientific works about the jury. The works examined below are works of social psychology, not, for instance, anthropology or economics; nevertheless they will be referred to broadly as "social science." By looking at this work, one can consider the extent to which assumptions in social research about law, knowledge, and community are compatible with the conceptions found in the legal texts discussed in the previous chapter. Insofar as courts—and others—consider adopting social research, one can also ask what is at stake in a social scientific or sociological perspective.

As this chapter shows, social scientific works about the jury, jury trial, and jury deliberation address important jurisprudential questions in particular contexts, constrained in particular ways. Analyses of social scientific approaches to the jury identify connections between law and social science and suggest that visions of a "sociological society" lie behind what are often taken for granted as the answers to many potential jurisprudential questions.

Again, this chapter is not about whether or how social scientific research actually influences courts. Social scientists acknowledge that even when their work is used by the courts, it does not necessarily influence them. One pair of researchers claims that the jury size cases mentioned in the previous chapter represent a typical instance of court use of social science. They argue that conservatives and liberals both opposed the small size juries of five: liberals because they thought such juries worked against the defendant; conservatives because although they generally favored the smaller, more efficient juries, they found five (unlike six) to be too radical a departure from the traditional number twelve. Where all sides want the same thing, these social scientists write, the court is willing to buttress its opinion with social science, but it only uses social science after already having made its decision. In most cases, they claim, the courts either do not rely on, or improperly rely on, social science research.[3]

Neither is this chapter about social researchers' intentions, psychological motivations, or potential misgivings about their own work. The chapter focuses on texts, and it explores the assumptions and implications of these texts. The texts are admittedly written by an "author" and referred to as so authored. But the stances and claims that the language of a text reveals are not necessarily attributable to the person who goes by the name of the author. In a way, then, the chapter may be said to take up what has long been considered a social scientific concern with unintended consequences—this time the unintended consequences of what six social studies say. Conversely, the chapter may be said to extend the claim that a work may reveal more or other than what its author intends, beyond literature, of which it is generally accepted, to nonliterary texts.

As a whole, the chapter calls for thinking about how conceptions of law, knowledge, and community articulated in social science texts are consistent with official legal conceptions described in the previous chapter. The call for thinking about sociological understanding of law indeed echoes, in some sense, the concerns of social studies that investigate legal assumptions about human behavior. But unlike such social research which, by and large, takes an interest in clarifying the empirical misassumptions of law in order to improve law, this chapter examines the foundations upon which social scientific claims about law rest, again not in order to improve law or social science, but to highlight the conceptions we, moderns, have of who we are.

1. Studies of Juries

In the 1950s and 1960s, in the wake of considerable skepticism about the role and capacity of juries, the Chicago Jury Project spawned numerous studies of the American jury. The 1966 publication of Harry Kalven Jr. and Hans Zeisel's "pioneering work,"[4] *The American Jury,* offered the first systematic study of jury decision-making. Kalven and Zeisel pointed to the "unsatisfactory debate" produced by a "long tradition of controversy over the jury system" (4–5). Much criticism of the jury, they wrote, "has stemmed from not more than the a priori guess that, since the jury was employing laymen amateurs in what must be a technical and serious business, it could not be a good idea. In comparable fashion, the enthusiasts of the jury have tended to lapse into sentimentality and to equate literally the jury with democracy" (5). Both sides in the jury controversy, assert Kalven and Zeisel, make the implicit assumption that "the decisions of the jury will sometimes and to some degree be different from those that would be given by the judge in the same case. . . . Critics point to these differences as evidence of the jury's fallibility and incompetence; . . . champions point to these differences as proof of the jury's distinctive function and its strength" (9).

"Much of the argument," Kalven and Zeisel continue, "appears to rest on assumptions as to what the facts are—the facts, that is, as to how the jury actually performs" (9). Hence, Kalven and Zeisel set out to investigate these facts. The thrust of their book is that judges and juries disagree a certain amount, which amount has been taken, and continues to be taken, as an affirmation of the competence of the jury.

Controversy about the jury after Kalven and Zeisel's study, writes Rita J. Simon in *The Jury: Its Role in American Society,* shifted from its competence to its representativeness and to its deliberative process.[5] Simon herself, seeking to organize and comment on major research concerning a broad array of issues about the jury, raises questions about the "implicit, if not explicit, assumptions about human social behavior" made by law and legal practitioners. She justifies social scientific investigation into jury behavior, in the context of jury size and decision rule (number required to render a verdict), asserting: "While one cannot discount the set of conventions and popular wisdom accumulated over several hundred years of legal experience, not all notions are so seasoned" (85). After examining empirical studies and some of the major political trials since 1945, Simon concludes that the jury "can perform its duty in a consistently responsible manner; . . . it can stand above popular prejudice and deliver verdicts that experts steeped and trained in the law respect" (147).

In *Inside the Jury,* Reid Hastie, Steven D. Penrod, and Nancy Pennington present the findings of a mock jury study that focuses on the effect of decision rule and the juror's behavior during deliberation. Their study also deals with the influence of individual differences in background on juror decision-making and develops a theoretical framework within which to view juror and jury behavior. "Such a theory," they claim, "grounded firmly on systematic empirical research, can reduce the dependence of legal policy makers on the vagaries of intuition and personal experience."[6]

Valerie Hans and Neil Vidmar's 1986 *Judging the Jury* synthesizes "what has been learned" in the last several decades "about how the institution of trial by jury operates in our society."[7] It draws upon archival sources, court documents, appellate court opinions, writings and interviews with jurors, and Hans and Vidmar's own research, as well as that of others. The authors examine "how historical events pushed the American jury on a distinctive evolutionary path" (20) and explore issues concerning jury selection, jury decisions, and three controversial types of trials—those involving the insanity defense, charges of rape, and the death penalty. Hans and Vidmar's "final judgment on the jury system is a positive one. Despite some flaws, it serves the cause of justice very well" (251).

In *The American Jury on Trial,* Saul M. Kassin and Lawrence S. Wrightsman, characterizing jury trials as "very carefully controlled, well-orchestrated events that are based on numerous assumptions about human behavior," investigate the behavioral assumptions on which the "complex network of rules, constraints, and rituals" that structure jury trials are based.[8] They explore the legal community's "ideal" expectations for jury conduct, examine how "fair trial" translates into concrete behavioral terms, and ask about the extent to which juries can measure up to expectations, before suggesting how to improve jury performance in several areas.

Finally, John Guinther's *The Jury in America,*[9] funded by and apparently (despite a disclaimer [ix]) written for the Roscoe Pound American Trial Lawyers Foundation, is almost two books in one. The Foundation's president "first saw the need for a book that would objectively study the civil jury system in America," Guinther writes in his acknowledgments (ix), implying that this book is it. Guinther's 231-page narrative affirms the place of the civil jury in America, deflating charges that a "litigation explosion," "mega-awards," and complex litigation are creating crises in the jury system. Fifty pages of notes are followed by *The Civil Juror,* a 100-page report of what the cover of the book announces as "A Research Project Sponsored by the Roscoe Pound Foundation, Bettyruth Walter, Ph.D., Research Director." The project employed survey questionnaires to ask jurors "what they did and why they did it" (xvii). After describing the history of the jury system and the structure of the "present-day American justice system," Guinther draws on the findings of the project, as well as on many other studies, to describe "what we know about the jury as a fact-finding body" or to explain "how juries function," before he turns to "the role [juries] play in our society as an instrument of justice" (xv).

All six studies show awareness of debates in political philosophy and law about whether there should be juries and what juries should do. With the possible exception of Guinther, the authors claim that their own projects focus primarily on what the jury does, in order to see, only secondarily, whether it does what it should. All are careful, in this context, to distinguish factual questions from value questions (Kalven and Zeisel), empirical from political (Kassin and Wrightsman, 160) or ethical ones (Hastie et al.), the actual from the ideal (Kassin and Wrightsman, 172–75), the empirical from the theoretical (Hastie et al., 37). Even Guinther, "when possible," strives to "separate fact from fiction, and see where the truth lies" (xiv).[10]

The studies, on the whole, give the jury what Simon calls "high marks" (xii). The studies defend the jury against charges of incompetence and inefficiency, often claiming that a jury verdict turns on the evidence presented in a particular trial as much as on other factors.[11]

The studies thus appear to favor the jury as an institution and to do so on the basis of "systematic scientific inquiry" (Hans and Vidmar, 19). Yet, despite their attempts to get away from "images" (Kassin and Wrightsman, ix, x, 1–19), "intuitions and personal experience" (Hastie et al., 4), "collective prejudices" and ideology (Simon, 11, 123–47), "rhetoric" (Hans and Vidmar, 19), "anecdotes" (Kassin and Wrightsman, 14), "a priori guess[es]" and "sentimentality" (Kalven and Zeisel, 5), and their attempts to affirm the role of the jury on other grounds (that is, by facts about the jury), most of the studies express their views in normative or value-laden terms. "Despite some flaws, [the jury] serves the cause of justice very well," conclude Hans and Vidmar (251). Guinther's conclusion epitomizes the "sentimentality" that Kalven and Zeisel deplore: "We have given much of our democracy away. . . . But in one place we still have a direct voice and can be heard, and that is through our juries. Because of them we are still direct participants in our democracy" (231).

While Hastie, Penrod, and Pennington, and Kassin and Wrightsman express their views more moderately, their studies necessarily adopt certain standards, the outcomes of "value-judgments," to evaluate the jury; the studies propose modifications, in various degrees, to policies concerning jury size, decision rule, the appropriateness of death-qualified juries, jury instructions, and allowing juries to hear complex cases. Kassin and Wrightsman consider such proposals for improving the law to follow "naturally" from the insights of social science. They write that "by bringing psychology to bear on questions of how the jury should function, we think certain modifications in trial practice and procedure naturally present themselves. It is a good system, but it can be better" (208). Hastie, Penrod, and Pennington's "basic argument" is that:

The behavioral sciences provide a new and useful source of findings and methods that are relevant to decisions concerning the right to trial by jury. Most of the fundamental questions concerning the proper form and function of the jury can be answered with reference to empirical facts about juror and jury behavior. Even those questions of ethics or values that are essentially undecidable with empirical findings can be sharpened or simplified when related empirical issues are resolved. (4)

Kalven and Zeisel's study is the exception to the claim that the studies explicitly affirm the role of the jury: "Can we now at long last answer whether the jury is a worthy institution or whether it would be more sensible to have all cases tried to judges alone? . . . we cannot answer . . ." (498). Yet their study, more than the others, takes for granted the framework presented by law: "it is a special advantage of empirical studies of legal institutions that the law supplies a pre-existing framework of significance and expectation to which the quantitative dimension can be added; it permits, that is, measurement with meaning" (492).

All of the studies, Kalven and Zeisel's included, thus share in the presumption that science, distinguishing between fact and value, can serve to improve law (see, e.g., Hans and Vidmar, 247). All of the studies present social science as a tool, law as its object.

The sections that follow ask: what is this object that social science would improve? what is the tool to which we are to entrust our law? Section 2 begins with the conceptions of law implicated in the studies described above, and section 3 looks at the conception of the jury revealed in the studies' proposals to improve jury trial. Section 4 turns more generally to the understanding of society and knowledge manifest in modern sociological approaches to law.

2. The Law of the Officials

The conception of law in these studies is not the law of the community, on which one might suppose traditional defense of the jury would rest. The law, as Max Weber[12] and H. L. A. Hart[13] (discussed further in the next chapter) would tell us, is the law of the officials. Kalven and Zeisel's work—taking as a "special advantage" the "pre-existing framework of significance and expectation" supplied by law—makes such a conception explicit. Their study asks, "When do trial by judge and trial by jury lead to divergent results?" and it measures the jury's performance against that of "the judge as a baseline" (10). Its findings about the magnitude and cause of judge/jury disagreement in criminal trials derive from survey data provided by judges overseeing 3,576 jury trials.

Despite almost universal acknowledgement of the limitations of such an approach,[14] studies using other methods also presume that "law" is not the law of the community. While other studies may not go so far as to take the courts, judges, and officials as the standard against which to measure jury performance, they take for granted that "law" refers to rules of the court and to judges' instructions. Simon, for instance, mentions that "experts in law" respect the jury's opinion (147). Hastie, Penrod, and Pennington look to the record of decided cases to establish a systematic set of principles by which to measure jury performance. Kassin and Wrightsman construct their ideal of how the jury should conduct itself by looking at the opinions of the legal community. At one point they introduce a problem this way: "The courts want juries to comply with their judges' instructions. With that reasonable assumption as a point of departure, we ask: so why do they cling to psychologically unsound methods of communication?" (144).

Discussions of "jury nullification" especially point to research presuppositions that "law" means the law of the officials, a law that contrasts to the "beliefs," "sentiments," and "attitudes" expressed in jury verdicts. Kassin and Wrightsman set up a tension between "the law" and jurors' "feelings of what is right and wrong," between verdicts "that are legally accurate" and what seems "instinctively to be fair and equitable" (158). Guinther's ninth chapter, on "jury justice," looks at "the jury as purveyor of community (rather than legal) standards of justice" (108).[15] For Kalven and Zeisel "what emerges perhaps as something of a surprise is that this reality [of jury decision-making] has so legal a texture" (497).

In asking not simply, "What do juries do?" but "Do juries obey the law?" the texts reveal a particular conception of law. In formulating the question as

"How is it that we allow juries to nullify the law?" and going on to ask "Do juries, despite (occasional) disobedience to law, serve some (greater/other/useful/desirable) social function?" the studies reproduce legal positivism's distinctions between law and morality, law and justice, legal authorities and legal subjects.

Whatever the appeal of this approach for empirical jury studies, jurisprudential debates between positive lawyers and natural lawyers alert us to what is at stake in these ways of talking: such formulations preclude the possibility of asking the more radical question, "How is it that judges and legislators have come to lay claim to what is called 'law'?"

The bias against this question—or the presumption in favor of law as the law of the officials—is apparent not only in the studies' presentation of research and formulation of questions, but also in the (limited) histories they present. (Such presumptions also appear in more extensive legal histories.)[16] Insofar as Guinther's study, for instance, concerns itself with the history of the jury, that history presents "law" as the law of the king, the common law as the king's law or, even, "pretty much what judges say it is" (32).

Yet at the same time as law, in Guinther's study, is of the king and the officials, justice is not. And, given the history Guinther tells, it is no wonder he defends the justice of the community as opposed to the justice of law: law founds itself initially through the forceful imposition of order by the king or by officials on the "folk customs" or "ways of the people." Guinther at first characterizes these early ways as "justice-by-mob" on which kings and nobles unsuccessfully attempt to impose order (3). They are not immediately successful as "British kings, even in [Alfred's] day, had not gained the absolute power they were to wield later—nor was there a centralized justice system to carry out *anyone's* laws uniformly" (5). For Guinther, force and civil authority come together under the rule of William the Conqueror: "By cajoling or forcing everyone to cooperate—when many must have feared the king's real plan was to steal their lands through taxation—and doing so without bringing about a rebellion, William showed how a king could rule not only by force of arms but also through the establishment of civil authority" (8). And in 1166, according to Guinther, "the consolidation of Henry's law took place at the great Assize of Clarendon," where "for the first time since the heyday of Athens . . . those seeking redress of their grievances could have their case settled not by the king, not by baron, not by priest, not even by the king's judge or the king's commissioners, but by their own peers" (10–12).

The point here is not to dispute Guinther's account of history but to show that this account ostensibly contrasts the justice of peers to the violence both of mob rule (or custom) and of official law (or imposition of power) in order ultimately to defend the justice of peers. Yet for Guinther, the justice of peers occurs with the consolidation of official power or law that authorizes it. Guinther never explicitly faces the implications of his account: that the justice of peers itself, like the official power or law that authorizes it, relies on cajoling and force; that the justice of peers resembles an earlier "justice-by-mob" upon which kings and nobles have successfully imposed order.

Hans and Vidmar tell a slightly different story; for them, in contrast to Guinther, justice, like law, belongs explicitly to the officials. For them, like Guinther, though, the "jury system" (and the use of "system" is not accidental) "serves the cause of justice very well" (251); the question of whose "cause" justice serves, of how justice has come to mean the justice of the officials, of how officials have come to lay claim to justice, is never problematic. According to Hans and Vidmar, William the Conqueror made no "immediate sweeping changes in the legal institutions" of the conquered. "Rather, the institutions were used to support the goals of the Crown and were only gradually modified" (25). The jury system's ability to support the "goals" of the crown and to "serve the cause of" justice suggests that, for Hans and Vidmar, initial validation for the jury system comes, if not from the Conqueror, at least from the system's compatibility with his goals. To the degree that William *permitted* the institutions of a conquered people to continue, those institutions are authorized by him—and justice falls into the officials' jurisdiction.[17]

Hans and Vidmar's view of justice points to a second possible rationale for the jury, a rationale that, unlike Guinther's, does not rely on a strict opposition between the justice of the jury and the force of law. Whether or not particular jury verdicts are just according to the standards of official law—and most of the studies, including that of Hans and Vidmar, assert that they are most of the time—the jury performs another function vis-à-vis the law of the officials: the jury legitimates official law, and, insofar as it does, official law permits the jury system to continue. As social psychologists E. Allan Lind and Tom R. Tyler write:

If we think about why we want to have lay juries two rationales are apparent. One rationale focuses on the jury as a problem-solving group convened to attempt to reach a decision that is as accurate as possible given the facts in the case. The other rationale sees the jury as a political institution that is designed to increase the legitimacy of the justice system by allowing community participation and representation in legal decision-making.[18]

According to Lind and Tyler, we know a great deal about the jury's problem-solving ability but less about this legitimizing function. Yet it is this function that social scientific texts elevate to a standard of measure when they defend the jury by claiming that the jury system "has weathered criticism and attack, always to survive and to be cherished by the peoples who own it" (Hans and Vidmar, 25). Affirmations that people *believe in* the justice of the jury system or that the jury is just *according to the officials* come to the same thing when one understands law and justice as the law and justice of the officials: both claims privilege the belief in justice, or the appearance of justice, or justice from a point of view, over justice itself; they point to the emergence of "legit-imacy" as a value, a value that takes on meaning only in the absence of justice "itself."

It is one thing for social science to maintain a veneer of objectivity by seek-ing proxies for "big words"[19] such as justice; that is, for it to acknowledge that its claims about x refer to appearances of x (to the belief in x or even to the fact that people say they believe in x) and not to hidden realities—to x-in-itself. It is another thing for those proxies to take over the meaning of a word to such an extent that appearance and reality become interchangeable—as has be-come the case with justice. The appearance of justice is known as "legit-imacy"; legitimacy is thought to be justice.

A social study that defends *or* denies the legitimating function of the jury takes for granted that the issue is one of belief and that the official order, its justice and law, provides both the standard against which to judge and the authority for the jury. Insofar as discussions of the jury today are formulated in terms of legitimacy, they concern a "justice" grounded in the power of offi-cials, a justice that has meaning only as belief in—or against—a framework of official law. Such justice, such power, and such law—that of social science, that of the officials—risk becoming the only law.

Yet where are we to look for other possibilities? History? The history of the jury indeed suggests that law need not be viewed as the law of the officials. It suggests that law may be seen neither as the imposition of a power that con-trasts to the mob-rule or justice of the community nor as a framework that authorizes the institutions of others. As chapter 1 points out, early jury his-tory shows the jury to be a jury of neighbors, whose verdict or "speaking of truth" was law—and whose law, irrespective of distinctions between fact and law, was justice.

But, as Hastie, Penrod, and Pennington accurately note, such history is uncertain and "provides few clear guidelines for current procedures and standards" (3). Social science turns away from such history and turns toward clearer guidelines with which to judge and improve the jury. In denying or neglecting early histories that connected law, justice, truth, and knowledge, contemporary accounts of the jury not only provide useful policy guidelines, however; they also reveal the extent to which earlier notions have lost—or we have forgotten—their meanings.

3. Improving the Jury Trial

Although history may provide no clear guidelines for current procedures concerning the jury, social science does. Such guidelines refer to matters concerning the entire jury process, from jury selection, to trial, to jury deliberation. In order "to minimize bias and incompetence," for instance, Hans and Vidmar propose "in-depth, careful examination of prospective jurors that focuses on jurors' preconceptions or reactions to the specific case" (246). "Social science methods," they claim,

can probably be helpful in advancing the cause of justice in some cases. . . . Jury experts . . . can sometimes help to eliminate the most prejudiced persons, and thereby create more impartial juries. The use of mock juries can help lawyers devise more effective trial strategies. In the long run, however, the legal system may be better served by social science studies that shed light on issues such as jury size, jury competence, and methods of improving the performance of jurors. (247)

Hastie, Penrod, and Pennington affirm that "because jury performance of the factfinding task is so remarkably competent, few innovations are needed to improve performance." Because an "evidence-driven deliberation style produces more thorough and impartial assessment and integration of the evidence," however, they suggest that "an instruction to the jury to begin deliberation with a review of the evidence and to avoid early or frequent vote-taking might facilitate performance" (230) and would also help prevent deadlocked juries (232–33). They also indicate that improvements are needed in the way the trial judge communicates to the jury, suggesting the use of written transcripts or taped recordings of the final charge and the repetition of specific instructions (231). Kassin and Wrightsman propose reading instructions to the jury at the beginning as well as at the end of the trial (144–46), providing jurors with access to written or taped versions of the instructions (146–47), and rewriting currently incomprehensible instructions (147–56). As an example of an empirically demonstrable way of improving instructions, Kassin and Wrightsman recommend, based on knowledge of "the nonverbal communication of deception," that jurors' attention should be directed "away from facial-expressive cues and toward body language and vocal cues" (211). Hans and Vidmar, too, call for "developing more coherent legal instructions," as well as "allowing jurors to take notes or to ask questions, or providing some directions at the beginning of the trial" (246).

Kassin and Wrightsman would allow the use of videotaped testimony at trial (212), and Hastie, Penrod, and Pennington write that "a simple directory of witnesses, including a photograph and identifying information for each witness, could be useful, particularly when many witnesses testify" (230). They also write:

> The unanimous rule appears preferable to majority rules because of the importance of deliberation thoroughness, expression of individual viewpoints, and protection against sampling variability effects of initial verdict preference. Furthermore, because respect for the institution of the jury is a critical condition for public acceptance of jury decisions, the lower postdeliberation evaluations of the quality of their decision by jurors in nonunanimous juries and the larger number of holdouts who reject the jury's verdict under these rules greatly diminish the usefulness of the majority rule jury as a mechanism for resolving legal disputes. (229)

These proposals concerning jury selection, jury trial, and jury deliberation are all grounded in particular understandings of the jury and of its decision-making. The studies all reject what they consider to be the simplistic notion that with enough information one can accurately predict the decisions of juries.[20] The studies claim that attempts to connect demographic status, abilities, aptitudes, temperaments, and personalities of jurors to verdict differences have met with "limited success" (Kassin and Wrightsman, 29-30), and they argue that cases are decided by the evidence.[21] States Simon: "different issues, different defendants, different contexts, different evidence should and did make for different verdicts" (146).

At the same time, the studies maintain a view of the juror as the site of particular predispositions that follow from attitudes toward particular issues and that have implications for the outcome of a trial: "In contrast to the broad strokes of juror demography and the not-so-hidden hand of personality, there is reason to believe that individual jurors' predispositions do follow reliably from their attitudes on specific issues of relevance to their trial. It is the 'specific' part that is important," write Kassin and Wrightsman (35), before an analysis in which they conclude that "jurors' attitudes toward rape are the single best predictor of how they vote" in rape cases (36–37).

The individual juror in these studies serves not only as the site of particular "attitudes" and "predispositions," but as a part of a group. In this capacity, too, the individual is the focus of attention and is represented by particular characteristics: "Research studies show that the amount of group participation is related to the characteristics of the individuals themselves," write Hans and Vidmar (108). They add:

> Just as external status is reflected in the selection of the foreperson of the jury, it is reflected too in who participates the most during deliberation. On the average, men

speak more than women. . . . Those with more education and higher-status occupations also tend to dominate the discussion. Likewise the foreperson, usually male, is regularly one of the most active participants. (108)

The studies understand decision-making to mean "how juries combine their sundry, individual perspectives into a single verdict," as Hans and Vidmar put it (20). The studies assume that deliberation and its outcome both involve a "combination" of "individual" "perspectives." The juror is the site of characteristics and perspectives that contribute to (although ostensibly they do not determine) both the group interaction that constitutes deliberation and the outcome of such deliberation.

The "information-processing" model, described both by Kassin and Wrightsman and Hastie, Penrod, and Pennington, points to the way in which the studies approach the topic of deliberation. Kassin and Wrightsman describe the jury as "a human lie detector" (66) and as "a fact-finding machine" (120). Commenting on the jury's "computer-like role," they write: "Confronted with a vast array of input from the bench, the bar, and the witness stand, the jury must acquire, comprehend, store and retrieve all verdict-relevant information before it can dispense justice. It is no small feat to live the life of a flowchart" (119). Hastie, Penrod, and Pennington's turn to "the dominant theoretical paradigm in experimental psychology" means that "juror decision making can be analyzed within the information processing approach by describing the trial as a psychological stimulus, identifying the processing demands of the juror's decision task, and outlining the sequence of cognitive processes performed by the juror" (15).

Under this approach, "jury verdicts and individual jurors' intellectual and evaluative reactions to the stimulus trial and the experience of deliberation" are "products of deliberation," which "products are the focus of legal discussions of the right to trial by jury," according to Hastie, Penrod, and Pennington (59). The trial becomes "a search for probabilities" (Kassin and Wrightsman, 153), and jurors are understood to "define their task strictly in terms of the accuracy of their verdict" (Kassin and Wrightsman, 212; see also Hastie et al., 171).

In contrast to the jurors of which they speak, the studies evaluate verdicts in terms not of accuracy but of consistency. Hastie, Penrod, and Pennington, for instance, express concern about "deviations from the second-degree murder verdict" in their mock jury study, "because this [second-degree-murder] verdict is the 'correct' one on a number of grounds. First, the jury in the actual trial on which the case was based returned a verdict of second degree murder. Second, the legal experts who viewed the case consistently selected the second-degree murder verdict. Third, second degree murder is the modal verdict for the experimental juries" (62). They also explain that "the issue of the correctness of the final verdict cannot be resolved in absolute terms, for there are no ideal rational or empirical criteria for accuracy in jury decisions" (62).

These social scientific accounts of jury decision-making and jury verdicts differ dramatically from the earlier conception of the jury that viewed the jury as a community of neighbors gathered as one to speak the truth of a situation irrespective of the distinction between fact and law. No modern social study considers the jury to be the primary standard for determining the actual innocence or guilt of the defendant. None treats the verdict as the speaking of truth. Rather, a jury's determination of guilt is an official pronouncement, which may or may not be in accord with the facts that can be inferred from information presented at trial, and which may or may not be in accord with the law contained in judicial instructions.[22] For social science, the jury's verdict may be consistent with official law, or it may modify or even nullify such law, but it does not constitute the law. The verdict is the outcome of particular interactions among a group of twelve individuals, who process both evidentiary information and judicial instructions. The verdict's importance (irrespective of whether the verdict is discussed in terms of accuracy or consistency) lies in the consequences it entails.

The studies thus investigate the way in which the processing that leads to a verdict occurs and compare that process to an ideal attributed, correctly or not, to the courts. Kassin and Wrightsman, for instance, claim that the courts have articulated a "clear vision" of jury deliberation dynamics. The first component involves "independence and equality. . . . A 12-person jury should thus consist of 12 *independent* and *equal* individuals, each contributing his or her own personal opinion to the final outcome." The second component is "an openness to informational influence." This involves "a duty to interact and discuss the case" with an "open mind": "Jurors should scrutinize their own views, be receptive to others', and allow themselves to be persuaded by rational argument." The third component requires that "although juries should strive for a consensus of opinion, it should *not* be achieved through heavy-handed normative pressure" (172–73).[23]

Social science's "real juries" (Kassin and Wrightsman, 214) do not fulfill these "ideals of deliberation" (214, 174ff.) or match the "information-acceptance model" attributed to the courts (176). Instead, jurors may behave in accord with a "normative-compliance model of deliberation . . . characterized by the use of heavy-handed social pressure that leads dissenters to publicly support the jury's verdict while privately harboring reservations. . . .

In this less-than-ideal model, the jury completes its task unanimous in vote but not in conscience" (175). Because both models "rarely appear in their pure forms," a "jury verdict meets the courts' standards if, following a vigorous exchange of information and a minimum of normative pressure, it accurately reflects each of the individual jurors' private beliefs" (176). "Some degree of social pressure is inevitable," write Kassin and Wrightsman, "and perhaps even desirable. It is a fact of life not just on juries" (185).

For Hastie, Penrod, and Pennington, as for Kassin and Wrightsman, the "real jury" involves the interaction of social forces. The mock juries Hastie, Penrod, and Pennington studied decided differently, upon deliberation, than simple pre-deliberation polling of individual jurors would have suggested: "In view of the initial distribution of juror preferences, the shift can be best understood as the natural resolution of social forces in the jury" (59).

For the social researcher proposing to improve the law, minimizing the inevitable social or "normative pressure" (Kassin and Wrightsman) and identifying and controlling natural "social forces" (Hastie et al.) becomes the issue. "How much pressure is too much?" ask Kassin and Wrightsman (185), before an investigation into the courts' "power to manipulate the often delicate balance between informational and normative influences" and into "the kinds of trial procedures that can promote and frustrate the ideals of deliberation" (186). Hastie, Penrod, and Pennington claim their findings "have significance in three conceptual domains: legal policy concerning the right to trial by jury, psychological theories of group decision making, and principles to guide attorneys in winning cases at trial" (211).

The promulgation of social scientific guidelines that aim to shape the jury process, seeking to reduce (otherwise "natural") normative pressure that interferes with the apparently judicial, social-scientifically sanctioned ideal of jury deliberation, or seeking to predict and allow for control of "social forces" naturally underlying group interactions, highlight the tensions inherent in a social science that proclaims its own neutrality. For the proposals of social science take for granted a particular model of the jury and of law that ultimately renders other ways of thinking about the jury and its law obsolete.

Proposals to strengthen jurors' memories, for example, (suggested by Hans and Vidmar, Kassin and Wrightsman, and Hastie, Penrod, and Pennington)— such as substituting written for oral instructions, allowing jurors to take notes, providing videotapes and charts, instructing the jury at the beginning as well as the end of trial—presume that the kind of knowledge these techniques promote is desirable. Like proposals to introduce social scientific findings about the reliability of eyewitness testimony to guide the jury in its decision-making, the particular proposals to strengthen juror memories presuppose that a jury informed by the truths of social science is preferable to a jury informed by "common sense."[24] They presuppose a jury whose verdict is the product of information processing that is very like the sort of processing that is believed to occur in the social sciences. Their ultimate goal becomes a jury whose "perception, memory, information and decision processes" best approximate the processes of social science, a science that serves to correct the mistaken assumptions of (an official) law.

Ultimately, the studies' articulation of these proposals, as techniques taken to be desirable, points to a presumption that law is manipulable and that its world can be mastered through the processes and truths of social science.

Donald Black's recent *Sociological Justice*,[25] points to the nihilism to which an approach that looks only to the truths of social science ultimately leads. Those interested in legal reform, Black writes, ought not seek to make law more equal (a sociological impossibility, Black claims, since law inevitably varies with social differentials) but to equalize social differentials or to "desocialize" law, or at least courts. Such desocialization, according to Black, ultimately requires "the exclusion of people" (their presence, their representation on videotapes, their voices) for people represent the "contamination" of trials with "social information" (or information about social differentials). The "final step in the desocialization of courts" involves eliminating judges and juries and "closing the courtrooms themselves," in favor of electronic justice or computers "programmed to process complaints and testimony and to select dispositions."[26]

The jurisprudential nihilism of Black's "sociological society" (Black, 103) looks extreme compared to the improvements suggested in the jury books discussed above. And indeed, the claim here, it must be emphasized, is not that the social-scientifically supported recommendations of the latter books are the same as Black's. Neither is the claim that the suggestions in these works ought not be adopted, nor is it that the studies themselves are inaccurate or inconsistent. Rather, the claim is that these studies presume a particular understanding of the jury, of law, and of knowledge that, if rigorously maintained, pushed to an extreme, or perhaps even simply allowed to develop "naturally," represents the denial or rejection of ways of thinking that we may not wish to give up thoughtlessly.

4. Sociological Society

The discussion so far suggests that social science texts are quite right that the historical account of the jury does not provide useful policy guidelines; it also suggests, however, that the historical account does tell us something: it tells us what our view is not. Gone is the juror as member of a community of persons who share the same law. In that juror's place is an individual who serves as the locus of (empirically observable, statistically identifiable, and above all manageable) attitudes and perspectives. Gone are the communities of early jury history, for whom law is knowledge of how to act and who one is. Such communities have given way to pluralistic societies, in which law is the law of the officials, and for which "there is only a weak statistical relationship between what we are and how we act" (Kassin and Wrightsman, 27).

This account of the jury, law, and knowledge—that found in social scientific texts about the jury—occurs not only in those texts but also in the society that those texts, if true, are about. That is, social scientific accounts provide access to certain societies: those represented in the texts and those for whom social science is knowledge. In these societies, law is the law of the officials, justice is what is agreed to (and not what is known, which is social science), juries are "representative cross-sections" of a population whose members represent individual perspectives.

In the society of which and to which the social scientific account bears witness, the juror standing in for a particular perspective is neither a person who is what s/he does nor a freely willing agent (or subject) nor a determined object. Instead, the juror (like the defendant and the jury of social science analysis) is an agent who wills yet has no control, who deliberates, but whose outcome is determined.[27]

In societies of which social science tells, the juror, as individual, is an object whose behavior is accessible to observation, at the same time as it remains unknown who the juror truly is (since one is not what one does). The juror is an actor whose agreement with others is of the greatest importance, yet whose speech is not to be trusted nor taken on its own terms.[28]

In societies where the verdict is the product of agreement among individuals with different perspectives rather than the truth of the community, the majority verdict and jury size become issues. For the verdict is not what twelve persons speaking as one know, but the product of a process of combining perspectives. How many perspectives must be, or can be, combined?[29]

In societies to which social science provides access, the desirability of the jury, its size, and particular jury regulations become policy questions susceptible of evaluation at two levels: First, what are the "facts" about jury verdicts, their accuracy and consistency, their conformity with official standards? And second, what are the political, legal, and educational "values," norms, or goals served by the jury system? In such analyses, the interest is in improving the law for the sake of empirical accuracy and/or normative standards. The modern jury and its law do not tell us who we are or what to do—instead the truths of the sciences of society inform us of the laws by which to manage the jury and with which to govern ourselves so as to maintain the utmost public confidence in the system. Social science becomes the science of government.

This analysis of the discourse of social scientific jury studies shows the extent to which jury studies adopt a particular moral—and amoral—view of the law and of the world. The law is the law of the officials, not that of the community. Such law finds itself in conflict with the morality of the jurors. While social science shows how legal institutions make mistaken empirical claims, social science analyses are themselves implicated in a view of law as positive law, distinct from morality, that bears reexamination—not to improve such analyses but to see what they say about who we are: a pluralistic society of non-individuated individuals, for whom law and justice have lost their meanings while social science speaks "truth."

4   A Matter of History

In order to look for beginnings one becomes a crab. The historian looks backwards; at last he also
believes backwards. . . .
   My objection to the whole of sociology in England and France is that it knows from experience only
the *decaying forms* of society and takes its own decaying instincts with perfect innocence as the *norm*
of sociological value judgement.—Friedrich Nietzsche[1]

How does the transition from the early mixed jury to the modern jury come
about? How does the transition from law as the practice of a community to
law as the valid declarations of officials come about? How does positive law
come about? These are matters of history, concerned in part with law that is
other than modern law. One cannot adequately get at these matters from
within modern positivism, for, as shall be seen in this chapter, the positivist
understanding of law and history precludes the possibility of any law other
than positive law. This chapter explores the positivist history of law to further
highlight peculiarities of contemporary positivism; in so doing, it sets the
stage for an attempt at another "history" of law.

   Historians of Anglo-American law commonly view communities governed
by custom as somehow non- or prelegal. At first this strikes one as odd, given
our culture's traditional reverence for the common law or for the judge-made
law which is said to have been passed down from time immemorial and is
sometimes referred to as customary or unwritten law.[2] On closer examination, though, one sees that English common law is official law, the law of the
king's courts, rather than custom. The king's law developed against a back-
drop of local custom and through the centralization of royal power into "a
particular system of rules, with their own rational coherence," as one historian describes the common law.[3] Since law "consists in rules laid down by
judicial or legislative authority," custom, though it may be accompanied by
good order and due deliberation, is "not quite the same as 'law'."[4] Custom
lacks, in part, the "judicial machinery" and "procedure" required for the pro-
duction of law and supplied by the king's courts.[5]

   In distinguishing custom from law this way, legal historians share the positivist conception of law held, as the preceding chapters have shown, by

Anglo-American jurists and social scientists. Without accepting an explicitly Austinian view of law as the command of a sovereign, legal histories of the common law, like modern legal texts and social research about juries, grant primacy to the law of officials in their understanding of law. They characterize law as a system of propositional rules promulgated by officials through legitimate processes and distinguish it from morality and custom.

H. L. A. Hart's *The Concept of Law* provides the clearest theoretical articulation of this positivist understanding of law and alerts us to important aspects of the modern—sociological—understanding of law and history. This claim too at first may seem surprising, for, just as contemporary policy makers and social researchers find little use for history, social scientists often dismiss not only history but also jurisprudence as tangential to their concerns. Moreover, contemporary philosophers of law generally also show little concern for history. *The Concept of Law,* as a work of jurisprudence, is remarkable in this context not simply for its accurate portrayal of the current sociological understanding of a legal system, but for the account of the emergence of a legal system which it simultaneously presents.

Section 1 briefly discusses accounts of the origins of the common law before turning to Hart's account of the emergence of positive law—the step from a "simple" "pre-legal" society to a "mature legal system," as he puts it. Section 2 shows how the "moment" of origin of positive law—a moment whose location in time historical accounts continually defer and a moment Hart conceives of as the acknowledgment of a mark of authority—is rooted in conquest. That is, understanding law as positive law commits one to law that is founded in conquest or force of will. Section 3 exposes the presumptions which enable positivism—both as history and jurisprudence—to reach this point, before it returns to the question of the transition from the customary law of the early mixed jury to the positive law of the modern jury.

1. The Origin of Positive Law

Accounts of the origins of the common law abound. These accounts often start with the Norman Conquest, but one finds that despite a common starting point, such accounts equivocate in their attributions of an origin to the common law. Some accounts indeed claim that the common law of later days was built upon a "Norman spirit of clever administration and orderly government, and [William's] own stern enforcement of royal rights."[6] Other accounts show, however, that William enforced "royal rights held by his predecessors."[7] They claim that the Norman spirit manifested itself by making use of an earlier "Anglo-Saxon administrative machine."[8] As one historian puts it: "The Conqueror took over a going concern."[9] In these latter accounts, the Normans encountered an already existing system of royal justice whereby, despite local differences, "proprietary justice and feudal government were in general harnessed by the royal power rather than opposed to it, and we simplify social and political facts but do not distort the pattern of events if we think of law and order as fundamentally residing in the courts of counties [or shires] and hundreds, and under the control of [royal] officials."[10]

Such accounts thus claim that even before William, in Alfred's time, "the conversion of the older organization by kindreds into that matrix of the medieval and modern society, the territorial community,"[11] had already begun. Neighbors were taking the place of kin, and tithings or townships taking the place of neighbors, in swearing oaths and waging law before the courts.[12] Historians seeking to rescue the Anglo-Saxons from the charge of "primitive" and to bestow upon them some credit for the achievement of the common law show also how Anglo-Saxon documents point to a culture where, already, kings enacted and inscribed laws. They claim that fragments show

a high measure of centralized government [whose] successful working was made possible by what Sir Frank Stenton has called 'the most efficient means of publishing the ruler's will which western Europe has so far known', that is the 'writ', a simple letter in the native language, authenticated by the king's seal, which gave instructions regarding the king's wishes or information regarding his acts.[13]

Still other accounts, however, find that even before Alfred, laws that had first "come with earlier conquerors" had been directed at "those who might be presumed to know the customs" and offered "fixed rules to govern situations which must previously have rested on discretion."[14] These earlier conquerors were not simply "rulers seeking control of an existing society," it is claimed, but "peoples seeking land and livelihood, largely destroying what was there before, and bringing with them their own ways." Those imported earlier ways, by these accounts, "refined and modified by Christian influence, by administrative needs, and by accident, had become the laws by which Englishmen were governed when the Normans came."[15]

No matter how far back one looks, then, it appears that the history of the law that will become the common law never *begins*. It is not with the Battle of Hastings, historians claim, nor even "with the reign of Edward the Confessor that 'the Norman Conquest really begins.'"[16] Invasions and the imposition of new ways, these accounts suggest, have always already interrupted and shaped the lives of the inhabitants of the British isles in such a way that any potential origin of law has another. And conversely, any potential origin gives way to the forces that follow. Before the conquering Angles and Saxons had pushed the Celtic people back into Wales, Cornwall, and south-west Scotland, the tribal inhabitants of Britain had had to contend with the Roman occupation.[17] After Roman withdrawal, the Christian Church "lingered on to vie with the druidical order for spiritual authority and ultimately to prevail."[18]

The shift from custom to law in common law histories appears, then, as a long continuum, to which no determinate origin can be affixed. By these accounts the fact of an official practice has always already begun to emerge, even as its power is continually contested and its emergence cannot be located at a particular point of time.

Moreover, no matter how free, how democratic, how peaceful or law-abiding the romantic historian makes an earlier community out to be, the critic of such an account points to the division of the free from the unfree, of those with status from those without, of the powerful from those who submit, of the king's law from the folk law.[19] Looking back, every society in English history can be characterized as already a system of coercive political power and of official or external rules, as too late to be a community living autonomously by a law that is independent of foreign influence or outside forces.

Starting with the Conquest, or with Alfred, or the Celts, or the Romans, these backward-looking histories, as Nietzsche might call them, thus document the sources of the past, tracing the development of the common law or official law as the imposition of rules. The fact of the power of the free, the strong, the invader simultaneously supplements the defective rules of the non-free with rules of authority, even as the fact or force of that authority suggests a lack that only subsequent rules of authority can rectify. Indicating how, through a series of events, what is about to become the common law becomes the common law, how the prelegal, which is never quite nonlegal, becomes the legal, these accounts reach backwards towards a forever inaccessible "moment" of origin. The origin of (positive) law is always already there and, what comes to the same thing, can never be situated at a determinate point of time.

If the origin of the positive law that is the common law occurs at every point in time and at no determinate point, how is one to understand such origin? *The Concept of Law* helps point to the answer. In a jurisprudential work whose preface declares that it "may also be regarded as an essay in descriptive sociology" (v), Hart seeks to provide an "analysis of the distinctive

structure of a municipal legal system and a better understanding of the re-
semblances and differences between law, coercion, and morality, as types of
social phenomena" (21). Hart faults the Austinian view of law[20] for failing to
account for the rule-like quality of law and for the sense in which law can be
said to be obligatory as well as coercive. Hart himself conceives of a legal system as the union of two types of rules and supplies a framework for understanding the process of unification of "primary" and "secondary" rules that
culminates in a "mature legal system."

"Secondary rules," for Hart, rectify the defects of "simple" societies living
only by "primary rules of obligation." Societies with "simple social structures" are those "where the only means of social control is that general attitude of the group toward its own standard mode of behavior in terms of
which we have characterized rules of obligation. A social structure of this
kind is often referred to as one of 'custom'; but we shall not use this term
because it often implies that the customary rules are very old and supported
with less social pressure than other rules" (89). In these "simple" societies,
the majority live by following rules which they accept, while a minority,
rather than following rules, conform to them through fear of social pressure.
One may be concerned with rules of conduct, Hart writes, in two ways, "either merely as an observer who does not himself accept them, or as a member
of the group which accepts them and uses them as guides to conduct. We may
call these respectively the 'external' and the 'internal points of view'" (86).
The internal aspect of rules refers to the fact that "if a social rule is to exist
some at least must look upon the behaviour in question as a general standard
to be followed by the group as a whole. A social rule has an 'internal' aspect, in
addition to the external aspect which it shares with a social habit and which
consists in the regular uniform behaviour which an observer could record"
(55). External points of view are the variety of vantage points from which one
may "from outside refer to the way in which *they* [the members of the group]
are concerned with them [the rules] from the internal point of view." An observer taking an extreme external perspective, for instance, need not refer to
rules as such, but may simply recognize "regularities of observable behavior."
Another observer may "assert that the group accepts the rules." The latter,
rather than simply understanding a red light as a sign that group members
will stop, for instance, may point out that members of a group look upon the
light as a signal to stop. While taking an external point of view, this observer,
Hart writes, "refer[s] to the internal aspect of rules seen from their internal
point of view" (87–88).

Any society, according to Hart, will contain some persons who "reject the rules and attend to them only from the external point of view as a sign of possible punishment" and others who "accept and voluntarily co-operate in maintaining the rules, and so see their own and other persons' behaviour in terms of the rules." The attitudes of the former will be expressible as "'I was obliged to do it,'" or "'You will probably suffer for it if . . . '" To "those who are normally the majority of the society," though, the rules will manifest themselves in statements of obligation that bespeak the internal aspect of rules. A legal theory "anxious to do justice to the complexity of the facts," Hart writes, must remember the presence of both points of view (88).

Hart, like historians of the common law, finds most "simple" or customary societies living by primary rules to be lacking. "It is plain," to Hart, "that only a small community closely knit by ties of kinship, common sentiment and belief, and placed in a stable environment, could live successfully by such a regime of unofficial rules" (89–90). All other societies living by primary rules will run up against three problems, according to Hart: the uncertainty of the rules, their static character, and the inefficiency of social pressure to maintain them.

These defects are rectified, Hart claims (90–95), by supplementing the primary rules with secondary or power-conferring rules of recognition, change, and adjudication, whose presence signifies the existence of a "mature legal system." The "rule of recognition" provides a procedure, by reference either to an authoritative text or to an official whose declarations on this point are authoritative, for settling doubts or uncertainty as to what the rules are, or as to the scope of a given rule. "Rules of change" provide the means, otherwise lacking, of deliberately adapting rules to changing circumstances, by either eliminating old rules or introducing new ones. And "rules of adjudication" empower officials to ascertain authoritatively and conclusively the fact of a rule's violation. "The introduction of the remedy for each defect might, in itself, be considered a step from the pre-legal into the legal world; . . . certainly all three remedies together are enough to convert the regime of primary rules into what is indisputably a legal system" (91).

The rule of recognition, in particular, "brings with it many elements distinctive of law." Sophisticated rules of recognition in "more developed" legal systems refer to "general characteristics possessed by primary rules," such as enactment by a specific body, long customary practice, or a certain relation to judicial decisions as criteria for identifying the rules. Yet even in simple form, as a list of rules acknowledged to be authoritative, for instance, the rule of recognition, Hart claims, provides "an authoritative mark." Its use as external criterion for the rules' authoritative identification provides "the germ of the idea of legal validity" and indicates the existence of a legal system (79). The mark introduces, "although in an embryonic form, the idea of a legal system: for the rules are now not just a discrete unconnected set but are, in a simple way, unified" (92–93).

In such a legal system, the mode of existence of primary rules is validity rather than actual acceptance. That is, questions regarding the existence of rules in this legal system, unlike in "the simple case of customary rules" (107), are decidable by criteria of validity, without reference to the acceptance of the rules. The rule of recognition provides the test of validity, a test whose "existence" itself, however, is ultimately a matter not of validity but of actual acceptance or use by officials—a matter of "fact": "For whereas a subordinate rule of a system may be valid and in that sense 'exist' even if it is generally disregarded, the rule of recognition exists only as a complex, but normally concordant, practice of the courts, officials, and private persons in identifying the law by reference to certain criteria. Its existence is a matter of fact" (107). The rule of recognition, in other words, ensures that the primary rules of obligation are no longer simply "the rules which a particular group of human beings accepts" (90). Instead, the primary rules become subordinate to the rule of recognition in that their authoritativeness depends on secondary rules that are accepted by officials, rather than on acceptance by the group of the primary rules as "right" in substance.

With this conception of a legal system, the lawfulness of the rules, or legality, depends on the fact of official practice. The resemblance between Hart's concept of law and an Austinian model of law as the sovereign's coercive orders becomes apparent, especially when law is considered from the subjects' standpoint. For neither Hart nor Austin *require* more from the subjects of an existing legal system than conformity to rules, regardless of the motive from which conformity proceeds.[21] Hart specifically identifies "two minimum conditions necessary and sufficient for the existence of a legal system." First, "rules of behavior that are valid according to the system's ultimate criteria of validity must be generally obeyed." Second, "[the system's] rules of recognition specifying the criteria of legal validity and its rules of change and adjudication must be effectively accepted as common public standards of official behaviour by its officials" (113).

Hart and Austin thus differ only in that Hart's officials accept their own rules as binding on themselves, while Austin's sovereign need not. This difference, upon which hinges all that is known as "the rule of law," is indeed important. The citizens of Hart's legal system, unlike those of Austin's, can console themselves that the law that may be imposed on them will also constrain the officials and so reduce the "arbitrariness" of official commands. But, from the perspective of the citizens, it remains that they, like the subjects of Austin's sovereign, may feel only forced or compelled to obey rules that they themselves, perhaps rightly, do not accept as right.

The minimal conditions of the legal system, in sum, are fulfilled by the imposition of official will upon the members of a society that admittedly had its own "social structure" of primary rules of obligation. Critics who claim that Hart fails to capture the "reality" of coercion in the modern legal system thus do not themselves realize what Hart's concept entails. To Hart, law is a "coercive system" (193) that accords exactly with presumed sociological "reality." Indeed, in doing justice to the "facts," the positivist concept of law, like the sociological understanding of law, is oblivious not to coercion but to the original morality of a society, to which it denies the power to found what it calls "law." For the legal positivist, it is precisely the fact of official practice— "the complex social situation" of acceptance and use of a secondary rule of recognition to identify the rules to which citizens must conform—which founds a legal system or which "deserves, if anything does, to be called the foundations of a legal system" (97).

The establishment of such foundations, or the "step from the pre-legal to the legal," for the positivist, occurs "no doubt as a matter of history," writes Hart, and "may be accomplished in distinguishable stages" (92). The first stage in the creation of a simple rule of recognition is "the mere reduction to writing of hitherto unwritten rules." The "crucial step," though, will be "the acknowledgement of reference to the writing or inscription as *authoritative,* i.e. as the *proper* way of disposing of doubts as to the existence of the rule. Where there is such an acknowledgement, there is a very simple form of secondary rule: a rule for conclusive identification of primary rules of obligation" (92–93).

Insofar as the rule of recognition provides the authoritative mark that "introduces . . . in embryonic form" the idea of validity and insofar as its emergence marks the moment of unification of rules indicating the existence of a legal system, its acknowledgment marks, as "a matter of history," the moment of origin of positive law. Sections 2 and 3 attend further to this "moment," a "moment" that legal history cannot locate at any determinate point of time. The discussion dwells on this moment in a manner legal historians may find strange; it seeks in this moment the essence of the origin of positive law, an essence which alerts us to important aspects of the "acknowledgment of authority" (section 2) and of the "writing of rules" (section 3) out of which legal philosophers, sociologists, and historians alike presume modern law emerges.

2. The Mark of Authority

What is the moment of origin of positive law? What, in other words, is the moment of the crucial step from "the pre-legal to the legal"? The moment, that is, in which "the germ of the idea of legal validity" appears and the authority of a rule of recognition is acknowledged? The moment which marks the difference between custom and a common law that is taken to be a "system of rules" having "their own rational coherence," "laid down by judicial or legislative authority," and accompanied by the "judicial machinery" and "procedure" supplied by the king's courts?

The story that follows takes up the acknowledgment of William's rule and the authoritativeness of his *Domesday Book* to explore the origins of a positivist legal system. Although this "history" conforms to the tendency of accounts of the common law to start with the Norman Conquest, its aim is not to render an account of chronological events in the common law's development but to inquire into the essence of the founding of positive law. It does not seek to locate origins at any particular point in time and it need not have started with the Norman Conquest, for, as section 1 has shown, the events of 1066 simply encapsulate a process which historians take to have always already begun, namely, the development of law as an official body of rules. The Conquest will do, however, for it extends and continues—just as its story repeats the story of—the unification of rules and establishment of authority that supplements a way of life itself perceived as deficient in authority; it epitomizes the unification that marks the emergence of a positivist legal system.

The Authority of the Domesday Book

Once upon a time, William the Conqueror (although he was not yet called the Conqueror or William the Great but only Duke William) "undertook the desperate adventure of invading England by transporting 5,000 men and 2,500 horses across the Channel, an astonishing performance in those days. The Battle of Hastings (1066) and the death of King Harold quickly settled him upon the throne of his new kingdom. Reforms began at once."[22]

King William reorganized the "the casual 'treasure of the Anglo-Saxon kings'" into "an Exchequer along business lines." He "insisted that the bishops should not transact ecclesiastical business in the hundred courts, but should hold their own Courts Christian for the purpose; and from that day to this the Church has maintained its separate system of courts administering canon law. Church and State which had been inextricably connected in the Anglo-Saxon age henceforth were strictly separate."[23] And finally, "his last years were absorbed in the great survey of the kingdom which is known as *Domesday Book.*"[24]

For two hundred years after its compilation in 1086, royal courts referred to the *Domesday Book.*[25] What provided the *Book* with such lasting authority? This question raises issues about the writing of law, the recognition of writings, and the development of a legal system.

Historians describe the *Domesday Book* as "a great rate book,"[26] "intended primarily to ascertain the assessments for the payment of the king's *geld* and to prevent evasion of its payment."[27] Natives called the book "Domesday," or "metaphorically speaking, the day of judgement," some suggest, because the Court of Chancery/Exchequer followed the book so literally.[28] As Richard fitz Nigel, the Treasurer of England, explained in about 1179, "the sentence of that strict and terrible last account cannot be evaded by any skilful subterfuge, so when this book is appealed to on those matters which it contains, its sentence cannot be quashed or set aside with impunity."[29]

The *Domesday Book* is a detailed record of the real property of the kingdom, its tenants, burdens, and values. The royal commissioners gathered information "in triplicate; that is at the time of King Edward [1065], when King William gave it [the land, to its present holder], and at the present time [1086]."[30] Royal clerks apparently compiled the main *Domesday Book,* the Exchequer Domesday, from summaries of surveys of seven or nine geographical circuits. Royal commissioners had prepared preliminary returns by taking evidence in local courts "on the oath of the sheriff of the shire, and of the barons and their Frenchmen, and of the whole hundred—priests, reeves and six villeins from each vill."[31] They did so before juries—half English and half Norman[32]—whose task was "apparently to approve and check the information variously assembled."[33]

The *clamores* and other entries in the *Domesday Book* indicate that disputes sometimes occurred before claims to property were recorded. The background to these disputes, as is explained below, lay in the transfer and uncertainty of holdings immediately following conquest by William the Bastard (as he was also sometimes called by his contemporaries).

Before returning to Normandy in February of 1067, William had granted land to the Normans who had helped him. While he might have known the names of the men who fought against him, though, he could not know the exact location or extent of their estates. In distributing these, therefore, he granted to individual Normans the lands held by particular Anglo-Saxons in specified shires, based on a rough idea of their value. The Norman grantee had to discover for himself what and where those lands were. But "a Norman could not very well ride round an English shire 'alone and palely loitering' asking in every village if Ulf or Tovi had held any land there; even if the villagers had been able to understand him, they would probably have done their best to cheat him, if not to murder him."[34]

Instead, grantees carried a sealed writ from the king to the relevant shire court for inspection and reading. There the whole shire witnessed the king's grant, "and would be held responsible for its execution; in this case [the shire] would have to inform the Norman what the lands of his predecessor were, and help him gain possession."[35]

The shire court usually met in the open air, away from towns so "it would not have been difficult for a body of Normans to arrive with a strong force of soldiers and surround the [meeting] place completely."[36] Furthermore, since William did not expropriate all the English at once, some were willing to collaborate in hopes of saving their own property. And while planned rebellions did occur in some shires in 1087, William had taken many of the natural leaders to Normandy with him—and when he returned to quash the revolts, he used the uprisings as excuses for further expropriations.[37]

"In the general confusion and terror of the Conquest," then, individual Normans sometimes seized more lands than they had been granted.[38] But twenty years after the Conquest, the Domesday Survey provided a way of "examining the details of the ruthless spoliation, and approving them only when they had been done by authority."[39] Because of this, according to one historian, the *Domesday Book* got its name: "Every Norman had been forced to account for the way in which he acquired his English lands; and if it was approved, his name was inscribed and his claim upheld for ever by the hundred, the shire, the king's justices and the king."[40]

Whether the original reference to the Book of Judgement arose from the Exchequer's use of the Domesday Survey for taxation, or from its validation of property claims, the *Book* served both purposes. It recorded the customary holdings and liability for *geld* in the past, and resolved the nature of such holdings, while ascertaining capacities for payment in the future.[41] In doing so, the Survey, on the one hand, recorded Anglo-Saxon customs and newly settled claims as fact; at the same time, the inscription of these facts imbued them with authoritativeness.

Understanding this transformation of custom or law simultaneously into fact and into the authoritative rules of the *Domesday Book* requires an inquiry into the writing of the *Book*. First, the king—or, in later periods, his predecessor—and his men had authored the *Book*. The king's men had done so in the sense of physically compiling and writing the *descriptio*. But the king "authored" the *Book* in another sense, as the ostensible source validating Norman—and Anglo-Saxon—claims appearing in the document. Edward A. Freeman writes that "from the beginning, [William] dealt with all lay estates in England as land forfeited to the Crown, which [he] granted out afresh, whether the grant was to the former owner or to some new grantee." Thus:

> The foreign soldier who received his reward in a grant of English land held that land, as a plain matter of fact and without any legal subtleties, as a personal gift from King William. The Englishman who bought back his land, or received it back again as alms, did not hold it as a gift in exactly the same sense as his Norman neighbor, but it was a royal grant by something more than a mere legal fiction. His land had been, if only for a moment, in the King's hands to be dealt with as the King chose; and the King had chosen to give it back to him, rather than to keep it himself or to give it to anybody else.

Consequently, Freeman points out that

> the lawyers' doctrine that all land must be a grant from the Crown is thus accidentally an historical truth. It became true by virtue of a single act of William's reign, which no law-book records, and which most likely no lawyer ever thought of. In this way William became systematically to every landowner in his realm, what earlier Kings had incidentally been to many of them, a personal grantor as well as a political chief.[42]

Freeman himself was concerned to depict the Conquest as an evolution, rather than a revolution, in Anglo-Saxon institutions, from which feudalism gradually emerged. Later scholarship has heavily contested his interpretation, which controversy need not delay us here. One can put aside the questions of how William "held" the land, of the extent to which the Normans adopted traditional Anglo-Saxon patterns of landholding, and of the extent to which William's grantees foisted themselves upon, or maintained themselves in, the shire by force, threat, or trickery. The point remains that William at once claimed to be, in some sense, the "source" of law while recording the law, in some sense, "as it had been in the days of King Edward."

Whether William inherited his authority directly from Edward the Confessor, as he sometimes claimed,[43] William continued—or appears to continue—some of Edward's law. In a charter to the City of London, for instance, he recognized Edward's law explicitly. He did so, nevertheless, as the source of law—by his "will." Addressed to "William the bishop and Gosfrith the portreeve, and all the burgesses in London, both French and English," the charter stated: "I let you wit that I will that you two be worthy of all the laws that you were worthy of in King Edward's day. And I will that every child be his father's heir after his father's day, and I will not endure that any man offer any wrong to you. God keep you."[44]

Yet even as William extended recognition to older laws, his knowledge of those laws depended on the Anglo-Saxons. His men necessarily inquired of the locals in compiling the Survey. Since local customs about the land were recorded as facts in the *Domesday Book,* its authoritativeness, like William's own claim to legitimacy, points to at least partial Norman acknowledgment of Anglo-Saxon customs. Such customs did not govern the Normans, who kept their own laws for relations with one another,[45] while special laws governed their relations with the Anglo-Saxons. (*Wilhelmes cyninges asetnysse,* of between 1067 and 1077, for instance, regulated the method of proof in trials between an "englisc man," and a "frencisc man" of "nordhmandisc lagu" or Norman law.)[46] But William did recognize at least some Anglo-Saxon customs for the Anglo-Saxons.

Several private treatises of the late eleventh and early twelfth centuries support this point. They suggest that the laws and customs granted by King William to the Anglo-Saxons after the Conquest were the same as those that his cousin King Edward had administered before him. The first part of the *Leis Willelme,* for instance, contains Anglo-Norman laws based in part on the genuine statutes of William I, some of which can be traced back to Cnute's code. The *Leis* take account of the Danelag and also regulate the liability of the hundred (a subdivision of the shire) for the killing of Normans.[47] The *Articuli Willelmi,*[48] written between 1110 and 1135, contain laws going back to William, in part based on the *Instituta Cnuti,* which is itself a twelfth-century Latin compilation of the Anglo-Saxon laws of Cnute with excerpts from Alfred-Ine and other sources.[49]

Further documentary analysis suggests, however, that although the Normans may have referred to Anglo-Saxon customs, they did so only as pretense or "to produce [an] impression." According to one historian, the *Articuli* were joined under Stephen with the *Leges Edwardi Confessoris* and another work to form the *Tripartita,* which, together with the *Quadripartitus* and other sources, were again compiled, in about 1210, into a document "containing interpolations and falsifications in the interest of the city of London."[50] The so-called *Leges Edwardi Confessoris,* written about 1130 to 1135, this historian writes,

presents itself as the result of an inquest concerning the Anglo-Saxon law which William the Conqueror undertook in the fourth year of his reign, by summoning from each county twelve notable Anglo-Saxons as jurors, who were to give evidence regarding the law. The law thus alleged to be proven is taken to be the law of Edward the Confessor. . . . The chequered contents of the book show that we have before us a private treatise, which presents the law in force toward the end of the reign of Henry I, and attributes to Norman institutions an Anglo-Saxon origin.[51]

The fabricated *Constitutiones Cnuti regis de foresta,* prepared by a high forest official with the aid of the *Instituta Cnute,* also sought "to cover the harsh and unpopular Norman forest law by the name of Cnute, and to produce the impression that it was customary Anglo-Saxon law."[52]

In the face of apparently conflicting documents, then, some historians argue that Norman laws for the English actually diverged from older Anglo-Saxon ways. *Willelmes Lad,* for instance, effected a "radical change in English procedure" which had "implications beyond the mere matter of pleading and proof" with which it was ostensibly concerned:

By undertaking to regulate the method of trying the major crime the crown here begins the process of absorbing full cognizance; and further, by the very method of regulation implicitly establishes in England the inevitable concomitants—the Norman judgment and that part of the Norman sanctions connected therewith. We say implicitly, for such a judgment would be a tacit incident of the Norman form of proof, and there is no direct evidence of special legislation on punishment. . . . [Two other] documents make it clear that afflictive punishment has been made general, but neither allow the inference that this was done by any formal act, although this seems probable because the Norman Kings would never have been satisfied with the Anglo-Saxon rules for failure at ordeal.[53]

Other historians argue, on the other hand, that "only a few changes had been introduced by William I," who, they claim, acknowledged the Anglo-Saxon law. They point, for instance, to "the continued respect paid to Anglo-Saxon law . . . strikingly illustrated by the bringing of the aged bishop Aethelric of Selsey to the plea held on Pinnendon Heath in 1075 or 1076 in order to answer questions on Anglo-Saxon law."[54]

The discussion so far shows a Norman acknowledgment of Anglo-Saxon law that on its face expresses, even if the Normans themselves did not carry out, an attitude of respect toward the law of the other. The legal historian's concern at this point is to ascertain the good faith or pretense of Norman actions or to discern the extent and manner of Norman adoption and adaptation of Anglo-Saxon customs. The discussion below takes up a different although related concern: how do historians come to understand a situation in which one group confronts and acknowledges another group's law simultaneously as the origin of a legal system and as conquest? The discussion first shows how the process of unification of primary and secondary rules whose occurrence marks the existence of a positivist legal system corresponds to a conqueror's view of the unification of law that occurs at the moment of conquest—at the moment when the authority of one group is acknowledged by the other, the moment when the rules to be obeyed are recognized to be those which accord with the conqueror's will, itself acknowledged as the source or criterion of law.

The Law of the Other

William and the Norman Kings who followed him were not the first to express respect for the customs of others in England. Fifty years earlier, upon his victory in England, the Dane, Cnute, exhorted the people to observe ecclesiastical and secular law, referring to the recognition given to "Eadgares *lage*" by both Anglo-Saxons and Danes.[55] Edgar (958–75), fearing the establishment of another Scandinavian king in Northumbria, it is claimed, had "used a conciliatory policy, admitting the right of the Danes to their own laws: 'I have ever allowed them this and will allow it as long as my life lasts, because of your loyalty, which you have always shown me.'"[56] An Anglo-Saxon diet of "Dunsaete," too, with the concurrence of Welsh *consiliarii,* in about 935 enacted a law regulating "the legal relations between the Dunsaetes of Kymric and English nationality separated from each other by a river, especially with reference to fresh pursuit, anefang, wergild, procedure, and international jurisdiction."[57] And the Elizabethan scholar, Lambard, states too that among the Saxons the practice existed that "viris duodeni jure consulti, Angliae sex, Walliae totidem Anglis et Wallis jus dicunto." ("Let twelve men versed in the law, six English and an equal number of Welsh, dispense justice to the English and Welsh.")[58]

In all these instances, what we might call an "acknowledgment" of another law appears. In the acknowledgment of another law comes a distinction between one's own law and that of the other. Such acknowledgment may be of two types. First, it may accompany respect both for one's own law and for that of the other. In this case, whether two groups live independently, compromise, enrich one another with their presence, make war or are enemies,[59] the practices that emerge toward the other, like the practices within the group, constitute each as a people. As such, the respectful acknowledgment of the law of the one and of the other precludes the ultimate dominance of either group and its authority over the other.

Second, should domination occur, or authority emerge, the two groups become one society. Their laws require unification. The story of the unification of the "separate" law of the new society will be the history of the emergence of a legal system and will point to a situation in which the two groups acknowledging one another's law stand in a relation, not of reciprocal respect, but of governor and governed. Historians—and sociologists—often point to the complexities of actual relations of this sort, arguing about the extent to which a particular group or class in society is governor or governed and the manner in which one group imposes its own law or is forced to adapt to a law that is not its own.

William's acknowledgment of Anglo-Saxon customs points to the existence of two groups: the Normans and the Anglo-Saxons. William's acknowledgment could be construed as pointing to a situation of reciprocal respect. It could also be construed as pointing to a situation in which one group, in some sense, dominates the other, leading to a "unification" of the two. Historians would then ask to what extent William imposed the rules of the Normans on the Anglo-Saxons or, conversely, to what extent the Normans themselves were forced to adopt Anglo-Saxon customary law. Insofar as histories of the common law address just such issues, their accounts of the development of a unified system of law present William's acknowledgment of Anglo-Saxon law as involving relations of governor and governed.

In simplest terms, this relation between governor and governed corresponds to the relations between a group accepting its own law and a group conforming to the law of another. Probing such relations in the context of history, though, reveals the more complex situation of a divided society of unified law, in which, as shall be seen, both—or all—groups tell and are told rules. Such a society displays the positivist distinctions between fact and law and law and morality. For, from the governors' standpoint, the governors' own laws are the law or rule; the governors' law is "what we do and what others *should* do." From the same standpoint, the law of the governed is mere custom or fact; it is "what the others *in fact* do." The governors' understanding transforms the law of the governed from law into fact. Conversely, from the other standpoint, that is, from the standpoint of the governed, their own former customs remain law, but they become the "old law"—or perhaps a new "morality." This law remains "what we *should* do," while the new rules of the governors ("what they do") become the new law or "what we are *required* to do." With the appearance of governors and their law emerges the possibility of distinguishing between law and morality.

So too comes the formulation of law as rules and the acknowledgment of the mark of authority, or what Hart calls the "germ of the idea of legal validity." For when the practices of the governed no longer constitute the law of a people, the governed depend on the other for knowledge of what to do. Insofar as the governors hope to impose their own practices, they must explain what these are to the outsiders—the former people. This telling of law takes the form of statements of rules. Insofar as the governed demand the retention of their practices, they too must formulate their practices as statements articulating their claims to the outsiders—the rulers: "The conqueror wishes to enforce his customs upon his new subjects. He must needs explain what they are. The conquered demand the retention of their ancient practices. They are compelled to formulate their claims. So it is when . . . William conquers the English, when the English conquer India."[60]

Conflicts between the rules of the former people and those of the rulers will arise. How are these resolved? Recall the example of William: William did not simply claim to inherit from Edward. He asserted—as the source of law—that *by his will* particular customs stood. In this assertion, he provided an authoritative and external mark that decided between the conflicting claims of Anglo-Saxons and Normans—the mark of royal power. Insofar as Anglo-Saxons and Normans alike acknowledged William's authority to determine law, the potentially conflicting rules of behavior of Anglo-Saxons and of Normans were no longer "just a discrete unconnected set" of propositions (much less of practices); they became, in Hart's words, "in a simple way, unified" (93).

William's authoritative mark indeed cured the set of primary rules of the Anglo-Saxons and the Normans of their "defects." The *Domesday Book* first recorded—to stick to Hart's two stages—"hitherto unwritten rules." More crucially though, the acknowledgment of the *Book* as authoritative, as the proper way of disposing of doubts as to the existence of a rule, pointed to an acknowledgment of William's will as the source of law which would henceforth serve as the criterion for recognizing rules; insofar as William's will was acknowledged to be the source of law and to constitute an authoritative mark, rules could be changed and William's mark would provide a way of identifying which ones would be enforced.

William's authority, of course, came not only from the Norman officials who respectfully acknowledged or accepted his rule, but also from the ability of those officials to enforce Anglo-Saxon obedience to the rules William identified. That is, William's will, the authoritative mark by which William unified the Anglo-Norman legal system, established itself over the Anglo-Saxons by force. As it did so, the "Conquest," the acknowledgment of the authority of William's will, marked the destruction of the Anglo-Saxons as a people.

No longer would Anglo-Saxon practices constitute them. With the acknowledgment of an authoritative mark external to their practices for identifying rules of behavior, the Anglo-Saxon way of life fragments into the realms of the moral, the legal, and the ambiguous "political"—in which one does what one "must." What one "must" do may be what one *ought* to do (the actions now prescribed by the moral, the old law) or what one is *forced* to do (the behavior sanctioned by officials). Insofar as one has a capacity to "do" anything, however (and the meaning of "action" becomes the great issue of politics and philosophy), one has potential for constitutional definition as a member of a "law"-governed society.

The moment of conquest captures precisely the acknowledgment of the mark of authority comprising the origin of positive law. While all groups in a situation of government may tell and be told rules, some group will dominate. The "conqueror" refers to the group whose rules are *acknowledged* as dominant. Should this group differ from the group whose customs *indeed* predominate, "conqueror" nevertheless refers to the former: to the group to whom the mark of authority belongs, the group who accepts the secondary rules and enforces the primary ones they mark.

Examining "the specific method of social control to be seen in a system of primary and secondary rules" shows the positivist legal system to correspond to a "law" in which, as a matter of "fact," officials impose their will on a conquered people. The unification of the propositionally articulated customs of a (former) people with the similarly propositional secondary rules of the outsider occurs with the citizens' acknowledgment of an external mark that identifies the rules they must obey. The authority of the mark is decided, for the positivist, by the facts: the existence and content of a rule of recognition presents "an empirical, though complex, question of fact."[61] According to this view, in other words, William's authority is determined by the acceptance of William's kingship by the Normans (or official class) and the success, or effectiveness, of Norman rule over England.[62]

To summarize, in a positivist system of law, where, as a matter of fact, officials accept secondary rules and citizens obey the rules of behavior that are valid according to the secondary rules, the externality to the rules of the mark of authority reveals a situation of domination over, rather than respect for, the law of the other. This is not to say that positivism condones "morally iniquitous law"; Hart, for one, emphatically does not (cf. 203–7). (Further, should the conqueror, like the officials, become citizen, the "rule of law" requires obedience to the primary rules.) Nevertheless, the unification of law whose origin lies in the acknowledgment of an external mark of authority lies in an imposition of will that completes itself in the conquest of a people—all of which is inscribed in accounts of the Norman Conquest and of the common law's development.

3. The Writing of Rules

By inquiring into the "crucial step" establishing a positivist legal system, that is, into the acknowledgment of a rule of recognition, section 2 has shown how the "moment of origin" of positive law coincides with the moment a conqueror imposes his will on a conquered people. Section 3 now turns to the presumptions that allow one to consider such imposition "law" and, conversely, that serve to deny the status and the name "law" to the customs of a people. From what ground does a conqueror perceive the practices of a people as incomplete and in need of a mark of authority? On what grounds—or from what ground—does the positivist find the rules of societies with simple social structures to be defective? And from what ground does the common law historian assert that custom is not quite law?

These questions again lead to history, this time to the "very important" first stage in establishing the foundations of positive law, a stage which Hart, for one, describes as "the mere reduction to writing of hitherto unwritten rules." To presume, as Hart does, that rules are writable, projects a particular understanding onto rules, which understanding need not be shared by those living by the rules. Insofar as an observer's presumptions about rules are not shared by those in the society whose rules are under consideration, that society's attitude toward its "rules" will appear inadequate to the observer. The rectification of such inadequacies, understood as the deficiencies of primary rules, begins with the "mere reduction to writing of hitherto unwritten rules" and leads to the prospect of a system of propositional rules, which prospect raises more difficulties, as shall be seen, than one might at first suspect.

Propositions and Practices

The phrase, "the mere reduction to writing of hitherto unwritten rules," which, for Hart, characterizes the first stage in establishing the foundations of positive law, seems to refer to the writing of previously existing law. But early written law did not always codify existing rules. Ordinarily, it addressed matters where law was already questionable or changing. Some ancient codifications occurred when particular groups grew dissatisfied with the established order and became strong enough to challenge its customs. Others occurred when particular unwritten laws became disputed. Rather than codifying existing rules, then, early codes are characterized by their "omission of the obvious."[63]

Thus, in Anglo-Saxon law, "written laws and legal documents being written for present use and not for the purpose of enlightening future historians, assume knowledge on the reader's part of an indefinite mass of received custom and practice."[64] The earliest collections of German written laws are "not comprehensive codes, designed to cover the whole region of law, but in the main only records of new principles introduced by specific legislation or through the medium of the courts."[65] Similarly, early Anglo-Saxon laws "do not form a complete codification of law, but comprise those portions that were changed, amended, or newly enforced: the greater part of the law remained unwritten."[66] In England, the conversion of the Anglo-Saxons to Christianity occasioned the first written laws, the dooms or judgments mentioned in chapter 1. Aethelbert set down, in English, a code of laws establishing, in part, "what restitution must be made by anyone who steals anything belonging to the church, the bishop or the other clergy."[67] At that time, "homicide, theft and other injuries were compensated by a tariff of emendations, adjudicated by a man's neighbors in the moot. The amount of the 'wer' or payment for killing a man, or the 'bot' for injuring him, depended on the social rank of the man injured or killed, and the gravity of the injury."[68] Aethelbert's laws thus protected the new missionaries and their churches by assigning them a social rank.

The West Saxon Code of Ine, resulting from that king's deliberations with the *witan* of his people in the late seventh century, also concerned "the salvation of souls and the condition of the kingdom."[69] Thus Anglo-Saxon acceptance of Christianity had "revolutionary consequences in the world of law," in that "it is likely that heretofore the traditional customs, even if they have not been conceived as instituted by gods who are now becoming devils, have been conceived as essentially unalterable. Law has been the old; new law has been a contradiction in terms. And now about certain matters there must be new law. What is more, 'the example of the Romans' shows that new law can be made by the issue of commands."[70]

If, as the examples above suggest, early written laws did not codify existing rules, how is one to understand the "hitherto unwritten" rules that a positivist account attributes to prelegal society? And how is one to understand the writing that constitutes the first step toward a positivist legal system? The phrase, "the mere reduction to writing of hitherto unwritten rules," points to a presumption that rules—that which is about to become written—*already* are writable; "hitherto unwritten" rules have "merely" to be "reduced" to writing.

The presumption that rules are writable, however, need not be shared by those who *live by* the rules of a simple society. For such persons, rules may exist as practices rather than as propositional statements. Recall Hart's characterization of primitive society as a society living by rules of obligation. Proper conduct within this society is understood neither as "habit," in the sense of mere convergence of observable behavior, nor as "conformity" to rules due to pressure or coercion. Instead, members of the community, taking an internal standpoint toward the rules, follow rules through a sense of obligation. The community's stance toward its own rules consists in the members' shared knowledge of *how to* act, a *practical* knowledge that need not be formulated as statements of rules or as propositional knowledge.

To an observer or outsider—one taking a point of view external to the community—obligation or the internal aspect of rules manifests itself, in Hart's words, as "a critical reflective attitude to certain patterns of behaviour as a common standard . . . that . . . display[s] itself in criticism (including self-criticism), demands for conformity, and in acknowledgments that such criticism and demands are justified, all of which find their characteristic expression in the normative terminology of 'ought', 'must', and 'should', 'right' and 'wrong'" (56). The projection of the writability of rules onto the practices of a simple society or onto the obligations of those who take an internal standpoint toward the rules reveals the distinction between an external view—in which statements of rules expressed in normative terminology "display" the internal aspect of rules—and an internal standpoint requiring no such display. From a standpoint internal to the community, unwritten practices do not need propositional articulation to be rules of law or obligation. Law appears before those taking an external standpoint, by contrast, as a phenomenon before an observer, as a graspable representation.

The introduction of temporality invoked by the "hitherto" of Hart's unwritten rules points to a peculiarity in the positivist's view of law, however, that goes beyond the difference between those within and those outside a community, the difference between the actor who follows the rules and the observer who notes what conformity to the rules entails. The positivist historian adopts a standpoint which is not simply the external perspective that a community member could after all adopt, but is a standpoint from which one *presumes* that practices (or rule-following or what to do) are writable, even *before* adoption of an external point of view. The positivist historian presumes that, even before the writing of rules, practices *already* take propositional form as articulable and transcribable knowledge "*that* such and such is a rule."

The positivist historian committed to producing an objective representation of the past treats rules as observable facts, to be represented propositionally. In presuming that rules can be represented propositionally, the historian somewhat resembles a new anthropologist, an outsider who, arriving in a foreign culture, believes the natives to have readily articulable explanations of what may otherwise seem (to the anthropologist) to be incomprehensible practices. While explanations of native practices may be forthcoming, the native, in acting, has no need for them. Until pressed by the outsider to describe how and what and why she does what she does, the native just does what natives do. The articulation in propositional terms, for the outsider or the observer, of the native's practical knowledge of what to do (whether by native, anthropologist, or both) entails a *shift* to an external view of native practices, in which the "fact" that the community thinks from the internal standpoint is acknowledged from outside. This shift or transformation of practice, apparent to the sophisticated anthropologist who no longer expects natives to have readily articulable explanations of their practices, is nevertheless invisible to an anthropologist who, like Hart's historian, continues to expect *already*-existing propositional articulations of law.[71]

In considering "the mere reduction to writing of hitherto unwritten rules" which is the first step toward a positivist legal system, one can now distinguish two possible transformations. One consists in a transformation of law (written or not) into rules graspable as propositions; the positivist *assumes* that rules are graspable as propositions, and hence fails to understand that grasping rules as propositions involves a transformation of practice or an imposition of positivist assumptions onto native law. The second transformation consists in the writing of law, whether or not that writing takes a propositionally rule-like form. Because the positivist's understanding of the development of a mature legal system begins with a prelegal society in which rules are already taken to be propositional, for the positivist the writing of law necessarily means the writing of propositions or of statements of rules. (One who does not presume that law is propositional—in other words, who does not assume the first transformation—could think the writing of law— the second transformation—differently or nonpositivistically, on the other hand, as the nonpropositional writing of law that occurs, for instance, in the poetic expression of practices.)

The positivist here emerges as an outsider to practices and as a particular sort of outsider at that—an outsider who neglects or forgets the shift or transformation in practices that the very commitment to an enterprise of propositional representation has wrought. That commitment, manifest in the presumption that rules are already propositional, leads the positivist observer of practices to conceive of those practices as propositions, while simultaneously viewing the native attitude toward these propositionally understood "primary rules" as defective or incomplete, insofar as the native attitude—a concern from within for the "internal aspect of rules"—fails to coincide with the observer's attitude toward propositional law. Grounding his or her understanding of law in that of the present age, in which rules are thought as propositions, the positivist observer measures native practice against modern law and, noting difference, projects onto practices a lack—the need for remedies to transform those practices or primary rules into a unified set of statements of rules, a positivist legal system.

The Defects

In other words, the outsider's perception of the defects in native practices or in a people's customs is grounded in the privileging of a particular understanding of law. For the outsider, knowledge of law is a propositional knowledge; a people's customs are not law in part because they lack propositionality. But, as the outsider also recognizes, propositions alone are not necessarily rules of law. Knowledge of law, for the outsider, consists in propositional knowledge of *authoritative rules* and authority consists in the power to enforce general obedience to the rules authority indicates.

Recall how, in the story of the Conquest, propositional knowledge of former customs now identified by external criteria together with the rules of the official class *replaces* the people's practical knowledge; this propositional knowledge, accessible to all who recognize the mark of authority, *becomes* "law." In a similar way, under positivism, the propositional knowledge of authoritative rules identified by the observer replaces practice or custom; practice gives way to positive law.

Just as, in the story of the Conquest, the articulation of conflicting Anglo-Saxon and Norman claims pointed to the need for an external mark to identify the rules, so too, in the account of the positivist observer, propositional knowledge of law requires more than propositions.

The positivist, recall, observes practices from outside the community which shares in those practices and, grasping those practices as propositions, considers these propositional "primary rules" defective. The articulation of propositions of law—like early written laws or codifications—may initially dispel doubts or announce or create change, as the positivist sees, but later formulations or articulations of "new law" compete with earlier formulations and with one another. As when governor and governed articulate their claims to one another, procedures and standards are needed to resolve the disputes expressed by competing propositions. The adjudication of claims may itself take propositional form, but the proliferation of such propositions accompanies the need for means of identifying and remembering authoritative statements. When authoritative statements take the form of writing, a means of identification that is not itself a written proposition is required. For, on the one hand, writings may continue to proliferate and compete with one another. And, on the other hand, writings ostensibly stay the same while societies change; the static character of once authoritative writings means that writings and circumstances must be adjusted to one another. Where law consists of propositional rules or writings, then, the uncertainty of statements of rules and the static character of writings (understood propositionally) reveal the need for procedures to settle doubts about the rules and to adapt rules to changing circumstances. In addition, in a society where propositional knowledge guides conduct, guidelines for ascertaining the fact of a rule's violation are needed.

For those living by customary or nonpropositional law, on the other hand, knowledge of law consists not in propositional statements of rules, articulable in writings, but in practical reason, in knowing what to do. Disagreement and uncertainty about what to do is resolved through action, through what is done. Such action does not, of course, preclude speaking, so long as speech is properly understood as irreducible to a codified set of rules. Changes in customs may emerge through changes in actions. Practices change gradually and in keeping with other aspects of society, as individuals and households, subject to common influences, make similar decisions.[72] The particular customs of medieval England's rural markets or fairs changed over time to fit changes in the types and quantities of goods that villagers produced and exchanged. Farming, property-holding, and social arrangements also adjusted in various ways to changes in the number and status of residents in an area. No one mandated particular changes in custom, such as the value and variety of goods produced or the treatment granted a particular person or status. Even in highly literate cultures, as words become obsolete, they stop being spoken, or their meanings change to fit new conditions; similar changes occur in customs.

That the observer perceives "the slow process of growth" in customary society as inadequate to adapt the "rules" to changing circumstances reveals the distance between the observer's standpoint and that of those for whom law is practice. For the latter, the customs they pass down among themselves remain current. Memory maintains the "records" of custom and keeps them "up to date." Although assertions may not always accord with "facts" or "historical truth," no older or other records contradict them or to render them uncertain. In 1127 in England, twelve jurors from Dover and twelve from Sandwich settled a dispute between St. Augustine's abbey at Canterbury and Christ Church about customs dues at the port of Sandwich. They swore in turn on a Gospel in public that the tolls belonged to Christ Church, "saying: this, 'I have received from my ancestors and I have seen and heard from my youth up until now, so help me God and these Holy Gospels'."[73]

The point is not that there are no conflicts in customary society, nor that such societies never change. The point, rather, is that conflicts do not consist of inconsistencies among written propositions or between writings and practices and that addressing conflict does not entail identification or interpretation of authoritative writings. Although some may perceive "the rituals, myths, beliefs and practices of the simpler societies . . . as static, as persisting unchanged over the generations, handed down in a fixed (at least underlying) form from one to another," customs in the form of myths, oaths, vows, practices, and prayers change character over time.[74] The use of particular labels to name cultures actually "conceal[s] considerable shifts from one decade to the next, even though this ethnic way of labelling, of talking about things, appears to assume a continuity, a homeostasis, an assumption that also underlies many scholarly discussions of non-literate religions."[75]

While explicit decision-making *may* accompany change in customary societies, societies with codified laws *require* rule-making or legislation to bring written law into agreement with practice or to change the practice itself. In societies with ostensibly complete codes, uncertainty about whether something is obvious or unthought pervades legal matters. "Completomania"[76] presumes that guidelines for action are either in the text of the law or to be added to it. When a "complete" code exists, new situations raise uncertainties about written law that must be addressed either through interpretation or further legislation. Whether a statute providing benefits for spouses of public employees extends to homosexual cohabitants of such employees, for instance, may be "obvious" one way or another, to some, but unthought by others. Resolving the issue, though, will not simply entail providing or not providing such benefits; it requires an authoritative interpretation of the text showing that a particular understanding was apparently in the law all along or requires additional legislation to change the law (or what skeptics about the completeness of the code will consider making "new law" where "no law" was before).

Any particular society with written law may not meet the requirement to adjust its statements of rules and its practices to one another, of course. Disparities are perceived, sometimes humorously, sometimes pejoratively, as "gaps" or "lapses" in the law.[77] Stories abound of unenforced laws currently on the books requiring men on horseback to go with lanterns before automobiles driven at night or making what is considered trivial misbehavior serious crime. Obsolete written laws may be revived occasionally to harass an otherwise "law-abiding citizen" or to "set an example." While the presence of anomalies in the law may provide the impetus and justification for legislative reform, it need not always do so.

In societies with written laws, then, writings endow laws with existence independent of practice and hence provide standards. But while the autonomy of a text provides something constant against which to consider claims, the appropriateness of using a particular text as a standard may be brought into question. Statutes, for instance, "cannot be freed from the letter of legal texts, until a new text has replaced an old one, even though life has long since condemned the old text to death; in the meantime the dead text retains power over life."[78] Former customs, on the other hand, do not come back to life as easily as statute law, for once past, they tend to be forgotten. Alfred's reenactment and repetition, in an attempt to unify the country in 896, of the three-century-old Kentian laws of Aethelbert, the two-century-old West Saxon laws of Ine, and the century-old laws of Offa of Mercia, could scarcely have occurred without writings.

In sum, because *any* "mere writing" may be of indeterminate or misleading origin, appear static, and call for interpretation, a society whose primary rules are written propositions of law appears lacking when it has no way of addressing these problems. The propositional writing of rules carries with it "defects," which defects consist in the difficulties that accompany reliance on statements of rules or written propositions for knowledge about what to do. These problems, absent in customary societies for whom the reconciliation of writings with practices is not at issue and for whom the determination of law is not mediated through the correct formulation of propositions, call for secondary rules whose ultimate appeal must be to something "beyond" writing. For those living by practice, though, the uncertainty that accompanies propositional rules of behavior or the lack of a final and authoritative determination of the "fact of violation" of a stated rule is without import. The practical "what is to be done?" refers to "what to do in this case" as well as to "what we do and have done." The customary "what we do and have done" may at first seem to imply a proposition or statement of a rule, but it refers to the action to take, the practices and traditions that constitute a people, rather

A Matter of History   93

than to the truth of a proposition or to the authoritativeness of a stated rule. The doing of law signifies the "ought" of the rule or Kant's categorical imperative, the (nonlogical) universalizability of an instance, rather than the statement or proposition of a rule. Disagreements are not, and cannot be construed as being, about the validity of a "rule" of law or its precise scope, or about the meaning of words in a text. In customary culture, where a question of law is a matter of practice or action, the Benthamite statement, "All questions of law are no more than questions concerning the import of words,"[79] is incomprehensible.

The Quest for Authority

With the "mere writing" of rules, questions of law become questions of words, of their meanings and authority. Controversies over the authenticity of documents and their value for ascertaining "law" abound. Early deeds and early charters illustrate the problems that accompany the identification of writings with law or the association of writings with certainty. Writing may record and "certify," without making law—or its history—certain. Deeds ostensibly secure claims to land. But the possibility of alienating land which develops in part with the technology of title-deeds, throws patterns of landholding and inheritance into uncertainty, as does the written testament or will that cancels more general customary kinship rights.[80] The "false certainty" of writings means that students of property law even today learn to establish titles and to cure recording problems.

Statements of rules alone or "mere writings" do not contain their own authority, then; but—what the positivist who presumes that rules are propositions and that laws are authoritative rules fails to see—writing need not show itself as this defective "mere writing." Custom may remain law and "truth" may attach to practice even in literate cultures. In the early period of writing in England, for instance, documents now known as inauthentic were not necessarily false. "Truth" came from a document's being worthy of use, rather than from the "authenticity" modern law requires and historians attribute to it. By the eleventh century, the king's courts often relied on seals and sometimes charters used by those who could not even read as evidence of transactions. "Forgers" prepared illegitimate charters, often based on earlier authentic documents or on good oral tradition, to produce records that looked acceptable for the time. These "forgeries" recreated the past in what would pass in the courts as an "acceptable literate form."[81] And the still existing late thirteenth-century *Mirror of Justices,* "the most fantastic work in our legal literature,"[82] was used to explicate both the law of its period and the Anglo-Saxon law, from the sixteenth century until 1787 when it was denounced as "satire" and "forgery."[83]

That not all documents are equally acceptable to courts and to historians[84] shows how writings introduce the possibility of a distinction between law and history that custom denies. For unless practiced, unwritten customary law "becomes history" and disappears. Custom can only *be* as current tradition; custom recalls the past and sends into the future a people who, through customs, remember who they are and whose customs determine who they will be. Written documents, authentic or not, on the other hand, leave histories, in both senses of "leaving history": they allow histories to be made from them even as they depart from traditional practice. Written law and history require a present verification of the accuracy of references to a past, which present and past each differ from the future. Thus written records, unlike custom, "retain a half life in archives and can be resurrected to inform, impress and mystify future generations."[85]

Unlike a people's knowledge of custom, then, knowledge of propositional law requires a determination of the appropriateness of the facts about which a writing speaks: determination of the authority of propositions in a legal case, of the authenticity of writings in a historical one. Such determinations require appeal to standards other than the mere existence of the writing or even of other writings. For without standards external to propositional writings, disputes—about the violation of rules, about the interpretation of statements, about their authority—will continue interminably, as Hart writes. The interminability of disputes, Hart claims, points to a need for an "agency specially empowered to ascertain finally, and authoritatively" a "fact of violation." (91). Yet the authoritativeness of the declarations of this "agency," too, if not the agency itself, requires guarantee so as not, in turn, to be subject to interminable dispute. An authoritative mark, a "rule of recognition" whose existence is itself a matter of "fact" rather than validity, is needed to stem the infinite regress into which the searches of the conqueror, the positivist, and the common law historian, for ultimate determination, certainty, or meaning, otherwise lead.

This need for authority, for standards beyond the rules, is a quest for origins: the mark of authority fulfills the quest. Yet, the authority of this mark, like the historical "moment" that fulfills the historian's quest for the origins of the common law, proves elusive. Factual accounts of history point continually to the origin of law in moments of conquest that can never be located at determinate points in time; similarly, positivist accounts of law locate the source of authoritative propositional rules in the fact of a rule of recognition, in the effectiveness or force of a conquering will. Factual histories, seeing other law as pre-mature versions of the law of their own time, recognize only the facts of positive law; positivist accounts of law, locating authority in the effectivity of force and will, fail to see law in the passing traditions of a people.

The reduction of rules to propositional writing means that just as knowledge of law becomes a matter of propositions rather than practices, so too does knowledge of history become a matter of fact rather than tradition. But another history is possible. Turning away from the positivist history that sees in every past a distorted precursor of the present toward a history that recognizes a radically different other, one can ask again the questions laid out at the beginning of this chapter. How does the change from the customary mixed jury to the modern jury of legal doctrine come about? How does the shift from law as practice to law as the valid declarations of officials come about? How does positive law come about? These are still matters of history, but no longer of history in search of an inaccessible origin. Rather, like the story of the mixed jury that follows, like traditions passed through time out of memory, such history tells of where we are going. It does so not by predicting future occurrences, but by relating a tale, a tale not of facts, of what exists and has existed looking back, but of who we are.[86] It speaks of what happens: the eternal disappearance, in the light of positive law, of law as practice.

The story that follows presents the mixed jury neither as a factual instantiation of, nor as a nonexistent model for, that towards which one must strive. Rather, the early mixed jury opens the possibility that law may be other than the fact of what presently exists. Its story reminds us of the possibility of respect for another law, without asserting the actual existence of that particular possibility. That the mixed jury is a practice almost without history is not coincidental. For the relation between early pre-fourteenth-century practice and the history of the mixed jury that begins and ends with statutory enactments resembles the relation between custom and the official law that abolishes it, between tradition and the positivist history that both tells of tradition's displacement and displaces it. These relations point to the limits of positivism at the same time as they recall another, nonpositivist law.

5   The Writing of Law

If men learn [writing], it will implant forgetfulness in their souls; they will cease to exercise memory because they rely on that which is written, calling things to remembrance no longer from within themselves, but by means of external marks. What you have discovered is a recipe not for memory, but for reminder. . . .

Then anyone who leaves behind him a written manual, and likewise anyone who takes it over from him, on the supposition that such writing will provide something reliable and permanent, must be exceedingly simple-minded; he must really be ignorant of Ammon's utterance, if he imagines that written words can do anything more than remind one who knows that which the writing is concerned with.
—Plato, *Phaedrus* 275 a-d

The 1353 Statute of the Staple was the first enacted law to allow suits in England to be judged by juries composed of aliens. Together with a 1354 statute, it made official what had already been happening in local courts and in some cases in royal courts: aliens were entitled to be judged by juries made up half of aliens and, implicitly, to judgments informed by their own customs or laws. The Statute also established a royal system of staple courts in which the privilege was available.

Ironically, the statutory establishment of a judicial system in which mixed juries were available marks the beginning of the weakening of the principle of personal law represented by the mixed juries discussed in chapter 1. The statute signals the development of conceptions of law and community that ultimately prove incompatible with the principle of personal law and with practices of a mixed jury. This chapter focuses on changes in conceptions of law. Chapter 6 explores changes in conceptions of community, and chapter 7 describes the abolition of the mixed jury.

Section 1 describes the 1353 and 1354 statutes. They transferred to royal control disputes involving aliens away from the hands of local courts that followed local customs and practices. Royal control meant that future statutes, such as that of 1362, could dictate changes in a practice that had once belonged at the local level. It also meant that the law of the alien took on a different character. In local courts, an alien's law and the law of the local community converged in the decision of the mixed jury. Once brought before the higher authority of the royal courts, the law of the alien, as well as the law of the community, lost its character as law. That is, juries testifying in royal courts and at common law can no longer be said to "know the law," for "law" is the law of the king's justice. In the separation of the jury from its own court—the local court in which custom is law—the community's law or custom becomes the "fact" that the jury is now "likely to know." In the royal courts, the mixed jury becomes a "special jury" like any other special jury, likely to know the facts about a particular situation—this one involving foreigners. Insofar as the statutes set the stage for the separation of matters of fact or custom from matters of law, the mixed jury can no longer be construed as a practice whereby a person is judged by the particular law that attaches to that person as a member of a community.

Section 2 looks at the difficulties facing interpreters—both practitioners and historians—of the written law of the mixed jury. As written law, the statutes leave a history or, more specifically, records of law. As these records gain in authority, practitioners interpret them to justify their views. Historians and those recording later statutes and reporting cases turn to the early statutes as reference points for understanding the law of the mixed jury. In doing so, they move away from, and forget, the customary past that is integrally related to the personal law basis of the mixed jury.

Section 3 turns to a mixed jury case that shows how, by the sixteenth century, concerns related to writing the law have become central to conceptions of law. The emergence of these concerns in the context of the development of the common law means that the jury takes on a new role which throws into question the original ground for the mixed jury.

1. The Statutes of Edward III of 1353, 1354, and 1362

"Staple" refers not only to the principal raw commodities of the kingdom—wool, woolen goods, leather, tin, and lead—but also to the market towns to which the staple wares of England were brought for sale and exportation.[1] Until the time of Edward III, wholesale as well as local business had been transacted at fairs held throughout the kingdom, which aliens were free to frequent. Indeed, aliens held monopolies on the export of raw goods and the import of manufactured ones, thus placing them in a very powerful position, since the English at this time manufactured little. The intermittent fairs provided only occasional opportunities for trade, however, so fourteenth century policy funneled the wholesale and foreign trade into selected towns where continuous markets were established.[2] The staple was sometimes situated in foreign towns (Bruges, Calais, Antwerp, for instance), sometimes in English towns, and sometimes in both at once.[3] The 1353 Statute of the Staple, made in the twenty-seventh year of the reign of Edward III, brought the staple home to England,[4] where it remained until 1363, when a foreign staple was established at Calais.

The 1353 law also provided that if a plea or debate between merchants or ministers of the staple (or royally designated market towns) came before the mayor of the staple, to try the truth thereof, "if the one party and the other be a stranger, it shall be tried by strangers, and if the one party and the other be Denizens, it shall be tried by denizens: and if the one party be denizen and the other an alien, the one half of the inquest or of the proof shall be of denizens, and the other half of aliens."[5]

One year later, another act extended the privilege of a mixed alien-denizen jury to "all manner of inquests and proofs which be taken or made amongst aliens and denizens." The mixed jury was no longer restricted only to suits between merchants, nor only to those before the mayor of the staple: "be they merchants or other, as well before the mayor of the staple as before any other justices or ministers although the king be party, the one half of the inquest or proof shall be denizens, and the other half of aliens, if so many aliens and foreigners be in the town or place where such inquest or proof is to be taken."[6]

The 1353 enactment is the earliest statute explicitly to allow aliens on juries. Both the statute and the staple court to which the statute refers were products of fourteenth-century royal power. The royal ordinance provided, nevertheless, that within these royal courts, merchants, and their servants and "meiny" in the staple, were to be governed, not by the common law, nor by royal declarations, but by the "law merchant." Town usages and practices that had governed when the staple courts were local were also to give way to the law merchant.

Within staple towns at this time, two *local* systems of government overlapped. Both alien and denizen merchants annually elected the mayor and constables of the staple who, at least until 1373, were not necessarily identical to the mayor and sheriffs of the borough. Sometimes though, staple and borough offices were combined. Since the 1353 statute specified that the mayor of the staple be familiar with the law merchant, the head of the burgesses would most likely possess the necessary qualifications for mayor.[7]

Staple courts were apparently mixed; one was composed of two English merchants, two Germans, and two Lombards.[8] And, according to the statute, these courts had "jurisdiction and cognizance within the towns where the staples shall be, of people and all manner of things touching the staple" (s. 1).[9] Neither the king's officials nor town customs or usages were to interfere with the operation of the staple court,[10] which was to rule by the law merchant, "and not by the common law of the land, nor by usage of the cities, boroughs or other towns" (s. 2). (The provision, that all cases falling within the jurisdiction of the staple should be tried by law merchant, whether the persons concerned were merchants or not, led to a petition by the Commons that the laws and usages of the staple were unknown and should be set forth in writing. The king agreed but it is unlikely that this was ever done.)[11]

Although many local matters fell exclusively within the jurisdiction of the staple, other matters "touching the staple" did not necessarily come before the staple court. While pleas of debt, covenant, and trespass were not to be brought before the town, the party plaintiff could "chuse" whether to "sue his action or quarrel before the justices of the staple or in other place of the common law: and he shall be thereto received" (s. 5). It was not unusual for such cases to be brought in other courts. Pleas of land and freehold had to be at common law (s. 7). And while, according to the Statute of the Staple (s. 6), pleas touching the king's house were to be brought before the mayor of the staple, a later statute revoked the staple court's exclusive jurisdiction by providing that nothing in the statute was to infringe upon the jurisdiction of the king and the nobles.[12]

By the terms of the Statute of the Staple, felonies also fell under the jurisdiction of the staple court; this power too was later withdrawn. The 1353 statute had provided that where felonies were charged against those of the staple, or where those of the staple be "slain, robbed or maimed" by any persons, the mayor of the staple and other meet persons shall "hear and determine the said felonies and maims within the staple without delay, according to the common law" (s. 8). Indictments outside the staple for trespass or felony by people of the staple, or by others against them in the staple, "shall be sent before the said mayor, and them which shall be assigned justices with him to do right in this party" (s. 9). The 1362 statute[13] withdrew the jurisdiction of the staple courts to try felonies committed by or against merchants of the staple or their servants, however, so that the staple court had no cognizance of criminal offenses, unless the "avenger of blood chose to prosecute at his own peril."[14] Cases of trespass arising in the staples involving merchant aliens could still be tried before the staple by merchant law, or elsewhere by the common law, as had been provided in 1353.

The Statute of the Staple made a mixed jury available in all pleas that came before the staple court. Like the 1303 Carta Mercatoria,[15] the Statute of the

Staple allowed mixed juries in an even wider range of cases than those to which the *lex mercatoria,* as defined by Pollock and Maitland, would apply. It established a broad jurisdiction for the mayor and court of the staple and provided that all that "touched" the staple was to be governed by law merchant. The extent to which it was actually used and the way in which it worked remain unclear, however. How were trials conducted? Was the jury limited to particular issues? In what language(s) did the jurors communicate with each other and with the court? And who counted as alien, who as denizen, for the purpose of claiming the privilege, and again in the composition of the jury? Even where information is available, it may not provide satisfactory answers. Regarding the latter question, for instance, it appears that at least one "alien" on a mixed jury was both citizen and denizen.[16] And while information is available on merchant juries in the Admiralty court through the sixteenth and seventeenth centuries, these juries apparently were limited to the narrower determination of mercantile practice and thus do not exhaust the category of mixed juries.

The 1354 statute expanded the privilege of claiming a mixed jury trial to, among other things, cases before non-staple courts. Already by the late fourteenth century there are instances of the use of mixed juries in a broad range of courts and cases. The Statute of the Staple, as mentioned, had permitted appeal from the staple court to the Chancellor and the King's Council.[17] Special privileges had also entitled alien merchants to bring suits directly before the Exchequer and the King's Council (later split into Chancery and Admiralty).[18] Dissatisfied aliens or those distrustful of local court actions did indeed bring such suits.[19]

In all the king's courts, as well as in local courts, the use of mixed juries after 1354 was not expressly restricted to issues concerning the law of mercantile transactions. In London, mixed juries were used in inquisitions and in cases before the mayors and commissioners, despite protests that it was contrary to the franchises of London that matters done in the city should be tried by men of foreign countries.[20] In the royal court of Exchequer too, where suits for debt were brought, an objection to a mixed jury on the ground that the privilege applied only in local and fair courts was disallowed.[21] Of some 60 cases in the King's Bench to which alien merchants were parties between 1350 and 1375, mixed juries were summoned in eight. These eight cases involved mayhem, abduction, trespass (assault), trespass (to chattels), and resisting collectors.[22]

In many sorts of cases, and in all courts, then, under the 1354 statute, aliens were entitled to mixed juries. Even where such juries were not used, aliens sometimes got special judges. In a King's Bench case, for instance, in which the defendant was an alien and four triers were appointed, two of the four were aliens.[23]

But despite the fact that the statutes of 1353 and 1354 ostensibly enlarged the privilege to apply in royal courts, making official what had already been practice in local courts, the statutory establishment of a staple system signals a change. It marks a weakening of the principle of personal law implied by the early mixed jury. The story of the decline of personal law parallels, roughly, the story of the decline of the law merchant.

Historians generally agree that by the fifteenth century, if not sooner, merchants, like the members of other communities residing in England, no longer administered their own law. From the local courts of non-staple towns, mercantile matters moved to courts in which the steward or chief officer of the royal court, rather than the merchant jury, was judge.[24] Gradually, common law courts took over mercantile affairs from Admiralty and the Exchequer. While common law courts would give full recognition to the law merchant, they would do so not by way of judicial notice of a proposition of law but by receiving evidence of mercantile custom as a question of fact.[25] And as commercial law became part of the common law, it would no longer be limited to members of "merchant communities" but would be extended to all who were engaged in trade. Although the English would maintain the notion that it was necessary to be a merchant to claim the privilege of being judged by the principles of the law merchant, at least in part, until the late seventeenth century,[26] the idea that the law merchant was the personal law of a community disappeared.

This account of the law merchant links its decline to several factors: the rise of the common law courts and their jurisdiction over commercial matters, the concurrent development of the separation of mercantile custom (fact) from law, and the expansion of manufacturing in England, which extended the class of persons involved in activities of trade and commerce beyond the narrow or identifiable class of alien merchants.[27] Similar factors underlie changes in the principle of personal law embodied by mixed juries. The Statute of the Staple provides a convenient landmark from which to trace the decline of this principle, a decline that entails not only a change in a rather particular doctrine but also a reconceptualization of law and community.

Before the Statute of the Staple, English kings, following what had been both local practice and the "international" law merchant, extended to foreigners and merchants a recognition of their own law—whatever the royal reasons. Although the Statute of the Staple declared that matters before the staple courts were to be governed by the law merchant, before mixed juries, and not by the common law, the establishment of staple courts transferred disputed matters from the hands of local courts to the control of the king. The statutes showed that the king had assumed the authority to assign all matters to jurisdiction, although he could still, of course, assign some matters to the local courts. The king's assumption of authority cleared the way for later statutes to undermine the jurisdiction of even the staple court over what had formerly been local matters.[28] The 1362 statute, while not explicitly mentioning mixed juries, reserved to "the King and all other lords, . . . their franchises, jurisdictions and privileges, as they had been before" the Statute of the Staple. It required that "process of felonies, and all other pleas, as well within the staple as without," be "at the common law, as they were before the statute of the staple, notwithstanding the said statute."[29] The 1362 statute, then, ostensibly returning privileges to the kings and lords, conspicuously failed to recognize the customs of the towns as they had been before the Statute of the Staple.

The 1354 expansion of the use of mixed juries to non-staple courts and to common law cases reveals a change in conceptions of law. Where the jury and its knowledge had formerly been associated with local practices and customs, the jury's knowledge now becomes dissociated from law. Jurors may still have special knowledge, but it is not that of the law. The common law is distinct from custom and community, that of which and from which the jury speaks. Instead the jury now speaks about facts. Jurors from particular communities are chosen, not because they know the law, but because they are "likely to know"[30] about the facts. "Thus we have a jury of Florentine merchants living in London summoned to decide as to an act alleged to have taken place in Florence; and a jury of cooks as to the quality of food sold."[31]

And finally, as the English become involved in manufacturing and take over functions formerly carried out exclusively by aliens, and as more foreigners who are not merchants come to England, the "other" loses not only his or her "law," but also his or her definition, as shall be seen in chapter 7.

2. Interpreting the Language of the Law

Written law raises problems distinct from those of customary law. These include the problems of change and of interpretation. Thus when a 1414 statute changed the property qualification for service on juries, a 1429 statute was required to clarify that the 1414 statute referred to common juries and was not intended to change the mixed jury provisions of the 1354 statute described above. In referring to the provisions of the 1354 statute, the 1429 statute interpreted it as applying to "merchants aliens." This terminology, however, differed from that of the mid-fourteenth-century statute itself.

The 1353 statute speaks of juries of "strangers" in suits in which both parties are strangers, juries of "denizens" in suits in which both parties are denizens, and mixed juries of "aliens" and denizens, where one party is alien and the other denizen. The 1354 statute speaks of mixed juries in suits involving "merchants or other," although elsewhere it refers to "merchant denizens and aliens." While the 1429 statute refers to the 1354 mixed jury provisions as applying to "merchants aliens," one hundred years later, in 1536, the 1354 statute is said to govern and to apply broadly to cases involving the "alien born." By the end of the sixteenth century, merchant status alone, and even alien merchant status, does not entitle one to a mixed jury. Nevertheless in the seventeenth century, it is established that the privilege applied and does apply to aliens generally. To what extent can one rely on changes in language to document changes in practice?

Despite the generality of the language of "aliens" and "denizens," the context of the fourteenth-century Statute of the Staple suggests that the practice of the mixed jury was connected to the presence of mercantile interests in England. Yet both before and after the Statute, non-merchant aliens had claimed the privilege and merchant aliens had claimed it in non-mercantile cases. The 1328 confirmation of the 1303 Carta Mercatoria quoted in chapter 1 suggests that *any* merchants, not just foreign ones, were entitled to mixed—half-foreign-merchant or at least half-merchant—juries.[32] And information about the early Gild Merchant suggests that for some time an expanded notion of "merchant" included all trade and crafts people.

The ambiguity about the class to whom the privilege statutorily applies after 1354—merchants, alien merchants, or aliens generally—continues well into the sixteenth century. That the privilege remained in use throughout this period is borne out by several Year Book cases,[33] and by the 1429 statute.[34] That statute confirmed the 1354 statute and provided that a 1414 statute from the time of Henry V requiring jurors to "have lands or tenements to the yearly value of forty shillings above all charges" did not apply to alien merchants.[35] According to the 1429 statute, because of the "restraint and impeachment so made to divers merchants aliens" by the 1414 statute,

many of the same merchants aliens have withdrawn, and do daily withdraw them, and eschew to be conversant on this side the sea, and likely it is that all the same merchants aliens will depart out of the same realm of England, if the said last statute be not more plainly declared, and the said merchants aliens ruled and governed, and demeaned in such inquests, according to the first ordinance aforesaid, to the great diminishing of the king's subsidies, and grievous loss and damage of all his said realm of England.

The 1429 statute stated that "it was not the meaning of the said late king, nor of the lords spiritual and temporal of the said parliament" to hinder the 1354 statute by the 1414 statute, since the latter was prompted by the mischiefs arising from the false oaths of the "common jurors of the realm of England." Since "said merchants aliens be not common jurors, nor inhabiting the said realm, nor may purchase nor enjoy any lands or tenements in the same, without the king's license," the statute declared that the 1414 statute extended only to inquests to be taken "betwixt denizen and denizen."

The 1429 statute speaks of "merchants aliens" throughout. It describes the 1354 statute as ordained "in favour and liberty of the merchants strangers repairing into the realm of England." But although the 1354 statute is juxtaposed to provisions about merchants and the wool trade, its language leaves open whether it applies only to merchant aliens or to all aliens—an opening of which later interpreters will take full advantage. The 1354 statute had provided for mixed juries in all manner of inquests and proofs "taken or made amongst aliens and denizens, be they merchants or other," and merchants are not mentioned again in that passage.[36] "Merchants or other" in the 1354 statute may modify only denizens, and it may have been taken for granted that the aliens who were mentioned could only be merchants (implying that the privilege applied only in cases involving alien merchants). On the other hand, "merchants or other" could also modify aliens, meaning that the privilege applied in all cases involving aliens.

The immediately preceding section of the same ordinance states that "no man, *other than a merchant denizen or alien,* that knoweth the laws and usages of the staple, . . . shall be charged by the same laws and usages till they be declared in parliament" (emphasis added).[37] In this section, too, it is unclear whether "merchant" describes only the denizen or both the denizen and alien. The statute seems to mean that no man shall be charged under staple law until that law be declared in parliament, except merchant denizens and aliens because merchant denizens and aliens know the laws of the staple. Because later sections of the same ordinance refer explicitly to aliens other than merchants—servants, mariners, masters—all of whom would be familiar with customs of trade, the most likely explanation of the statutory usage of the term "alien" in the context of the staple is that "alien" included all those familiar with trade. It was thus unnecessary in this context to distinguish among aliens in the same way one distinguished among denizens. Although some discrete groups of religious and artisan aliens resided in England during the fourteenth century, in the context of the staple court, merchants (and seamen and those connected to them) would most readily come to mind. It seems that at the time of the 1354 statute, the question of whether the privilege applied to aliens generally or to alien merchants was moot, since aliens in England most likely were trade-connected (or else, as had been the case with the Jews and earlier French immigrants, were associated with other religious or secular communities with their own privileges).

Although it seems likely, then, that "alien" referred to all manner of trade-connected foreigners, the extent to which the 1354 statute was actually applied, to aliens or to merchants, remains unclear. The 1362 statute shows the problem in interpreting "merchants." Recall that the 1362 statute does not mention mixed juries, but it refers to the 1353 Statute of the Staple. Despite the fact that the 1362 statute reserved to the mayor of the staple the power "to take recognisances[38] of debts of every person, *be he merchant or other,* in the same manner as is contained in the same statute of the staple,"[39] a 1532 act[40] circumscribed the use of the Statute of the Staple on the ground that mayors had broken the law by extending the Statute to non-merchants. Only after the 1532 act, writes one historian (and also under the ordinances of 1311, which had attempted to nullify the Statutes Merchant of the late thirteenth century and to limit the number of staple towns to twelve, before being repealed in 1322), were "'merchant and merchant' regarded as essential parties to a statutory recognizance."[41] Thus, by 1532, the language, "be he merchant or other," that appears in the 1354 statute is also problematic.

The 1429 statute discussed above clearly describes the 1354 provisions for a mixed jury as relating to alien merchants. By the sixteenth century however, this focus on merchants, if indeed it had been practiced as such, had disappeared. In Fitzherbert's *Abridgement* (first edition, 1514 or 1516), the statutes of Edward III are claimed to "have been put in use always generally, s.[42] as well where aliens, who are not merchants of the staple, sue, or are impleaded, &c. as merchants, by the trial *de medietate linguae.*"[43] The apparent expansion of trial *per medietatem linguae,* as trial by mixed jury had come to be called, to a broad class of aliens corresponded to the waning of the influence of foreign merchants relative to English ones and to the influx of more permanent foreign settlement in England.[44]

By the end of the sixteenth century, merchant status alone and even alien merchant status did not entitle one to trial *per medietatem linguae,* yet, at the same time, the statute was held to apply to aliens generally. In *Barre's Case*

(1598), Barre and other merchants, both English and alien, prayed for trial *per medietatem linguae* but were denied it, because it was held not to be required for aliens, and prohibited to English, be they merchants or not.[45] *Barre's Case* confirmed a query raised in Sherley's non-merchant case (1557), where a reporter had asked: "Whether the court *ex officio* ought to award the special writ above [venire facias[46] *de medietate linguae*] by reason of the above statutes, [when] it does not appear to them by the record that one party is an alien." Dyer, the reporter, presented a broad interpretation of the class to whom the mixed jury privilege applied under the statute. He answered the query, "it seems not, for by the common law the trial was by all English, and the statutes were made for the benefit and in favour of aliens, if they will accept it but they are not compellable thereto."[47]

Another case, *Heyward v. Lypson,* in 1601–2, also held that a named "mercatur extraneo," although declared as such in the pleas, was not entitled to trial *per medietatem linguae* since he had not prayed for it. (Chief Justice Popham dissented and thought the merchant should be able to challenge the array the way knights could do).[48]

These holdings, that trial *per medietatem linguae* could not be had by all merchants and that alien merchant status alone was insufficient to qualify for the privilege, were possible because just as trial *per medietatem linguae* was being expanded to apply to a broad class of aliens, the view was developing that certain procedural requirements—for the prayer for a jury *de medietate linguae* and its timing—had to be met. Both the revision of the interpretations of the fourteenth-century statutes to permit non-merchant aliens a mixed jury, pointed out above, and the holdings restricting the use of the mixed jury in merchant cases on procedural grounds, discussed further below, point to the increased role of writing and written records in ascertaining the law. Many of these elements crystallize in *Sherley's Case.*

3. Sherley's Case

Dyer raises the query above, and one other, in the context of *Sherley's Case* (or *Sherleis Case,* or *Sherris Case,* depending on which of three reports one reads), dated 1557.[49] John Sherleys, a Frenchman accused of treason for being "one of the rebels with Stafford, who rebelliously took the castle of Scarborough" prayed for trial *per medietatem linguae,* which was denied him. Dyer explains that "the precedents have been searched for the trial of an alien for treason, and none can be found *de medietate linguae.*" In addition, a 1554–55 statute[50] had provided that "all trials of treasons to be awarded, had, or made, shall be made and used only according to the counsel of the common law of the realm, and not otherwise,"[51] and, as explained by another reporter, "there was no *medietas linguae* at common law; it was introduced by statutes made in the reign of Edward III, both for felonies and contracts" and so it could not be had in a trial for treason.[52] The court held of "no signification" that Sherley "was not a subject of the realm"; the indictment for treason brought against him was "against the duty of his allegiance," for "this [was a] time of peace between England and France; to levy war with other English rebels was sufficient treason; and if it were time of war, he should not be arraigned but ransomed."[53]

The dual claim that the jury *de medietate linguae* had been introduced by statute and had been unavailable at the common law runs counter to the evidence discussed in chapter 1, showing the customary nature of the early mixed jury. At the same time, the statutes of Edward III did indeed make the use of mixed juries in the royal or common law courts official (although they did not use the *medietas linguae* terminology, which is discussed further in chapter 6). *Sherley's Case* thus illustrates a "new" perspective on law—and on history. This perspective focuses on law as what occurs in central courts rather than as local practice, and it exhibits a concern with the writing of law that accords historical primacy to statutory records rather than to custom or even charters. It places an emphasis, too, for judicial purposes, on the written records of the court and on precedent, neither of which had been possible in the previous era of oral pleadings and manuscript records.

In those earlier times, parties had taken turns narrating, denying, admitting, and introducing new facts, until the "issue" was reached, a decision on which was the jury's responsibility. Pleadings were exchanged orally by the serjeants at bar, and only at the end of the term would the clerk record, in Latin, what then became the binding and unamendable pleadings. Until the pleadings were recorded, lawyers would discuss flexible, tentative, and hypothetical pleas.[54]

Rough records of these pre-sixteenth-century oral pleadings are available from Year Books. These compilations of notes on cases, taken in law French on manuscripts, only began to be printed after 1481. They were kept not for citation as precedent in later cases, but more likely "as prompt-books for the benefit of counsel who wished to get some idea of the best procedural points to make in the cut-and-thrust of actual litigation."[55]

In the mid-sixteenth century, after the introduction of paper pleas, tentative pleadings also disappeared. Pleadings were prepared outside the courtroom, and serjeants in the courtroom shifted from oral pleading to the skilled examination of witnesses, no longer having to vouch to the court for the facts as well as the law of their cases. The clerks' records had "once reported—in the third person—what the serjeants had said"; now written pleadings "recited with the impersonal third person of the record what the parties contended."[56] Or as one historian writes, by the seventeenth century "the science of pleading had begun to degenerate from its primitive simplicity and to become a piece of nicety and curiosity."[57] A concern with the form and manner of pleading arose, which at times displaced questions about the matter itself.[58]

The new system of written pleadings was "intended to reduce decision to a single point. And this decision became—word of words—a *precedent.* The word (from the French for *preceding* in time) is not used in its law sense before the late sixteenth century."[59] The sixteenth-century concern with "precedent," however, is not yet committed to the modern doctrine of *stare decisis.*[60] In what "Sir Carleton Allen thinks is the first occurrence of the word," Dyer uses "precedent" in reporting a 1557 case, "merely to tell us that in spite of two 'precedents' the court adjudged the contrary."[61] In *Sherley's Case* of the same year, as well, Dyer uses the word twice. He states that the precedents have been searched in cases of treason for trials *per medietatem linguae* but none have been found. And he notes that in the "attainder of Charles Gavare for the death of Gambe in the 3d year of E.6" and "in divers other precedents, the trial of aliens for felony and murder has been *per medietatem linguae,* and still shall be."[62]

The first edition of the well-respected Dyer's *Reports,* from which *Sherley's Case* is taken, covers 1537 to 1582 (and includes a few cases from 1512–13, 1516–17, 1527–28, and 1532–33) and appeared in 1585.[63] It represents one of the first law "reports," as opposed to Year Books, annals, commentaries or cases, that began to appear in the late 1500s. These early reports were not official. They contained personal notes and comments by the reporters and, despite the fact that all statutes had been in English since 1489, appeared in law French.[64] Many of them overlapped in coverage. Unlike the Year Books, the reports contained references apparently intended for citation.[65]

Although the last Year Book case is from 1535, the Year Books "did not cease to be read or to be printed at that date."[66] Four sixteenth-century Year Book abridgements are generally treated as authority: Stathan, of which only one edition appeared, in 1495; the *Abridgement of the Book of Assises* of 1509 or 1510; Fitzherbert, first published in 1514 or 1516, with later editions appearing in 1565, 1573, 1577 and 1586; and Broke or Brooke, whose abridgement first appeared posthumously in 1568.[67] Staunford's 1557 *Les Plees del*

Coron, although not itself an abridgement, was compiled from Fitzherbert's *Abridgement.* That work suggests a "departure" from earlier "textbooks" like Littleton's *Tenures:* "no longer, it seems, could a judge write on his own authority from well-known first principles. He must instead digest authorities."[68]

In the context of these changes in the practice and learning of law, Dyer's report of *Sherley's Case* indicates a new way of presenting and looking at law—as the recorded business of royal courts. The two queries raised by Dyer in *Sherley's Case,* the first of which has been mentioned above, highlight a concern with judicial records. Although *Sherley's Case* was not the first to raise the issues presented by either query, Dyer's report of *Sherley's Case* addresses the issues in a way that they would not have been addressed in earlier times.

As mentioned above, Dyer asks "Whether the Court *ex officio* ought to award the special writs above by reason of the above statutes, and it does not appear to them by the record that one party is an alien." He answers that a venire facias *de medietate linguae* need not be granted, for it was up to the alien to affirmatively claim his privilege, and since it was a privilege, lack of it, when it was not requested, could not constitute error.[69]

The issue in this query is also raised in a case occurring twenty years earlier. In *Abbott of Westminster v. Leman Clarke* (1536–37),[70] trial *per medietatem linguae* was used as an example of the rule that "where a statute is made for the benefit of a man, if he will not use his advantage of it by showing it, it is at his peril: as if the king would pardon a man by his charter, he shall not have the benefit of it, unless he also wills it himself: so is the statute which says 'that when the matters of alien born are in trial, 'it shall be tried p.m.l., yet if the trial be by Englishmen only the judgment is not erroneous.'"

The text of *Abbott of Westminster,* read in light of our modern standards of punctuation,[71] is problematic. If anything, it seems to suggest that it follows the wording of the statute it cites. In fact it does not; the 1354 statute says nothing of trial by Englishmen only, while the 1353 statute suggests that such trial would occur only between denizen and denizen. By the mid-1500s, though, it is taken as established that the 1354 statute, rather than the 1353 statute, governs, and that it applies solely to trials involving an alien against a denizen. Fitzherbert,[72] Brooke,[73] and Staunford[74] agree also that since the 1354 statute fails to mention trial between two aliens, neither a mixed jury nor an alien jury can be had in such instance (although Staunford allows that an all-alien jury may be had in a case between two aliens in a staple court).

Abbott of Westminster also takes the "alien born" and not mere "aliens," nor alien merchants, as the subject of the 1354 statute, despite the text of the 1354 statute and the interpretation given it in 1429 as applying to alien merchants (discussed in the previous section).

Finally, the test for whether trial *per medietatem linguae* should be granted is not the same in *Abbott of Westminster* as in *Sherley's Case*. *Sherley's Case* reformulates the test for granting trial *per medietatem linguae* from whether the alien born "wills it himself" to whether alienage appears "by the record." This subtle shift points to the beginning of a concern with the record, a concern reflected in many of the reported cases about trial *per medietatem linguae* between 1550 and 1700.

The 1663 case, *Vangangel v. Browning*,[75] for instance, follows the same approach as *Abbott of Westminster,* as the response to the first query in *Sherley's Case,* and as *Heyward v. Lypson* (mentioned previously, holding that being named "mercatur extraneo" in the declaration was insufficient to entitle a foreign merchant to a jury *de medietate linguae* if he had not specifically prayed for it).[76] In *Vangangel,* the Court refused to award a jury *de medietate linguae* to a defendant based on his affidavit that he was an alien, as "the plaintiff ought to enter it on the roll, to have trial de medietate at his peril" on notice given by defendant's attorney to the plaintiff or to plaintiff's attorney.[77]

Dyer's second query in *Sherley's Case* expresses concern also with establishing proper procedure. Dyer asks, this time without reply, "But *quaere* if the alien be plaintiff and omit such advantage of request, whereby a general venire facias issues, and is returned &c. whether by this he has not let slip his time." The question is not merely whether an alien must affirmatively claim the privilege, but whether he must do so by a particular time.

Before *Sherley's Case,* indeed until *W.D.'s Case* in 1571,[78] the law on this point remained unclear. In a 1463 case,[79] an action of debt was brought against a Lombard. After the venire facias had been issued and returned, the jury did not appear and defendant asked that the tales (the bystanders from whom jurors were chosen) be half denizen and half alien, as he was an "alien born." But it was held that since the defendant had not prayed *medietas linguae* at the first, he could not have it later. Brooke cites a case forty years *later,* though, where, after the venire facias issued, and after a *distringas juratorum*[80] where the plaintiff "shewed" the matter, the defendant prayed *supersedeas* to the sheriff to stay it and requested a new venire facias *de medietate linguae,* as he was an alien, a Lombard. And although he had not prayed *medietas linguae* at the first, writes Brooke, "he had the moiety of strangers, according to the statute."[81]

The question of timing arose again in 1571, in the case of W.D., a Scot charged with the rape of a seven-year-old girl. W.D. pleaded not guilty and after the venire facias was awarded, the panel returned, and three of the jurors sworn, W.D. pleaded that he was a Scot by birth and asked that his trial be *per medietate linguae*. The Justices of both benches denied his prayer for three reasons: (1) "because a Scot was never here accounted an alien, but rather a subject"; (2) "and also the Scottish language is not a strange tongue, but mere English"; and (3) "besides he had passed the advantage by the general issue above."[82] This third reason for denying trial *per medietate linguae,* that W.D. had "passed the advantage," became precedent[83] and was cited in later treatises. Thus Mortimer Levine writes that "from a strictly legal point of view, [it was] probably the most impressive ground given by the justices of their ruling."[84] (The other grounds will be discussed further in the next chapter.)

The concern in *Sherley's Case* with creating a proper record before granting trial *per medietatem linguae* fits into the context of broader changes, not only in the sixteenth century nature of pleadings, but in the nature of law. Law, including entitlement to a mixed jury, has become written. Records—of statutes, of pleadings, of cases—are now the sources of law and its history. The interpretation of records has become all-important in ascertaining the law, the written law of a centralized government that has assumed authority over law. Henceforth juries, as spokespersons of communities whose knowledge is law, become obsolete. The jury's new function will be to ascertain the facts, for the law is written and knowledge of it is a matter of interpretation and precedent. Concurrent with the jury's new role, the original ground of the mixed jury—that as a community member, one is entitled to one's own law, the law of one's community—will be thrown into question, for law no longer attaches to a person or class of persons; rather, as shall be seen in the following chapters, it extends to all who come within the bounds or the jurisdiction of the state.

6   The Jury *de Medietate Linguae*

The naive discourse of savages obliges us to reflect on the thing that poets and thinkers alone remember: that language is not simply an instrument, that man can be on a level with it, and that the modern West loses the sense of its value through the excessive wear it subjects it to. The language of civilized man has become completely *external* to him, for it is no longer anything for him but a pure means of communication and information. The quality of meaning and the quantity of signs vary in inverse ratio. Primitive cultures, on the contrary, more concerned to celebrate language than to put it to use, have been able to maintain that *internal* relationship with it that is already in itself an alliance with the sacred. For primitive man, there is not poetic language, for his language is already in itself a natural poem where dwells the value of words. And while I have spoken of the song of the Guayaki as an aggression against language, it should henceforth be understood as the shelter that protects him. But is it still possible to hear, from wretched wandering savages, the all too strong lesson concerning the proper usage of language?—Pierre Clastres[1]

The previous chapter explored the relation between writing the law, particular changes in the conception of law, and the decline of personal law that accompanied mixed jury legislation. Writing the law played a key role in moving from an older conception of law that attached to the person to a conception of official or authoritative law that accorded the status of "fact" to the jury's knowledge of the community and its law. This chapter examines an accompanying change in the conception of community. Language plays an important role in displacing the earlier community or personal-law ground for the mixed jury.

In the sixteenth century, a new name emerges for the mixed jury; the mixed jury becomes the jury *de medietate linguae* or "of half tongue." With the new terminology come new answers to the old questions: Who is an alien for the purpose of claiming the mixed jury? And who is an alien for the purpose of serving on the mixed jury? Changes in the link between the alien claimant and alien jurors bring the question of the reason for the mixed jury to the fore.

With one exception, references to mixed juries before the sixteenth century do not mention juries "half of one tongue and half of another." Instead they refer to the jurors of two communities—who happen to speak different

languages—or to the jurors of the international merchant community—
who, incidental to their identity as members of the merchant class, may
speak different languages. In either case, like the early assemblies of neighbors and the precursors of the modern jury, such early mixed juries represented gatherings of members of one or two communities—who shared
customs and laws with the parties or who knew the parties or the situation—
to speak on the matter.

By the end of the sixteenth century, mixed juries were continually referred
to as "juries *de medietate linguae*" or "of a moiety of tongues." But the jury of
half-tongue was not composed half of jurors who spoke English and half of
jurors from the alien party's country, or even speaking the alien party's language, as the phrase "de medietate linguae" might suggest. Instead, the alien
half of the jury could ostensibly be composed of "any alien whatsoever."

Section 1 introduces the term "de medietate linguae" and shows how the
use of the phrase raises questions about the reason for the mixed jury. Section
2 traces sixteenth-century changes in ideas about the composition of the
mixed jury and shows how such changes correspond to a "half-tongue" perception of the mixed jury. Section 3 shows that, by the end of the seventeenth
century, for the purposes of the mixed jury, the earlier identity of community
and language has broken apart. Before the sixteenth century, such identity
was taken for granted and thus not discussed. In the sixteenth century, the
relation between language and community broke down. At the end of the seventeenth century, the identity of language and community was asserted, but,
paradoxically, in the explicitness of that assertion, the earlier identity was
lost.

1. The Introduction of "Linguae"

Fourteenth-century statutes did not use the terminology "trial per medietatem linguae" or "jury de medietate linguae." First, such statutes were written in law French. But even the Latin of the charters that preceded the
statutes and the Old English and Latin of local bylaws failed to use such terminology. Instead, they referred to "denizens" and "aliens," "privatu" and
"extraneos," "burgenses" and "forinsecos," and so forth. The earliest Year
Book cases spoke of jurors "de lour marchantz, et lautre moyte des autres,"[2]
or simply of "aliens" and "indigenis," sometimes adding "according to the
statute." As late as 1501, a venire facias in a suit involving a Florentine-born
party issued "quorum una medietas fit de indigenis and altera medietas de
alienigen nat. in predict. civitate Florenc."[3] Some documents specified the

allegiance as well as the birth place of alien jurors: "altera de alienigenis, videlicet natis in D in partibus A sub obediencia Imperatoris A."[4]

No reference to mixed juries as "de medietate linguae" appears before 1500. A single 1494 statute, published in 1496, mentioned, in English, trial by "half-tongue" (or rather "tryall and enquest" by "half toge").[5] Later collections of statutes would annotate the 1494 statute as "medietas linguae," but in its early version it appeared without Latin cross-reference.

In the sixteenth century, use of the Latin "per medietatem linguae" to refer to the mixed jury became widespread. The first printed use of the term occurs in the 1542 *Great Abridgement of Statutes,* referring to a 1530 statute.[6] The 1530 statute, "concerning outlandyshe people calling themselves Egyptians," declared that if "suche stranger hereafter to commyt within this realme any murder, robberye, or any other felonye," the inquest shall be "all to gether of Inglyshmen." It specified that the inquest should be all English "all be it that the party so indicted pray medietatem linguae, according to the Statute of Anno viii H.vi."[7]

Since the text of the statute of 8 Hen. VI (1429), written in law French and described in the previous chapter, does not itself use "medietate linguae," the text of the 1530 statute provides a valuable clue as to the origin of the term: it suggests that "medietatem linguae" was used in court pleadings. Indeed, this seems the case, although one cannot ascertain exactly when the phrase began to be used. Certainly, fourteenth-century Latin court rolls and law French transcripts of pleadings during this time employed a variety of terms to refer to the composition of the mixed jury—none of which mentioned the language of the alien claimant or jurors or suggested that language was an issue.[8]

Historians writing in the late nineteenth and twentieth centuries have argued, nevertheless, that language underlay the concept of trial *per medietatem linguae,* not only in the sixteenth century but also earlier. For example, James Oldham writes: "Thayer [1898] is undoubtedly correct in suggesting that the concept [of *medietas linguae*] grew out of notions of fair dealing, spurred primarily by the idea that some members of the jury should speak the defendant's language."[9] Oldham acknowledges that the practice whereby half a jury spoke the defendant's language did not persist after the sixteenth century. It would eventually suffice, he writes, that each of the six alien jurors be from a different nation. "This ludicrous image of jury members wholly unable to communicate with each other, much less with the defendant," he continues, "obviously contradicts the original justification for this type of trial."[10]

Oldham's remarks about the jury *de medietate linguae,* admittedly marginal to his own project, serve as a useful focus for the remainder of this chapter. The discussion below challenges Oldham's view that notions of fair dealing, in the sense that some members of the jury should speak the alien's language, formed the justification for the notion of trial *per medietatem linguae,* either in the sixteenth century or earlier. On the contrary, as chapter 7 will show, this notion of fair dealing, broadly expressed as primarily requiring linguistic communication among all parties, is a "modern" view and, insofar as it is linked to the modern notion of the "indifferent" or impartial jury, it lies behind the eventual nineteenth-century abolition of the institution known as the jury *de medietate linguae.*

Language admittedly does play an important role in the sixteenth to the seventeenth centuries, but it is not as a reason for the mixed jury. During the sixteenth century, printing enables words—if not language—to be mass-produced.[11] Paper pleadings change the nature of the trial process.[12] *Sherley's Case* showed a concern with the form and manner of pleading that illustrated a "new" perspective on law. And writers referred for the first time to a jury *de medietate linguae.*

Concurrent with these changes, the English language came into its own, "colonializing" England. Before the fifteenth- and sixteenth-century emergence of standard, literary, and official English, great variety existed not only in spoken but in written English.[13] In the sixteenth century, local dialects began to give way to standard English. Not only did Englishmen set about unifying the British Isles,[14] but the English language came to predominate over the languages of the Cornish, the Scots, the Welsh, and the Isle of Man, at least for official use and in publication.[15] Although, in 1600, only a fraction of the population spoke dominant London English,[16] English was rapidly becoming the language of government and administration.

Before the sixteenth and seventeenth centuries, regional variations in dialect and administration meant that the alien half of a jury that was composed of community members or fellow countrymen was composed not only of those who shared in the alien's laws and customs but also of those who were steeped in the alien's way of life, including the alien's language.[17] Language might seem a plausible proxy for community, when community boundaries were vague. Those who did not speak one's language were "other," yet they too were identified and identifiable by their language.

After the spread of more uniform English, however, language could no longer serve to identify the community in the same way. For insofar as English became standardized, it pointed to a single "community" of English speakers. Although standardization was not achieved until after the nineteenth century,[18] the sixteenth century marked significant development toward it.

In *W.D.'s Case* (described in chapter 5), then, one reason for not according a mixed jury to Scottish-born W.D. was that "the Scottish language is not a strange tongue, but mere English."[19] Like *Sherley's Case, W.D.'s Case* was ostensibly concerned with the question of who was entitled to a jury *de medietate linguae*. In using the English language as a test for the alienage of the claimant, *W.D.'s Case* raised questions about the reason for such a jury, implicitly challenging, as shall be seen, the older personal-law or fellow-community-member basis for the mixed jury.

Recall that, in *Sherley's Case*, French-born Sherley was charged with treason. The Court denied him trial *per medietatem linguae*, because of the nature of the crime with which he was charged. The Court noted also that although Sherley was not a subject of the realm, the indictment against him was "against [contrary to] the duty of his allegiance," for in time of peace, levying war with English rebels was sufficient treason. The jury found Sherley guilty of treason, but he was reprieved and afterwards pardoned.[20]

Mary Queen of Scots, mentioned in a footnote added to Dyer's report of *Sherley's Case*, was not so fortunate. For her too, an indictment of treason would be "contra ligeanciae suae debitum." The footnote reads: "Holden clearly in parliament 29 Eliz. that Mary queen of Scots being in this realm under the protection of the queen, and compassing the destruction of queen Eliz. was a traitor like another person who is a mere subject, and if she were indicted of this treason, the indictment should be as here, against the duty of her allegiance."[21]

Presumably following up on this footnote, Mortimer Levine speculates that the first ground for the holding in *W.D.'s* (rape) *Case*—that a Scot was not an alien, but a subject—was politically motivated. He writes:

The only possible basis for maintaining that a Scot was a subject was the old English claim of suzerainty over Scotland. Although Elizabeth I probably had no imperial designs on Scotland, she did not abandon her claim of suzerainty. During the conferences held at York and Westminster in 1568, when the commissioners of Mary Queen of Scots denied the authority of Elizabeth's commissioners to judge the question of Mary's guilt in the Darnley murder, the English invoked the claim of suzerainty to assert their jurisdiction. By Michaelmas term of 1571, the Ridolfi plot had been unfolded and it might prove necessary to try the Queen of Scots for high treason. To do this in the face of Mary's inevitable denial of any English jurisdiction over her would have to be justified before the world. W.D.'s plea to be tried *per medietatem linguae* offered an opportunity to make a seemingly unconnected ruling which would support an English claim to try Mary. This potential political motive, as well as the difficulty of the point of law involved, may explain why it was deemed necessary to make the ruling more impressive by requiring the opinions of justices of both benches. All this is speculation incapable of proof, but, considering the political situation, it seems a distinct possibility.[22]

Levine thus declares that, while "the first part of the ruling of 1571 [of W.D.'s Case] may have been expedient politically, it was hardly sound legally," as "the claim that a Scot was never accounted an alien in England is more than doubtful."[23] The second ground, that the Scottish language is not a strange tongue but mere English, supports the doubtful claim that a Scot is not an alien, however—if one applies the pre-sixteenth-century identification of language with community to the situation in Scotland, where English spread from the fourteenth to the sixteenth centuries. (*Sherley's Case* suggests additional grounds—or at least precedent—for an English claim to try Mary, based not on the doubtful non-alienage of Scots but on the indictability of aliens in England for treason. Mary's claim, as a Queen, to be subject only to the judgment of God, as well as other factors in her case, make this tangent too complicated to develop here.)

Of greater interest than Mary for the purpose of this chapter is Levine's suggestion that, according to the contemporary sixteenth-century understanding of a jury *de medietate linguae* as "half of one tongue and half of another," the second ground in W.D.'s *Case,* that the Scottish language is not a strange tongue, might be a better justification for denying trial *per medietatem linguae.* As mentioned in the previous chapter, Levine ultimately finds the third ground, that W.D. failed to pray for trial *per medietatem linguae* in a timely fashion, the most impressive legally.

Of the second ground, Levine writes: "In the days before modern means of simultaneous translation, the mere mechanics, to say nothing of the fairness, of a trial of an alien whose understanding of English might be poor or nonexistent was reason enough for selecting half of the jurors from among his own countrymen."[24] The second ground was thus "a justification according to the contemporary understanding of a jury *de medietate linguae. . . .* This would not be true for the statute on which the privilege was based which speaks of aliens generally, not only the accused's countrymen."[25] The contemporary view, he notes, was that "the alien half of a jury *de medietate linguae* should be made up of the accused's countrymen," but that "later, and perhaps earlier, the prevalent view seems to have been that the aliens need not come from the country of the accused."[26] He thus suggests that in the sixteenth century, at least part of the test for whether one got a jury *de medietate linguae* was whether one was a member of a group that spoke a foreign language, in which case one would be entitled to a jury composed half of one's countrymen.

Historians such as Oldham and Thayer, on the other hand, maintain that language itself, rather than "nationality" identified by foreign tongue, was the test of whether one was entitled to a jury *de medietate linguae,* not only in the sixteenth century, but also earlier. Despite recognizing that juries *de medietate linguae* had origins in merchant-related practices, they argue that language underlay the concept of trial *per medietatem linguae.* As mentioned above, Oldham writes that Thayer correctly suggests that the concept of *de medietate linguae* "grew out of notions of fair dealing, spurred primarily by the idea that some members of the jury should speak the defendant's language."[27] But Thayer himself, cited by Oldham, writes only that "the jury of the 'half tongue,' *de medietate linguae,* was founded on considerations of policy and fair dealing, rather than a wish to provide a well-informed jury. See 'Ordinance of the Staples,' 27 Edw.III. st. 2, c. (1353); and St. Edw.III. c.13 (1354)."[28]

Levine's claim that the early statute does not mention countrymen is correct. But neither do early charters or statutes of the fourteenth century specify that alien jurors must speak the same language. And at the same time, there is no evidence that the early mixed jury, like Oldham's later "ludicrous" mixed jury, could be made up of "any" aliens. On the contrary, both types of early mixed jury—the merchant jury and the jury from two communities— were composed of alien jurors familiar with the alien party's customs, the parties themselves, or the circumstances under which the action arose.

On the first type of early mixed jury, that is, on the merchant jury, jurors— whether alien or non-alien—were knowledgeable about the trade practices of a number of places. At their most diverse, they might speak different languages. (Even English merchants from the four main ports of England spoke different dialects.) But differences in native languages spoken by jurors do not mean that the English of the thirteenth and fourteenth centuries were unaware of the need for a common means of communication. Such awareness would seem to have been especially great in the merchant courts, which were characterized by their "speedy justice." As a twentieth-century editor of "a mercantile case involving a Lombard plaintiff relying on ledger accounts" points out, "it was clearly essential (if justice was not to become a farce) that not only half the jurors, but also at least some of the auditors . . . and of the arbitrators . . . should speak the language that was before them in written form."[29] The existence of this particular case, though, involving written accounts,[30] does not prove, as Oldham claims, that language, fair dealing, or communication, as such, was the "original justification for this type of trial."[31] On the contrary, the example muddies the distinction Thayer, whom Oldham cites, makes (in the quotation above) between juries *de medietate lin-*

guae, justified by policy reasons or by notions of fair dealing, and juries with special knowledge or information. A jury chosen for policy reasons or for fair dealing to read a foreign language will *also* be a well-informed jury, able to understand accounts written in that language and to speak the truth of the matter.

The second type of early mixed jury was composed of the members of two groups. Although members within each group shared a common language, language did not provide the basis for the mixed jury privilege in these instances either. The early mixed jury of Solomon de Standford, for example, was half-Jewish and half-Christian. Its justification, like the justification for allowing the Jews their own courts, was that the Jews constituted a distinct people or community, with their own laws and customs. During the medieval period, charters extended the privilege of a mixed jury not only to religious groups like the Jews, but also to the Flemish, the Lombards, the Hanse, the Almains, and others, each of whom were a "people," bound together by and bound to their own law and, it then happens, their own language.

The argument so far shows that language necessarily played a part in both types of early mixed juries, although it provided the primary justification for neither. If the original justification for a mixed jury had been to understand the alien's language, or for the alien to understand English, one wonders why translation or interpretation would not have sufficed. The idea was not foreign: in a fifteenth-century Year Book case, a Lombard who spoke no English or Latin was read the pleadings "in son language desmesne"[32] and went on to wage his law in his own language.

If understanding language had been the main concern in providing mixed juries, a possible reason for alien jurors might have been that fellow aliens could speak and understand the nuances of the alien's language better than "non-native" speakers. Under this reasoning, though, language is still more than a matter of mechanical translation or modern "communication." It is tied to belonging in a community and sharing an understanding or a common world that is expressible in—although not necessarily through—language. Only if language were thought of in this way could a poor understanding of English be "reason enough," as Levine claims, "for selecting half of the jurors from among [an alien's] own countrymen."

Language alone cannot serve as the reason for the early mixed juries. Instead, the general notion that one should be tried by those who share in a knowledge of the practices of one's community underlay the use of mixed juries in early merchant and non-merchant cases. Justice required, in regard to both types of mixed jury, that members of a community following their own laws or customs while in England be judged, at least in part, by those of their own community and law. Language was integrally intertwined with community and custom. Yet early references to mixed juries of both types speak of aliens and natives, of place of birth and allegiance, while never explicitly mentioning language. Whether political motivations or respect for the law and customs of merchants and others provided the impetus for the early privilege of claiming a mixed jury, language seems only to have played an incidental role in the early formulation of the privilege.

2. Sixteenth-Century Changes in Mixed Jury Composition

In the sixteenth century, the mixed jury came to be referred to as a jury of half-tongue. By the end of that century, language, like community, seemed irrelevant to the composition of the alien half of the mixed jury, in that alien jurors could come from any country. They did not need to speak the alien party's language or to be from the alien party's community. This section explains how language came to displace, without replacing, the more fundamental ground for the mixed jury: that a person be judged by the laws and members of that person's community.

The situation developed through an apparent confusion between the two types of early mixed juries. (Recall that mixed juries could be juries composed of the members of two communities or could be juries of merchants from a single merchant community coming from several different countries.) The confusion between the two sorts of juries came about following the introduction of the "of half tongue" or "de medietate linguae" terminology.

As mentioned above, a 1530 statute employed "per medietatem linguae" to refer to the type of jury denied to the gypsies (most, if not all of whom, were trilingual, speaking Romany, English, and Welsh).[33] The "half-tongue" appellation seems appropriate, in light of the identity of language with community, for such juries and for the other dual-community mixed juries that were claimed to have "been put in use always" since the statutes of Edward III.[34] The "half-tongue" terminology, although not appearing in any court records, had been used in the 1494 statute mentioned above, and, by 1530, had probably been in use for some years to refer to dual-community juries.

With the application of the "de medietate linguae" label to mixed merchant juries, complications arose. Such usage may have seemed natural since, by the early sixteenth century, both types of mixed juries were thought to have the same source: if not the fourteenth-century statutes of Edward III, then the grants by the king. "Medietate linguae" appears in the margins of

Rastell's 1557 *Colleccion of Statutes* next to the statutes of Edward III, as well as the statutes of 1429, 1494, and 1530. In 1560, Staunford even described the inquests provided for in the charters that preceded the "universal" law of 1353 as half "of their tongue." He wrote:

Al common ley devant cest estatute [28 Edward III], & lestatute fait anno 27.E.3.cap.8. cest trial per Medietatem linguae puissoit aver estre ewe, per grant le roy. Come si le roy per ses lettres patents ussoyt graunte a ascun company des aliens, come le company de Lumbards ou Almaignes, ou auter tiel company que quant ascun de eux serroit impledus le moity de lenquest serroit de lour langue. Et ceo appiert M.22.E.3.fo.14. Et puis de faire ceo un ley universall: le dit statute de anno 27.E.3. fuist fait.[35]

At the common law, before this statute [of 28 Edw. III] and the statute of 27 Edw. III, the trial p.m.l. could be had, by a grant of the king. As when the king by his letters patent issued a grant to any company of strangers, such as the society of Lombards or Germans, or other such company, that when any of them be impleaded half the inquest shall be of their tongue. And this appears in [the case] Mich. 22 Edw. III, fol. 14. And then to make this a universal law, the said statute of the year 27 Edw. III was made.

By the late sixteenth century "medietas linguae" was being used for both sorts of mixed juries. But this factor alone cannot explain the change in the composition of the mixed jury to "any aliens." That change occurred because *both* types of mixed jury were traced back to the statutes of Edward III, which provided generally for juries composed of "aliens." Further, mixed juries was not simply "traced back" to such statutes; rather, the authority to grant the privilege of a mixed jury was attributed to the king. The customary basis for the mixed jury was forgotten.

In the second half of the sixteenth century, Brooke attempted to show that the "medietas linguae" terminology was inappropriate for mixed *merchant* juries. He did so in the context of a 1505 Year Book case on an action for debt. Three versions of the case published in Year Books present (Justice?) Tremaile asserting that an alien defendant, claiming he was from Lombardy, could have "le moity del estrangers accordent al statute" (although the alien had not asserted his claim until after the *distringas*).[36] The Year Books did not mention "language," "tongue," or "country."

In his 1573 Abridgement, Brooke cites the 1505 case, noting that, according to the 1354 statute of 28 Edw. III:

que est malement pleder adire, per medietatem lingue, car il navera eur de son langue demesne, mes de ascun maner de aliens, & sic ponit in usu.[37]

It is badly pled to say "per medietatem lingue," for he will not have them of his tongue, but of any manner of aliens, and so it is put in use.

Citing the same case elsewhere in the same edition, he writes,

Tremaile, al contrary, et puis il au medietatem lingue accordant al statute, tamen le statut est per medietatem alieneginarum & non lingue.[38]

And then he had trial by medietatem linguae according to the statute, although the statute is by half aliens and not tongue.

Brooke's 1586 text adds:

. . . vide que il navera moitie de son countremen, mes dascun estraungers, car le [statute] nest per medietatem lingue, mes per le moytie des aliens, quod nota, car est fauxement abridge en labridgement de statutes.[39]

. . . saw that he did not have half of his countrymen, but of any strangers, for the [statute] is not by half tongue, but by half aliens, which note, because it is falsely abridged in the abridgement of statutes.

The point to note is Brooke's claim of false annotation in the 1542 *Great Abridgement.*

In asserting the inappropriateness of the "medietas linguae" terminology, Brooke presumably had mixed *merchant* juries in mind. He turned to the original language of the fourteenth-century statutes, which provided for juries of "aliens" generally, to make his point. But because the statutes now served as the authoritative source for *both* types of mixed jury, without distinguishing between them, the provision that juries were to be made up of unspecified aliens was in effect transferred to what had formerly been dual-community juries.

By the beginning of the seventeenth century, then, not only were both types of early mixed jury called "de medietate linguae" and traced back to the statutes of Edward III, but, because those statutes referred to "aliens" generally, the distinction between the two types of mixed jury broke down: the alien part of either type of mixed jury was to be composed of "any" aliens.

Thus Staunford, who used the "de medietate linguae" terminology to refer to the fourteenth-century statutes, declared that it was immaterial from what nation alien jurors came:

Cel statute [28 Edw. 3] parla generalment des aliens. Et pur ceo il semble nyent material de quel nations les aliens sont quix serront de lenquest, issint que ils sont aliens, s. non obstant que ils sont dauter nation: que nest la partie al action.[40]

This statute speaks generally of aliens. And for this it seems immaterial to which nations the aliens belong who will be on the inquest, as long as they are aliens; one can know that it is not an obstacle that they are from other nations than is the party to the action.

Staunford's view, apparently, was that the king's earlier grants to companies of strangers provided for juries half "of their language"; the fourteenth-century statutes made such grants "universal," not only by allowing mixed juries to all aliens, but by allowing any aliens on all mixed juries.

By 1607, John Cowell, defining "medietas linguae" in his *Interpreter* and citing Staunford on the issue, found no need to address the question of who the alien jurors were to be: "Medietas linguae—signifieth an enquest empaneled upon any cause, whereof the one halfe consisteth of Denizens, the other of straungers. It is called in English the halfe tongue, and is used in plees, wherein the one party is a straunger, the other a denizen."[41] In its 1672 edition, *The Interpreter* refers to a "Jury" rather than an "enquest" and states that "this manner of Tryal was first given by [1353 and 1429] statute of 27 E. 3, st. 2, c. 8 & 8 H. 6, c. 29." It continues: "Before the first of these statutes was made, this was wont to be obtained of the king, by grant made to any company of Strangers, [citing Staunford]."[42]

The transformations traced above in the doctrine are, no doubt, much neater than those in the practice that the doctrine was intended to record. The dual-community mixed jury did not immediately disappear. In 1602, in *A Tract on the Succession of the Crown,* Sir John Harington referred to W.D.'s *Case* to support James of Scotland's right to succeed to the crown of England upon Elizabeth's death. ("And this judgment given with these reasons is extant and to be seene in Mr. Dyer's cases as the meanest student in the Innes of Court knoweth," he wrote.) Harington was interested in the first ground of W.D.'s *Case*—that a Scot was not to be counted in England for a stranger. But he described the case generally and explained "the benefitt which by our LAWES is afforded to Strangers, to witt, to have MEDIETATEM LINGUAE," as "that is, half of the jurors to be of his own countrymen."[43]

The view of the mixed jury as a jury of "countrymen" made sense of earlier cases and explained some late sixteenth-century holdings. Under this view, an alien-born party was presumably entitled to a jury of countrymen identifiable by their common language. A jury composed half of such countrymen would not only "be able to know something of how I have lived hitherto"[44] but would judge the fellow-foreigner's case according to standards derived not only from the English "pais," but also, perhaps unconsciously, by the norms of the alien's country. In 1580 and again in 1592, for instance, the Court held, consistent with a "countrymen" view of the mixed jury, that where an alien sued as administrator for an English intestate,[45] or where an alien was executor,[46] the trial should be by all English, for in these situations the alien sued *en auter droit* or in another Englishman's right. Conversely, the "countrymen" understanding of the mixed jury supports the ruling that where an alien was testator or intestate, trial should be had *per medietatem linguae,*[47] for it suggests that an alien's property should be governed in some sense by the alien's law.

In comparison to the "countrymen" view of the mixed jury, Brooke's position, that the alien half of the jury is to be composed of "any" aliens, may appear "ludicrous," as Oldham put it.[48] But Brooke's view, too, had non-ludicrous origins in the notion of the merchant jury, where an internationally mixed jury was the mechanism best suited to declaring or determining the practice of an "international merchant community." (Brooke himself wrote that no jury *de medietate linguae* was available in cases of contract not made at a fair or market, fairs and markets being where merchants transacted business.)[49]

Indeed, Brooke's position, that in an action of debt an alien was entitled to a jury of any aliens according to the statute, represents a last attempt to recapture the consistency of the early reason for a mixed jury of merchants. For Brooke also argued against using "medietas linguae" to refer to a mixed jury which was neither of half tongue nor half of countrymen. *W.D.'s Case,* with its three grounds for denying W.D. a mixed jury, pointed to the ambiguity which surrounded the reason for the mixed jury following the adoption of the term "de medietate linguae" in the sixteenth century.

3. Language and Community

In 1685 the second edition of *Tryals per Pais,* a work attributed to Duncombe and believed to have been published first in 1644 or 1645, devoted several pages to the jury *de medietate linguae.* The trial "called in Latine, Triatio b linguis, or per medietatem linguae," now originated in the common law: "this Tryal by the Common Law was wont to be obtained of the king, by his Grant made to any Company of Strangers."[50] Furthermore, citing a note from a later edition of Dyer's *Reports,* Duncombe wrote that "it matters not, whether the Moyety of Aliens, be of the same Country as the Alien, party to the Action, is: for he may be a Portugal, and they Spaniards, &c. Because the [1353] Stat. speaks generally of Aliens."[51] "So that Brooks says," continued Duncombe, "it is not proper to call it a Tryal per medietatem linguae, because any Aliens of any tongue may serve. But under his favour, I think it proper enough." He added: "For people are distinguished by their Language, and Medietas Linguae, is as much as to say, half English, and half of another tongue or Country whatsoever."[52]

With this claim, Duncombe returned to the pre-sixteenth-century equation of language with country. But in the meantime, an important change had occurred: the alien party—the "other," who is not of the country of England and who speaks a foreign tongue—had been stripped of community. Duncombe's only disagreement with Brooke was in vocabulary, but in vocabulary that said much in allowing for a jury composed half of "any" aliens and that pointed to a shift in sixteenth- and seventeenth-century understanding. In maintaining that "medietas linguae" meant half English and half of any language or country, Duncombe showed (as was suggested in section 1 above) that the spread of the English language had indeed created a single community of English "speakers," for whom "others" were simply non-English.

By the end of the sixteenth century, then, the alien half of the jury "de medietate linguae," despite its name, was made up neither of those who spoke the alien claimant's language nor of the claimant's countrymen, but was made up of any aliens. Brooke, with the image of the early merchant jury in mind, had objected to this terminology, maintaining that a jury of "any" aliens was not "of half tongue." Duncombe's affirmation of the term signaled the end of the earlier reason for the mixed jury that had connected the alien with his community, language and law.

On the one hand, Duncombe maintained that "people are distinguished by their language" and he suggested the identity of "tongue and Country." On the other hand, he reiterated that the alien was not entitled to judgment by his "countrymen," but was to be judged by "any alien" or non-English. The bond of community between the alien claimant and alien jurors had been broken. The personal-law ground for the mixed jury had been lost, as the alien was no longer entitled to judgment by members of his or her community or according to its law.

Language, despite its conjunction with country in Duncombe's work, had become separated from community. That separation had occurred with the use of "de medietate linguae" to refer to merchant juries. Before then, at least in the context of mixed juries, language and community went together—and they did so in a way so deep and so inseparable that there had not even been the need to mention their unity. Duncombe's attempt to bring language and community back together, while retaining the "any" alien composition of the mixed jury, only pointed to the distance that had grown between them.[53]

Later writers followed in Duncombe's footsteps, attributing their stance on the composition of the mixed jury—that "any" aliens could comprise the alien half of the mixed jury—to Brooke, yet calling the jury "de medietate linguae." This combination—a jury known as "half-tongue" made up half of any non-English aliens—made the community or personal-law ground for the mixed jury obsolete. A new reason was needed.

Support for the "any" alien view of the composition of the mixed jury had come at first from reading the 1353 Statute of the Staple in the context of law merchant juries. Later such support came from interpreting the 1354 statute of 28 Edw. III to mean that *any* alien could be on the jury, since the statute did not specify *which* aliens. This reading represented a change from 1429, when the same statute was taken as referring to alien *merchants* (at least as claimants). This post-1429 line of reasoning paralleled the reasoning mentioned in the previous chapter regarding cases of English against English or aliens against aliens under the 1354 statute: because the wording did not specify trials of aliens against aliens, or English against English, such actions were held not to fall under the statute. The same sort of reasoning was used in 1593, in a case against an alien that held that a writ of inquiry for damages following an action of assumpsit was to be by all English as it was "out of the statute" of 1354.[54]

Hawkins also adopted this type of argument in his famous *Pleas de Corone* (1716):

Some of the precedents for the award of a *venire* of a jury of half denizens and half aliens, in pursuance of 28 Edw. 3. mention, that the alien shall be of the same country whereof the party alleges himself; and others direct generally, that one half of the jury shall be aliens, without specifying any country in particular. And this form seems most agreeable to the statute, which speaks of aliens in general; and it seems confirmed both by late practice, and the greater number of authorities.[55]

Hawkins is cited invariably on this point in all the works that follow his. Bacon (first edition 1736),[56] Viner (first edition 1742–46),[57] later editions of Dyer's *Reports,* and other works repeat Hawkins's assertion that the form of the jury whereby one half shall be aliens, "without specifying any country in particular . . . seems most agreeable to the statute, which speaks of aliens in general."[58]

Constructing the 1354 statute this way provided a reason for the "any" alien composition of the mixed jury, but it did not supply a justification for the mixed jury itself. The loss of the personal law or community basis for the mixed jury during the sixteenth century had left the institution bereft of meaning. Together with an influx of immigrants, who now came for purposes other than trade, the disappearance of a distinct class of merchants who could lay claim to their own law and the separation at trial of custom and fact from law, resulted in a decline in the principle of personal law embodied by the early mixed jury.

In its place would arise the impartial law of the state. That law, more uniform than local custom had ever been, would extend its reach to all who lived in the territory. Like the standardization and spread of the English language, the development of state law would promote a single "community," this time a community not only of those who spoke the same language, but of individuals who would be equal under the law. Unlike language, which had only displaced but never replaced the bond between "countrymen" or community members that lay at the heart of the personal law ground for the mixed jury, impartiality (described in chapter 7) would provide a justification—up to a point—for an alien claimant to have a mixed jury of "any" aliens.

7   The Indifferent Jury

"In this life, we want nothing but Facts, sir; nothing but Facts."—Charles Dickens[1]

The substitution of language for alienage to describe the mixed jury pointed, in the previous chapter, to a decline in the conception of community associated with personal law. With the disappearance of the community or personal law basis for the mixed jury, however, language did not replace the former countryman bond between the alien claimant and alien jurors. That is, the alien half of the jury was not composed of those (aliens or non-aliens) who spoke the alien party's language, nor even of those who spoke a language other than English. Nor did language itself become the test of whether one could claim a mixed jury. Instead an alien, as a member of a non-English speaking country (and not simply a non-English speaker), could claim a mixed jury composed of "any" aliens. A new justification was needed to make sense of this construction of the mixed jury. The link between the claimant and the jurors that would eventually replace the countryman bond was impartiality.

For a time before the full acceptance of impartiality to justify the "any" alien composition of the mixed jury, treatise writers and others would rely on the texts of the fourteenth-century statutes: the statutes do not specify what sort of alien; they refer only to aliens generally. Later, impartiality provided a justification which went beyond the language of the statutes. But once it gained in acceptance, it raised difficulties. For in the nineteenth century, citizenship or alienage became matters of statutory definition, and impartiality, which had provided a reason *not* to distinguish *among* aliens, could not simultaneously serve *to* distinguish *between* aliens and natives, either for the purpose of claiming or of serving on the mixed jury. An 1870 statute ultimately abolished the mixed jury.

Section 1 describes the emergence of impartiality as a replacement for the countryman bond between an alien claimant and alien jurors. Section 2 provides the eighteenth- and nineteenth-century background for the mixed jury cases discussed in the remainder of the chapter. It describes changes in the function of the common jury, the struggle to make English the language of the law, and the increasing codification of law. Section 3 focuses on the 1849 case of *Regina v. Manning and Manning* and looks at who counted as an alien for the purpose of claiming a mixed jury under nineteenth-century naturalization law. Section 4 turns to the composition of impartial mixed juries. The loss of difference between aliens and natives under impartiality corresponds to the demise of the mixed jury, described in section 5.

1. Impartiality and Suits among Aliens

Hawkins's assertion that "one half of the jury shall be aliens, without specifying any country in particular"[2] is cited invariably by later writers. But the reason he gives for "any aliens"—that the statute does not specify where alien jurors are to be from—gives way in the late eighteenth and nineteenth centuries to another reason for the "any alien" composition of the alien half of the mixed jury—that of the need for jury impartiality. The latter justification, jury impartiality, appears even earlier regarding another jury issue: whether, in a case between two aliens, they are entitled to a full alien jury.

In the 1500s, Fitzherbert, Brooke, and Staunford agreed, referring to the 1442 Year Book case of 21 Hen. VI 4, that the 1354 statute of 28 Edw. III, in Hawkins's words, "doth not extend to an appeal, or other action by an alien against an alien for the Words are, All inquests &c between Aliens and Denizens."[3] Year Book versions of this case stated that where both parties were aliens, the suit shall be tried by "ceo pais entierment" ["this country entirely"], although if an English and an alien joined in issue, it shall be tried "lun moity per ceo pais, et lauter moitie per laut" [one half by this country, and the other half by the other]. The reason given in the Year Books, like that given by Fitzherbert, Brooke, and Staunford, is "et ceo par le statute."[4] Hawkins and Bacon, too, followed on this point.

In the mid-1700s however, Blackstone and Viner, echoing Duncombe's (1685) view of the matter, provided another justification for the same holding. Duncombe had written that the inquest in a suit between two aliens shall be all English, "for though the English may be supposed to favour themselves more than strangers, yet when both parties are Aliens, it will be presumed, they favour both alike, and so indifferent. 21 H.6.4."[5] According to Blackstone (lectures first published 1765–69) "where both parties are aliens, no partiality is to be presumed to one more than another, and therefore by the statute 21 Hen. VI, c. 4, the whole jury are then directed to be denizens."[6] Viner describes the 1442 case of 21 Hen. VI 4: "Issue was joined *between two aliens,* and Markham prayed d.m.l., viz. the half of the persons of one country and the other half of persons of the other country, *et non allocatur,* but was *agreed to be all of English;* for they are as indifferent to the one as to the other."[7]

Comyn (first edition, 1800) took the seemingly contrary position of allowing all-alien juries, as opposed to requiring all-denizens, but his statement is noteworthy:

In an action by an alien against an alien, by the [1353] St. 27 Ed.3.8. the inquest shall be by all aliens. And by the same statute and the [1354] St. 28 Ed.3.13. if one party be alien, and the other denizen, the inquest before all justices shall be by half aliens, if so many be found in the visinage, otherwise by so many as are to be found, and the rest denizens. . . . And these privileges have always been allowed since these statutes in all pleas, and before all justices, if it was demanded.[8]

Comyn's endorsement of the all-alien jury in suits between aliens appears to reflect a reversal of the view (of the 1442 case of 21 Hen. VI, compatible with *Abbott of Westminster,* and running from Fitzherbert, Staunford, and Brooke, to Duncombe, Viner and Blackstone) that two aliens were not entitled to all-alien jury trials. That view was justified, as noted above, at one time by a textual analysis that referred to what was not said in the 1353 statute and, later, by appeal to the impartiality of English jurors judging a case between two aliens. (Staunford had qualified his position by saying that where two alien merchants of the staple brought suit concerning the staple *in the staple,* the plea should be tried by aliens "par le dit statute de Anno 27 E.3."[9] Duncombe merely cited Staunford.[10] Although the two thus suggested an exception to the all-English composition of a jury in a suit between two aliens, neither deviated from the scope of the language expressed in the 1353 statute of 27 Edw. III.)

It would, however, be a mistake to see Comyn as representing either a return to a community or personal law basis for the mixed jury or an extension of a reasoning that limited itself to strict statutory reading. Comyn's all-alien jury was not limited to the suits of merchants of the staple. Nor did he suggest that aliens, whether from a single alien "community" or from the communities of the two parties, would be best able to speak about alien matters. Comyn did not mention the composition of the jury; he took for granted, in 1800, that the jury was to be of "any" aliens, accepting without comment Brooke's, Duncombe's, and Hawkins's approach.

Although Comyn's all-alien jury thus was contrary to the traditional (sixteenth-century) understanding of the fourteenth-century statutes and of the 1442 Year Book case, and ran counter to Duncombe's, Blackstone's, and Viner's (seventeenth- to eighteenth-century) views on whether an all-alien jury could be had, it was compatible with the impartiality justification that had emerged in Blackstone and Viner. Blackstone and Viner, like Duncombe, had argued that in a suit between two aliens, English jurors would favor neither alien and would be impartial or "indifferent." Comyn, taking his cue from the practice of having "any" alien on the alien half of a half-English jury, could have argued that, in a suit between two aliens, having all alien jurors would ensure impartiality. Under both views—the all-English or the all-alien jury in suits between two aliens—the question of jury composition no longer turned on omissions of statutory language, not to mention community membership, but on impartiality. Whether aliens in suits between two aliens are entitled to all-English or all-alien juries, the alien's "countrymen" have been displaced from the jury—in one instance by the English, in the other by "any" alien.

The concern with impartiality that emerged, in discussion about juries in suits between two aliens in the eighteenth to nineteenth centuries, accompanied a change too in the conception of half-alien juries.

2. Eighteenth- and Nineteenth-Century Juries

Few secondary sources refer to the actual use of trials *per medietatem linguae* during the eighteenth century. Published reports of nineteenth-century cases and a footnote in a history of crime and courts in England indicate, however, that juries *de medietate linguae* did not disappear. Drawing from Surrey assize records from 1748 to 1802, J. H. Beattie writes:

An alien who could not speak English had the right to be tried by a jury "de medietate linguae," a jury composed of half denizens and half aliens. Such requests were not of course very frequent. It appears that on some of the occasions on which such a jury was requested, the jury was assembled immediately and the trial continued. (ASSI 31/8, p. 147 [Derien]). But if no preparations had been made a request for such a jury would likely result in the prisoner's being returned to jail to await the next assizes. Antonio Welpes, who was indicted for murder in 1771, requested an interpreter and a jury "de medietate linguae" when he came to trial; he was held until the court met for the Summer assizes some months later when he was provided with both. He was convicted, hanged and dissected (ASSI 31/10, pp. 117, 158).[11]

The Old Bailey Session Papers for 1802 show two cases during the seventh session in which "the prisoner being a foreigner, a Jury of half foreigners were sworn."[12] The first involved the theft of a silver watch by a "Hamburghman" who "understands English." The second involved fraud. At the Winchester Assizes in 1856, three Italian sailors charged with murder and piracy in the

Bosphorus availed themselves of a mixed jury.[13] Between 1828 and 1870, five mixed jury cases appear in the published law reports. All except one are discussed below.[14]

Beattie's footnote, admittedly minor in the context of his work, raises interesting questions. For although Beattie does not intend to produce an exhaustive catalogue of who is entitled to the privilege of a mixed jury, his statement, like that of Oldham in the preceding chapter, suggests that in the eighteenth century juries *de medietate linguae* were granted not to "aliens born" nor to aliens belonging to groups whose language was not English, but to *individual* aliens who did not speak English. If the individual's language was the concern though, as pointed out in chapter 6, why bother with a jury, much less an alien jury, when translators or interpreters would suffice?

An earlier view, also discussed in the previous chapter, pointed to the rootedness of language and community in each other to answer "Why provide for alien jurors when language is the concern?" But once a mixed jury could be composed of "any" aliens, as was the case by the late eighteenth century, this answer lost its force.

The breakdown of the connection between language and community indicated the need for a new approach to the mixed jury. Changes in the function of juries generally had been informed, in past years, by a concern with impartiality and objectivity, which concern contributed to the formulation of the new approach to mixed juries. A brief description of changes in the general jury follows.

Jurors, by the late seventeenth century, were no longer chosen for their knowledge of a party or of a case, much less of the law. But a juror's personal knowledge of a case did not yet constitute grounds for objecting to the juror.[15] The Court held that friendship between a juror and a prosecutor was not ground for an objection, reasoning that one did not choose jurors *wholly* stranger to the fact. On the contrary, the Court claimed, one would object if the juror were not from the district or vicinity.[16] For a long time, too, jurors "might bring in a verdict, although no proofs were offered on either side," for "the law suppose[d] them to have sufficient knowledge to try the matters in issue 'and so they must, though no evidence were given on either side in court.'" Furthermore, "acting upon their own knowledge, [jurors] were at liberty to give a verdict in direct opposition to the evidence if they saw fit."[17]

By the early nineteenth century, however, a different view of the jury had emerged. In 1816 the Court refused to sustain a verdict based on a juror's own knowledge rather than on the facts produced by evidence.[18] A discrete law of evidence governing the presentation of evidence and the testimony of witnesses at trial accompanies the distinction between a juror's own knowledge and the facts produced by evidence. Although "the transformation of the active medieval juries into passive courtroom triers is among the greatest mysteries of English legal history, still no better understood than when Thayer wrote,"[19] such transformation certainly corresponds not only to the development of a substantive law of evidence but also to the articulation of rules of law. During the nineteenth century, statutes codifying many areas of law were drawn up, and at the end of the nineteenth century the first of the "digests"— 'whose object was to restate in clear language the case law of the time"— devoted itself to the subject of evidence.[20]

The demise of the countryman rationale for a mixed jury combined with a belief in a jury that was not to bring its own knowledge of the facts, much less of the law, to bear on the issue made the interpreter's appearance, in nineteenth-century cases involving individual aliens who did not speak English, understandable. With the interpreter, language itself became impartial, completely severed from its former unity with community. (At another level, England's empire during the same period also illustrated the disjuncture of language and community.) In the context of the jury, language, through translation and interpretation, would henceforth serve its modern function as a vehicle for neutral communication among the actors in the court. So ingrained would this conception of language become that nineteenth and twentieth-century histories would attribute the origins of mixed jury trials to problems of communication with foreign-speaking individuals.[21]

In 1731, the king-in-Parliament had officially made English the language of the law.[22] The emphasis on the need for neutral communication carried over into provisions requiring sworn interpreters and translations of affidavits in legal proceedings. Even where aliens opted not to assert their privilege to a mixed jury,[23] they could not very well refuse an interpreter.

If the test for whether an interpreter was required was whether an individual alien understood English, the test for a mixed jury was still, in the eighteenth century, whether the claimant was an alien. Judging from the "any" alien character of the alien jurors which accompanied Duncombe's association of country with language, "alien" meant "non-English" or "non-English-speaking." With the more radical separation of language from community in the nineteenth century, the test for "non- English" became neither alien birth, language, or allegiance, but the provisions of British naturalization law.

The first evidence of the demise of national origin in identifying the alien claimant appears in two eighteenth-century statutes that explicitly took away privileges to juries *de medietate linguae*. A 1740 statute deemed foreign mariners and seamen serving on British ships "natural-born" after two years service and took away their mixed jury privilege.[24] The second statute, in 1749, naturalized foreign Protestants serving on British whale-fishing boats.[25]

The clearest instance of reliance on statutory British naturalization law to ascertain the right of claimants to mixed juries came in 1849, however, in the case of Swiss-born Maria Manning.[26]

3. The Case of Manning and Manning

Maria Manning, married to a "natural-born subject of this realm," claimed a jury *de medietate linguae*. She and her husband had been jointly indicted for what was perhaps a somewhat sensationalist murder.[27] Both pleaded not guilty and Manning's claim to a jury *de medietate linguae* was denied. The trial proceeded in the ordinary course and both prisoners were convicted. In its opinion, the Court declared that the issue was "simply this": "Was the prisoner, Mrs. Manning, an alien or not at the time of the trial? If she was, she would be entitled to that which she prayed—to be tried by a jury *de medietate linguae*. If she was a British subject, she would not be so entitled."

Maria Manning's attorney, Ballantine, argued in the appeal that an 1844 statute[28] providing that a woman married to a natural-born or naturalized subject "shall be deemed and taken to be herself naturalized, and have all the rights and privileges of a natural-born subject," did not affect Maria Manning's right to a mixed jury. An 1825 Jury Act[29] had reenacted the provisions of the 28 Edw. III statute granting aliens the right to juries *de medietate linguae* (although limiting the privilege to cases of felony and misdemeanor). In order to affect someone's rights under the 1825 Jury Act, claimed Ballantine, the 1844 statute would have had to refer expressly to those rights, which it did not do.

Ballantine's argument made use of ambiguities in nineteenth-century British conceptions of naturalization and Parliamentary power. By the seventeenth century, one could distinguish two legal procedures for incorporating aliens into the community. Parliamentary acts of naturalization adopted foreigners on terms that generally conferred full subjectship. Royal patents of denization, on the other hand, bestowed limited rights and placed the denizen somewhere between the natural-born or naturalized subject and the alien.[30] Since Manning had become naturalized by getting married, Ballantine argued that her status was *analogous* to that of the denizen, but *closer* to that of the alien, at least for purposes of claiming a mixed jury trial, since an earlier act had explicitly given her, as alien, the right to claim such a jury. Thus, Ballantine had suggested at trial, the real question was whether Maria Manning was a "denizen," and if not, he claimed, she was entitled to trial *per medietatem linguae.*

Parry, his co-counsel, had also argued that the privilege of a mixed jury was one which "could not be got rid of by mere implications in an Act of Parliament; but that if abolished at all, it must be abolished by express enactment." He argued further "that there was only one way that an alien could divest himself [or in this case, herself] of the capacity or status of alienage, and that was by the consent of the State or Government of which he was a subject." Asked by the judge, "Was it not rather that a man cannot get rid of the *allegiance* he owes to the country where he was born?" Parry repeated that a person could not divest himself of *alienage* without the consent of the country where he was born.[31]

On appeal, Ballantine grounded the *de medietate linguae* provisions of the 1825 Jury Act in something resembling the community rationale for the mixed jury, arguing that the Legislature "seems clearly to have intended to give all persons born abroad under another allegiance, habituated to other customs, and probably speaking another language, a jury *de medietate linguae,* some of whom might comprehend the customs, and understand the tongue of the country of which the prisoner was native." He suggested that the 28 Edw. III statute, referring to inquests "*amongst* aliens and denizens," and not "between" them, "may well have intended to give the right to all persons born abroad," since at the time that the statute was made the distinction between aliens and denizens was probably not very clearly marked. (Ballantine was correct that the distinction was not clearly defined and that the 1354 statute may not have been intended to distinguish between "non-naturalized" and "naturalized" aliens, but he argued mistakenly from the statutory language, because in 1354 "denizen" included those Ballantine would call "natural-born subjects." Thus by his interpretation of "amongst," the statute would give the right to everyone. The Crown does seem to have tried to point this out. The point here is only that reading the statute with different meanings of "denizen"—the nineteenth century "naturalized by the king" or the fourteenth century "native-born" as well as "naturalized"— changes one's understanding of the history of mixed juries.)

Ballantine described "the practice" this way: "if a party has a foreign name, the officer asks him if he will have a mixed jury, and upon his prayer it is granted to him. He is not asked whether he is an alien or naturalized, but his mere claim is sufficient. . . . Thus upon claim made, the mixed jury is awarded as a matter of course."

The Crown formulated two objections. It based the first on *Barre's Case* (1598), in which the Court had held that where defendants were both aliens and Englishmen, no jury *de medietate linguae* could be had, since the English could not be tried by a mixed jury. The Crown found support for the holding of *Barre's Case* in the language of the 1825 Jury Act, which omitted the word "denizen" and thereby restricted the right to jury *de medietate linguae* to non-naturalized aliens. Even if Maria Manning was an alien, she was not entitled to a jury *de medietate linguae,* the Crown argued, because she was jointly indicted with her British husband who could not have one. Ballantine, in response, questioned the correctness of the holding in *Barre's Case,* arguing that it virtually repealed Marian Manning's statutorily granted right.

The Court never reached the issue of *Barre's Case* directly, addressing itself instead to the Crown's second argument, that Maria Manning was not an alien. The right to trial *per medietatem linguae* attached to one's status as an alien and was not a personal privilege, the Court held. Maria Manning, it determined, had the status and the political and civil character of a British subject:

The ordinary effect of every naturalization bill, is to declare that by the naturalization, the party is and shall be taken and deemed to be a British subject. What did it give? It gave all that belonged to a British subject. What did it take away? It took away all that did not belong to a British subject, for it made the naturalized party *ipso facto,* a British subject to all intents and purposes.[32]

The Crown asked: "Can a person who is naturalized be treated as an alien?" And the Court answered:

A British subject might be subject to certain disqualifications, but the Court know of no instance in which the character of an alien and a British subject are united. The disqualification imposed was not a disqualification that resulted from alienage after naturalization by the Legislature, but was the disqualification imposed by the authority of Parliament on a particular individual.[33]

The Court also argued that the "natural effect" of the words, "the party should be taken and deemed to be naturalized," was "to enlarge and simplify the operations of the Act," and that they should not be construed "with the intention of restriction":

There are no words, from the beginning to the end of this Act of Parliament, which warrant any conclusion that it was intended to operate at all, by enlarging or limiting all that belonged to the status of British subject. It no more referred to the Jury Act than every naturalization bill referred to the Jury Act. With respect, therefore, to the prisoner, the court can discover no intention whatever in this Act of Parliament, more or less, than to make her a British subject; and if that be so, the whole question is at an end, and she was not an alien at the time she was tried, and being a British subject, she was not entitled to a jury such as she claimed.[34]

Thus, although the Court did not explicitly address the issue of the fairness of the joint indictments of an alien and an English subject raised by *Barre's Case* and left open the question of whether it would be a mistrial for any British subject to be tried *per medietatem linguae* (as the Crown had argued), the Court confirmed that a British subject, natural-born or *however* naturalized, was not entitled to claim a mixed jury. The Court's position made clear that aliens lost their alien status by British law, implicitly rejecting Parry's (perhaps singular) conflation of foreign allegiance with alienage. Likewise, the Court discarded Ballantine's interpretation of the 1825 Jury Act provision on juries *de medietate linguae,* harking back as it did to a community rationale for mixed juries. Instead, the Court favored a narrower, text-bound discussion of legislative intent which was "collected, not by travelling out of the Act, but at looking to the whole of the Act itself"—and only the Act itself.

In relying on the Act this way and in insisting on a strict distinction between "alien" and "British subject" for the purpose of claiming mixed juries, the Court also moved away from what, by Ballantine's description, was apparently the practice. Ballantine's description of the treatment of "a party with a foreign name" suggests a certain informality, or at least a less legalistic approach to the question of who is an alien than that adopted by the Court.

4. The Loss of Difference

Whether an "alien" was entitled to a jury *de medietate linguae* came to depend, in the nineteenth century, on the status of the individual under the (statutory) naturalization law of Britain, rather than on a person's allegiance to a foreign country or membership in another culture. The complementary issue of who could serve on a mixed jury, with the acceptance of the "any" alien composition of the alien half of the mixed jury, had already become disassociated from notions of country or community. What remained of the meaning of alienage for the purpose of serving on mixed juries? Answering this question involves a comparison of sixteenth- and seventeenth-century holdings on the composition of mixed juries with two nineteenth-century cases involving challenges to alien jurors in mixed jury trials. While earlier cases emphasized and maintained the different "quality" of the alien part of the jury, or of the mixed as opposed to the common jury, nineteenth-century cases eradicated the difference between alien and British jurors.

Coke had claimed that alien jurors were subject to challenge for *propter defectum patriae* although, after mentioning it, he did not elaborate.[35] He also noted the existence of half-alien juries (see chapter 1), to which he attributed the same early beginning as to the general jury. He failed to perceive the potential inconsistency of allowing half-alien juries if aliens were *all* subject to challenge, however. All the treatises that followed Coke cited him on the point that aliens were subject to challenge. The 1825 Jury Act, too, provided that "no man, not being a natural born subject of the King, is or shall be qualified to serve on juries or inquests, except only in the cases hereinafter expressly provided for," which exception included juries *de medietate linguae*.

Despite these provisions, aliens did sometimes serve on general or common juries. In 1828, for instance, in *King vs. Sutton and Others,*[36] Sutton had moved for a new trial after conviction, claiming that a special juror who served at the trial was an alien, which had not been known to Sutton until after the trial. The Chief Justice denied Sutton a new trial, since Sutton apparently had had the opportunity to challenge the alien earlier: "We ought to be very careful in giving way to such an application, for if we must grant a new trial at the instance of a defendant after conviction, we must, also, do it at the instance of a prosecutor, when there has been an acquittal; and it seems to me that, without a precedent, we ought not to interfere in this late stage of the proceedings."[37]

Sutton's case shows that although technically aliens and naturalized subjects were not to sit on common juries together, in at least some instances they did so. As far back as the 1500s courts had had difficulty finding sufficient numbers of qualified jurors, and they developed a number of techniques to ensure the presence and service of jurors. One of these techniques was the tales *de circumstantibus,* a writ awarded to the sheriff to make up a deficiency of jurors out of the persons present in the court.[38]

Several sixteenth and seventeenth century cases establish that the tales could be used in mixed jury trials. *Caesar v. Cursiny* (1592)[39] was the first of these. Admiralty Court Judge Julius Caesar had brought an action on the case for slander against Philip Cursiny or Curtine, a merchant-stranger, for saying that Caesar had given a corrupt sentence. A mixed jury found Curtine guilty and liable for 200 marks. Curtine sought to arrest judgment, claiming that the tales *de circumstantibus* which had been awarded, apparently of all strangers, went against a 1544–45 statute.[40] He argued that the statute referred to the use of the tales for "common tryals," and not for trials *per medietatem linguae;* that the statute spoke of a lack of "jurors," and in this case only one juror had defaulted; and finally, that the non-alien plaintiff was the party defending the use of the alien tales.

The Court upheld the use of the tales in this case because, according to Popham, returning aliens was neither against the spirit or the letter of the law. The power of the Justices of Assise or Nisi Prius to command the sheriff to nominate such other persons to the tales as before (on the original return) included aliens as well as English, where the case required it, "for expedition was as requisite in cases for, or against them [aliens], as it were between other persons." Gawdy analogized the situation to one "where [if] a thing is to be tryed by inquest within two counties, and those of the one county appear, but not those of the other, [then] the tales might be of the other county only."[41]

Coke, reporting *Denbawd's Case* (1612–13), listed five things to be considered in granting the tales. In discussing the fifth, the "quality of the *tales,*" Coke used *Caesar v. Curtine* for the proposition that the talesmen "ought to be of the same quality as the principals are; and therefore if the [trial be] *per medietatem linguae* of English and aliens, the *tales* ought to be so, so if the principal be out of a liberty, and all those things which are required by the law in the principals are required in the *tales.*"[42]

In *Goodwin v. Montenaigh* (1601),[43] the Court held that where tales were awarded in a case to be tried *per medietatem linguae,* aliens and denizens should be returned and identified, to maintain the quality of the original panel. Since such identification had not occurred, the judgment was stayed at the defendant's request, and a misreturn declared. Upon presentation of an affidavit that six aliens and six denizens were sworn, however, the plaintiff had judgment without a new trial (for the Court had declared a misreturn and not an arrested judgment).

In all three of these cases, the Court concerned itself, at least formally, with reproducing the "quality" of the original jury panel. The cases point to a belief in a "qualitative" difference between a common jury and a jury *de medietate linguae.* While it was important to preserve the "quality" of a mixed jury, *Goodwin* shows that the Court would not go so far as to require a new trial to do so, when the record could be adjusted easily to show that the proceedings were still "good."

These sixteenth- and seventeenth-century holdings contrast with two nineteenth century cases involving challenges to alien jurors in mixed jury trials. While the earlier cases emphasized the different "quality" of the alien part of the jury, or of the mixed as opposed to common jury, the latter eliminated the difference between alien and British jurors.

The holding on the first issue in *Regina v. Giorgetti* (1865)[44] retained some distinction between the foreign and English half of the jury *de medietate linguae*. The Court held that where six English jurors were already "in the box," the Crown was compelled to show cause of challenge to a foreign juror, after the panel had been "called over,"[45] although the panel had not been exhausted by formal challenges. It seems that normally, in non-mixed-jury cases, only after the original panel had been exhausted did the Crown lose its right to peremptory challenge. But "that case does not apply. The object of the statute is to give the prisoner the benefit of the attendance of the six foreigners." Eight Englishmen were already in the box but "the last two English gentlemen were inadvertently called and they should withdraw, and the jury should be made up to the number of twelve from six foreigners. I am of the opinion that the Crown cannot challenge without showing cause."[46]

The second issue discussed in Giorgetti's case involved the Crown's challenge to Dominic Maffia, an Italian who had been called from the supplemental panel. The Crown alleged that Maffia came from the same state as defendant Giorgetti and that he had publicly stated that if he found Giorgetti guilty (of the wilful murder of Thomas Kelly), his life would not be safe when he returned to his native state, to which he was about to return. After the Court appointed two triers to try the truth of this statement, and the Crown had put their cause in writing, the Crown discovered that its evidence referred to a statement made by the proposed juror's brother, Peter Maffia, and withdrew its objection. The court officer then "gave the book into the hands of the juror and recited the oath to him, when the juror himself, before kissing the book, stated that he had the same objection to serve which had been stated of his brother."[47] His Lordship ruled, however, that the objection came too late, for although the juror had not kissed the book, he had taken it into his hands while the oath was recited to him, so he had really been sworn.

The reporter of the case noted that although the judge had decided according to the authorities, the rule regarding the lateness of the objection seemed "very inconvenient" unless the Court adopted the precaution suggested in another case: that the Clerk of Assize ask each party whether they challenge or not. The rule seemed especially inconvenient where, as here, the objection would be "when he was called upon to contribute himself to the act of taking the oath, viz, when he is told to kiss the book." The reporter cited other opinions to the effect that "the case of a layman and foreigner having a conscientious objection which renders him an unfit juryman, and who makes his objection known before he has kissed the book, seems to have a favorable claim to the interposition of the Court."

According to the Court though, the "special" circumstance of a foreign juror appearing in court was no different from the appearance of any other layman. The foreign juror and the layman were similarly subject to established procedural rules. Yet Giorgetti, the alien claiming the privilege of trial *per mediatatem linguae,* was allowed to present his plea through a sworn interpreter. Though Giorgetti, as foreign claimant, thus appeared to be getting special consideration which his foreign jurors did not, both Giorgetti's interpreter and the ruling against Maffia's objection served to "neutralize," rather than to show respect for, perceived differences between the two Italians and the English.

The bond posited by the "countrymen" model, which once would have served to put one's fellows *on* the jury, had lost what little power or relevance it retained. In the face of a need for jurors and respect for established procedure, the weight given this bond was insufficient to establish the credibility of Maffia's claim of partiality, even under threats, to his fellow countryman. Maffia's claim pointed to the gap that had emerged between the law of the community and that of the court.

If *Giorgetti* exemplifies the dissolution of what remained of (any impact by the belief in) the countryman bond, *Levinger v. the Queen* (1870)[48] illustrates the change away from the earlier belief in the "qualitative" difference between aliens and English jurors that accompanied the impartiality rationale. *Levinger* involved an appeal to the Privy Council for the Supreme Court of the (Australian) Colony of Virginia. A mixed jury, half of British subjects, half of aliens, had already been empaneled to try a Bavarian, Hugo Levinger, when Levinger peremptorily challenged an alien by the name of Lord. The Attorney General of the Colony, on behalf of the Crown, demurred, on the ground that Lord, an alien, was not subject to peremptory challenge, and the Court ruled against Levinger. The jury found Levinger guilty and, after appeal to the Supreme Court on a different issue, the Court sentenced him to seven years imprisonment with hard labor.

Levinger argued that the Court in *Giorgetti* had recognized the right of peremptory challenge of alien jurors in favor of the prisoner. He asserted that the Australian Supreme Court case of *Reg. v. Ah Toon,* holding that a foreigner on trial by a jury *de mediatate linguae* had no right of peremptory challenge as to the foreign panel, was wrongly decided:

Now, it is a principle of English law that Prisoners shall be entitled to challenge from mere caprice. It is laid down by *Blackstone* (Comm. vol. iv, p. 353), with reference to peremptory challenge, "the law wills not" that a Prisoner "should be tried by any one man against whom he has conceived a prejudice, even without being able to assign a reason for such his dislike," and he gives a reason for such a rule.[49]

The Crown, on the other hand, argued that the 1865 Juries Statute (which it referred to as "the *Victoria* Statute") confined the right to challenge alien jurors to challenges for "cause certain."[50] It argued that since their establishment under Edward III, juries *de medietate linguae* had been under a footing different from that of ordinary juries, and it construed the language of the 1354 statute of 28 Edw. III as follows:

The second section of that statute, expressly required, as to the half of the denizen jury, that they should not be "suspicious to the one party nor to the other party," and by omitting that requirement as to aliens, indicated the intention of the Statute, that they should not be subject to peremptory challenge.[51]

The Court held that Levinger was indeed entitled to challenge an alien juror peremptorily. The common law rule, it said, as modified by the *Victoria* Statute, was that every person arraigned for any "Treason-Felony or Misdemeanor" shall be admitted to challenge peremptorily to twenty jurors. The "end of challenge," wrote Sir Joseph Napier in his opinion, citing Coke, "is to have an indifferent trial, and which is required by law." As Lord Campbell, Chief Justice, had written elsewhere:

Unless the power were given under certain restrictions to both sides, it is quite obvious that justice could not satisfactorily be administered; for it must often happen that a juror is returned on the panel who does not stand indifferent, and who is not fit to serve upon the trial, although no legal evidence could be adduced to prove his unfitness.[52]

(The limitation placed on the Crown's power to challenge in *Giorgetti* was consistent with this holding because the Crown could not be permitted to go so far as to make the empaneling of the appropriate twelve-member jury impossible.)

The prisoner could not be deprived by implication "of a right of so much importance to him, given by the Common Law, and enjoyed for many centuries," unless the implication was necessary for the interpretation of the *Victoria* Statute which, the Court argued over several pages, it was not. And, against the Crown, the Court read the 28 Edw. III statute as conferring a privilege (to a mixed jury) on aliens rather than taking away a right (to peremptory challenge) "confessedly material to" securing an indifferent trial, as required by law.

The grounding of peremptory challenges in the need for a legally required indifferent jury suggested a potential argument for an even stronger need for such challenges in the case of alien jurors:

In addition to what has been observed by Lord Campbell, C.J., as to peremptory challenge and which applies to all jurors impanneled on a trial for Felony, there may be
aliens with national prejudices and hostile feelings against the prisoner; and objections which he could not make out by legal evidence. There is not a reason assigned in
Books of authority in favour of the right of peremptory challenge that is not, at least, as
applicable (at least in some instances more so) to any alien as to any of the other jurors.[53]

But this suggestion that aliens might be susceptible to greater prejudice than other jurors was not so extreme that the law would consider alien jurors or juries *de medietate linguae* qualitatively differently from ordinary jurors or juries. In fact, the Court expressly declared that alien jurors were to be treated the same as the denizen jurors of ordinary juries and of mixed juries: "This section [of the *Victoria* Statute] places him [the alien juror] in the same position as if he had the qualification required by the Act, but leaves him sub-ject to be challenged for any other cause of challenge; that is to say for any personal disqualification at common law, except alienage itself."[54] The only difference between alien and denizen jurors involved the property qualifica-tion. And here, "but for the express saving in favour of the alien juror," the disqualification as to property would have attached to aliens.[55] As the Court wrote in *Levinger*, "in every instance where the Legislature has not in-terfered in his favour, it will be found that an alien juror is dealt with as if he were a denizen."

By 1870 then, no special quality attached or was attributed to the alien juror or to the half-alien jury, beyond the "fact" of alienage. The "indifferent" jury pointed to a loss of difference. Since one's fellow aliens, other aliens, and British jurors might all be equally prejudiced against one, there seemed little sense, given the aspiration of an impartial jury embodied in legal require-ments for an "indifferent" jury, in continuing to allow aliens the "privilege" of claiming a half-alien jury.

5. The Abolition of the Mixed Jury

The abolition of the jury *de medietate linguae* came, unsurprisingly, in the same year as the *Levinger* decision. In an 1869 Report of the Royal Commis-sioners inquiring into laws of naturalization and allegiance, the Commis-sioners had found it to be "settled law that those members of a mixed jury who are foreigners, need not be of the same nationality as the alien; they need not even speak the same language, but may each of them belong to a different nation and speak a different tongue." The Commissioners saw "no advantage in the maintenance of such a system," which it understood as originally "an encouragement to foreign woollen merchants to resort to the English market." Because "the inconveniences which may arise from [the maintenance of the system] are obvious," the Commissioners recommended the repeal of statutes authorizing trials by mixed jury.[56]

The Appendix to the Report contains Chief Baron Piggott's refusal in 1867 of a mixed jury to Irish-born John Warren, who had been formally naturalized in the United States, on the ground that "he who once is under the allegiance of the English sovereign remains so for ever. . . . It would be really almost pedantry for me to cite authorities on that subject. They are familiar to every lawyer." Piggott then draws on Blackstone's distinction between natural perpetual allegiance and local temporary allegiance, before turning to "some American authorities of the greatest weight and highest reputation,"[57] or to "Mr Justice Storey in his book on the Conflict of Laws, that is on the laws of nations as they relate to each other—and Chancellor Kent expounding the law of America, and expounding it, in the first instance by an exposition of the law of England, which is its foundation."[58]

Piggott quotes Storey's qualification of the claim that "every nation has a right to bind its own subjects by its own laws in every other place." The nation instead "possesses the right to regulate and govern its own *native-born* subjects everywhere, and consequently . . . its laws extend to and bind such subjects, at all times and in all places. This is commonly adduced as a consequence of what is called natural allegiance; that is, of allegiance to the government of the territory of a man's birth."[59] Thus, as in American law, which grounds itself in English law, Piggott claims, no citizen can renounce his allegiance without the permission of government, and Walker's application for a mixed jury, as that of a non-alien, was denied—as was Augustine Costello's in a similar case the same year.[60]

Upon second reading of the proposed Naturalization Bill in the House of Lords, mention was scarcely made of the jury *de medietate linguae*. The Earl of Derby declared its abrogation to be "an unmixed advantage. It is not always easy to find such juries; it is not certain that when found they will be the most intelligent or the most unprejudiced that can be found. Indeed, the probability is rather in a reverse direction, because in general the field of selection is so very small." But the issue of the justice of the mixed jury with which the Earl appears most concerned relates to the British nation. It concerns not the challenge the mixed jury could pose to British laws, however, but the implications of the mixed jury for British identity: "It seems to me, moreover, that it is stigmatizing ourselves as a nation very unjustly to assume that the prejudice against foreigners is such that an alien on his trial will not have a fair trial before British subjects."[61]

The Earl of Clarendon approved the comments of his "noble Friend (the Earl of Derby)" on "doing away with mixed juries, and for the reasons that he has stated," adding the now familiar claims that the principle was adopted in Edward III's reign and that jurors need not be of the same nationality of the alien tried. He concluded that "there is no longer any reason for continuing a system the inconveniences of which are manifest, and have long been experienced."[62]

In Committee in the House of Commons, the question of the necessity of a clause holding that aliens are not entitled to jury *de medietate linguae* was raised briefly. Mr. M'Mahon said there was no necessity for the clause, since the privilege was statutory, had been altered, and was not part of the common law. The Solicitor General said that the clause "said nothing about the common law" and the clause was agreed to.[63]

The Naturalization Act of 1870[64] thus not only permitted aliens to acquire, hold, and dispose of real and personal property "in the same manner in all respects as by a natural-born British subject," but also declared: "From and after the passing of this act, an alien shall not be entitled to be tried by a jury de medietate linguae, but shall be triable in the same manner as if he were a natural-born subject."

And, in the same year, Parliament took another step consistent with the interchangeability of aliens and denizens. While aliens could no longer claim the special privilege of trial *per medietatem linguae,* they now could serve on common juries:

Aliens having been domiciled in England or Wales for ten years or upwards, if in other respects duly qualified, shall be qualified and shall be liable to serve on juries or inquests in England and Wales as if they had been natural-born subjects of the queen: but save as aforesaid, no man not being a natural-born subject of the queen shall be qualified to serve on inquests in any court or on any occasion whatever.[65]

With the abolition of the mixed jury, the demise of personal law and the rise of the law of the state was complete. Law no longer came from the community or attached to community members; instead it issued from the state and extended to all those within its bounds, irrespective of who they were. Or rather, who they were now was by definition according to the law of the state. The impartiality with which the law of the state was concerned in the nineteenth century was not unique to that period. Even the earliest records declared that jurors were to be "senioribus and legalibus," "good and sufficient men," "not suspicious to the one party nor to the other party." But the "indifference"—the absence of difference—that characterizes the treatment of individuals in the law of the state was peculiar. Through it fairness and the rule of law indeed supplanted the harshness and violence of early communities. Yet the story of the mixed jury shows also that under state law the richness and complexity of persons and their law has given way to the sterility and fungibility of individuals.

Conclusion

The same never coincides with the equal, not even in the empty indifferent oneness of what is merely identical. The equal or identical always moves toward the absence of difference, so that everything may be reduced to a common denominator. The same, by contrast, is the belonging together of what differs, through a gathering by way of the difference. We can only say "the same" if we think difference. It is in the carrying out and settling of differences that the gathering nature of sameness comes to light. The same banishes all zeal always to level what is different into the equal or identical. The same gathers what is distinct into an original being-at-one. The equal, on the contrary, disperses them into the dull unity of mere uniformity.—Heidegger[1]

The history of the mixed jury points to the disappearance of difference. It tells of the decline of law as practice and of the rise of law as doctrine. On the jury, in place of alien and native who are the same, each a member of a different community, sharing in its laws and customs, appear impartial individuals, equals of all members of the population. The "loss of difference" articulated in chapter 7's nineteenth-century legal texts is not the "sameness" of chapter 1's early mixed jury, which treated both foreigners and natives as members of their own communities. On the contrary, this loss of difference points to an *absence* of community in which, the twentieth-century texts of chapters 2 and 3 suggest, all threaten to become outsiders to one another and themselves as well.[2]

A strange inversion has occurred: where once all were insiders of communities who knew their own law, all are now observers of a world that posits truth of fact. In place of the community's knowledge of what to do appear sciences of society and government, whose truths inform the judgments of state officials. The community has been turned inside out under a gaze that makes aliens of us all.

The story of the mixed jury shows how this inversion has come about. It relates the disappearance of community membership to the decline of personal law and to the concomitant development of an externally imposed, propositionally articulable, and recognizable official common law. Chapter 1 pointed to the earliest mixed juries and asked how legal scholars had missed the personal law implications of a practice that allowed members of other communities to participate in the declaration of law. Chapters 5, 6, and 7 told of the progressive demise of personal law in England. The story these chapters told, relying on what one could consider the most positivist sources of history and law, the declarations of written records, culminated in the privileging, as law, of an official system of rules to the exclusion of the customary law or practice of the mixed jury. The twentieth-century tendency in England toward "substituting trial by judges for trial by jury" has often been remarked. "But in another direction," as a 1924 article calling—to no avail— for the restoration of juries *de medietate linguae* in criminal cases notes, "trial by jury seems to have sustained as great injury by the abolition of the jury *de medietate linguae,* an element of the jury system that actually seems coeval with it." The tone of the article is grave. It seeks to avert the "remediless miscarriage of justice" of the sort that occurred when a Frenchman, "admittedly entirely ignorant of our language, was convicted of murder." It warns of "great danger" to trial by jury, "the 'bedrock and foundation' of all our criminal procedure whose certainty, expedition, and justice had been the admiration of jurists of all civilized nations" and cites "the eloquent apotheosis of this tribunal . . . in Sir James Mackintosh's defence of Pettier in 1803, when he urged that a jury was as inviolate as the country itself."[3]

The article links the mixed jury, the jury, and integrity of the country. And indeed, changes in the mixed jury point to changes in conceptions of law and membership in England. The transformation of the practice of the mixed jury into official doctrine in chapter 5 indicated the king's assumption of authority over law and revealed a weakening of the principle of personal law. The replacement of an alien's countrymen with "any alien whatsoever" on the jury in chapter 6 showed a further weakening of this principle. And the statutory abolition of the mixed jury in the name of its "inconvenience" and the value of "indifference" or impartiality in chapter 7 suggests the complete demise of law understood as the shared practices of a community's members.

Given this history, the neglect of the personal law implications of the earliest mixed jury seems more understandable. For the rise of positive law has meant more than the development, through the writing of law and the recognition of an external mark of authority, of a unified system of official rules whose validity is distinguishable from their morality.[4] The rise of positive law accompanies the transformation of practice into propositionally articulable rules and the growth of a pervasive concern with the facts of law, with the law that exists, with what is empirically verifiable, procedurally regular, and statistically probable. The positivist concern with fact characterizes not only modern law but much modern thought. Such positivism means the foreclosure of certain possibilities—among them the possibility that law could be understood as, or could indeed be, other than fact, other than the valid law that exists or positive law.

The tendency to view all law as positive law reaches its peak in a peculiarly modern version of positivism. Presuming that law is propositional, as discussed in chapter 4, modern positivism takes the factual character of law for granted, oblivious to the necessarily prior transformation of practice into fact.[5] While a nonpositivist history may suggest such transformation, positivist thought, as chapter 4 argues, finds itself constitutionally incapable of identifying an earlier law that is not already some version of positive law.

The origin or source of law, for positivism, lies in the perpetual imposition of human will—in an eternal reenactment of human conquest and command. Even when positive law does not manifest itself as the command of a distinct human sovereign, it appears nonetheless as the man-made creation of governmental policies of social control, as sociological norms.[6] The source of law, in the positivist jurisprudence and history described in chapter 4, as in the official legal texts and sociolegal studies discussed in chapters 2 and 3, may be acknowledged as just or may appear just, but can never be known to be so. Thus the modern verdict, the declaration of law that is a speaking of truth, no longer tells of the practices of communities. Instead it reveals the fact of the preferences of a cross-section of the population. Evaluated for its accuracy and consistency, a verdict reached through what are agreed to be fair procedures serves to maintain public confidence in the system, i.e., in the legitimacy or *belief* in the system's justice. Jurors become elements of a population whose acquiescence to ostensibly neutral procedures governs the determination of policies and which acquiescence is itself the subject of empirical investigation.

Investigation into such facts ostensibly maintains the positivist distinctions between law and morality and between fact and value. But sociolegal research itself, rejecting history for failing to provide clear guidelines for standards and procedures, often proposes improvements to law that threaten the distinction between "is" and "ought" upon which positivism ostensibly grounds itself. Proposals explicitly indicating the resemblance of law to fact, for instance, simultaneously take law to be a matter not simply of fact but also of will. They understand law as a matter of directing and controlling public perceptions, a matter rendered accessible through expert, even if diffuse, knowledge of social interests and policy.

Consider what such knowledge makes of the "commonsense of the layman," as one court has called it, whereby jurors are thought to use their own knowledge of the everyday world to deal with questions of credibility. Of many proposals to abolish the jury or to limit the matters on which juries may deliberate, a joint proposal by a lawyer and a social scientist stands out.[7] It suggests that judges should instruct juries as to empirical findings about the "background context for deciding factual issues"—the speed with which memory decays over time, the effects of stress on eyewitness testimony, or the relation between a witness's confidence in an identification and the accuracy of that identification, for instance. Sociological and psychological research about the state of mind of battered women, the typical behavioral traits of abused children, and the recidivism rates of convicted criminals, currently presented at trial by expert witnesses, would, according to this proposal, first be submitted to the judge to present to the jury.

One striking thing about this proposal is that the findings of "social framework" to be presented to a jury will not inform the jury as to whether a particular witness is to be believed or whether a particular person has committed a particular act. Instead, this research would inform the jury as to the probabilities that people *of this sort* did or will do *these sorts of* things. Supplanting what remains of the jury's own knowledge and judgment, the information supplied by such research would make verdicts more compatible with the empirical findings of social science research.

Even more telling about modern conceptions of law and knowledge than the proposal to inform juries about social framework, however, are the claims its proponents make about the character of social research. The social science research to be used to instruct juries should not be treated solely as fact, the authors claim. It should be considered as "more analogous" to law, "as a source of authority rather than as a type of fact." The authors propose that courts "deal with empirical research much as they now deal with legal precedent in a common-law system." They write that "the principal similarity between social science and fact is that both are positive—both concern the way the world is, with no necessary implications for the way the world *ought* to be." And, on the other hand:

The principal similarity between social science and law is that both are general—both produce principles applicable beyond particular instances. Until now, courts and commentators have attended to the similarity between social science and fact, and have largely ignored the similarity between social science and law. Yet jurisprudential considerations do not preclude pursuing the law analogy rather than the fact analogy, and there is considerable precedent for according positive materials like social science the status of authority in the law.[8]

According to these authors, then, the generalizable yet empirical findings of social science are closer to the generalizable assertions of law about how things ought to be than they are to the "specific empirical events" or facts of a case. For them, the crucial distinction between law and fact is not between "ought" and "is" but between dispositive generalizations (conclusions of law and empirical research) and specific descriptions (propositions of fact).

Analysis of twentieth-century American texts about the jury confirms the story of the earlier English mixed jury. It points first to the pervasiveness of a positivism that, in our time, threatens to make strangers of us all and to turn law into the fact of policies or into the outcome of the absolute if dispersed human will of social science. Yet the story of the mixed jury also suggests that law indeed may be other than positive law. Although based on the most positivist of sources, this work looks away from evidence of what exists and probabilities of how we are empirically, away from—in Hart's words—"the theoretical and scientific study of law as a social phenomenon,"[9] to the tradition of the early mixed jury. This tradition recalls what already is and the possibilities of what has been and could be. The story of the mixed jury reminds us of the world to which we belong as members of communities who, in acting, know what to do.

In restricting itself to texts, in treating official doctrine as law, in recounting history in documents, this work, on the one hand, epitomizes positivism and, on the other, reveals positivist jurisprudence for what it is: as so committed to what exists that it is in danger of completely forgetting both the possible, which may not presently exist, and the members of one's community who make any commitment possible. The sociological and positivist commitment of our age—to the human determination of guidelines concerning what exists—threatens to make us oblivious to any law that is not ostensibly within our control—including past law. This work warns of the danger of forgetting all other law, of denying to all law that is not our own creation the status of "law." It warns of letting the law of the other, like the justice that is respect for those who live by other laws, silently disappear, as we ourselves become strangers to the practice of law and experts at dictating, from outside, the terms of our own governance.

Hart writes of a particular chapter in *The Concept of Law* that in it "we shall not only carry this analysis a little farther but we shall make the general claim that in the combination of [the] two types of rule there lies what Austin wrongly claimed to have found in the notion of coercive orders, namely, 'the key to the science of jurisprudence'" (79). This work claims that in the combination of Hart's two types of rule, there lies not only "the key to the science of [positivist] jurisprudence," namely, the notion of law as the fact of imposition or the effectivity of will, but also an impoverishment of the possibilities of jurisprudence. Objecting not to the accuracy of the positivist description of the legal system that exists, this work carries the analysis further; it explores the implications of allowing the accuracy that is appropriate to evaluating propositions to become the sole truth of law.

The warning against forgetting that positive law is one possibility of law ought not be construed as calling for a return to natural law or to the so-called "communitarianism" that some will find in the early mixed jury. Nor ought it be construed as claiming that the possibilities for our law are infinite. To remember that positive law is but one possibility for law will not necessarily bring justice or community about, but to forget all other possibilities will certainly foreclose them to us. The possibilities to which the mixed jury bears witness, in its reminder that one's identity is limited neither to the facts of one's existence nor even to the interpretation of one's texts, do not demand of us particular changes or challenge us to devise an escape from positivism. For even as the absence of community revealed in our texts appears as a manifestation of positive law, attempts to create community or to escape positivism through policies, commands, or other acts of will reinforce the very positivism that they seek to overcome. Insofar as this work itself, in its attempt to write a history that is not simply of the facts and to avoid the habits of evaluating and prescribing that characterize the modern attitude toward law, seeks to escape positivism, it too manifests the paradoxical nihilism of a positivistic age, an age that seeks continually to become something else, to be other than itself, to perpetually overcome, thereby letting nothing be.

NOTES

Report Abbreviations

B. & C.   Barnewall and Cresswell's *English King's Bench Reports* (1822–30)
Co. Rep.   Coke's *Reports, King's Bench* (1572–1616)
Cro. Eliz. Croke's *English King's Bench Reports, tempore Elizabeth*
Den.   Denison and Peirce's *Crown Cases Reserved* (1544–52)
Dyer   Dyer's *Les Reports des divers matters & resolutions* (1537–82)
E. & B.   Ellis and Blackburn's *English Queen's Bench Reports* (1852–58)
F. & F.   Foster and Finlason's *English Nisi Prius Reports* (1856–67)
Maule & S. Maule and Selwyn's *English King's Bench Reports* (1814–29)
Pop.   Popham's *English King's Bench Reports* (1592–1627)
Vaughan   Vaughan's *English Common Pleas Reports* (1688)

Epigraph

1. W. H. Auden, "September 1, 1939," *Another Time* (New York: Random House, 1940). This poem was later supressed by the author and excised from collections of his work. From *The Collected Poetry of W. H. Auden,* by W. H. Auden. Copyright 1940 by W. H. Auden. Reprinted by permission of Random House, Inc., and by Faber and Faber Ltd.

Introduction

1. Frederick Pollock and Frederic W. Maitland, *The History of English Law before the Time of Edward I,* 2d ed. (Cambridge: Cambridge University Press, 1898), vol. 1, p. xxv.

2. Gerard Raulet, "Structuralism and Poststructuralism: An Interview with Michel Foucault," *Telos* 55 (Spring 1983): 210.

3. *Lex Ribuaria,* vol. 31, 4: "Quod si damnatus fuerit secundum legem propriam, non secundum Ribuariam damnum sustineat," cited in E.-M. Meijers, *L'histoire des principes fondamentaux du droit international privé à partir du moyen age, specialement dans l'europe occidentale,* in Hague Academy of International Law, *Recueil des Cours* (Paris: Librairie du Recueil Sirey, 1934), pp. 547–686, at 557–58.

4. H. L. A. Hart, *The Concept of Law* (Oxford: Clarendon Law Series, 1961), p. 2.

5. 27 Edw. III, st. 2, c. 8, ss. 12–14; referred to as 27 Edw. III, the Statute of the Staple, or the 1353 statute.

6. 28 Edw. III, c. 13.

7. *Report of the Royal Commissioners for Inquiring into the Law of Naturalization and Allegiance,* presented to both Houses of Parliament by Command of Her Majesty (London: Her Majesty's Stationery Office, 1869), p. xi.

8. Friedrich Nietzsche, *Twilight of the Idols,* trans. R. J. Hollingdale (London: Penguin, 1968), p. 65.

Chapter One

1. Otto Kahn-Freund, *The Growth of Internationalism in English Private International Law* (Jerusalem: Magnes Press, Hebrew University, 1960), pp. 10–12, 15–16; J. G. Collier, *Conflict of Laws* (Cambridge: Cambridge University Press, 1987), p. 9. Holdsworth calls private international law "the youngest branch of English law"; cf. Sir W. S. Holdsworth, *A History of English Law,* 16 vols., 6th ed. rev. (London: Methuen, 1938–72), vol. 15, p. 334. It first appeared as a distinct body of doctrine under the name "private international law" in the mid-1800s. Even then, its status was unclear and it might show up as a single chapter in a larger work on public international law. English private international law, unlike civil *droit international privé,* is synonymous with what civil lawyers consider the narrower area of conflict of laws, which includes questions of English court jurisdiction, choice of law, and recognition and enforcement of foreign judgments, but excludes the general topic of nationality and the treatment of foreigners. See Henri Battifol and Paul Lagarde, *Droit international privé,* 3 vols., 7th ed. (Paris: Librairie generale de droit et de jurisprudence, 1981), vol. 1, p. 4. For the history of private international law on the Continent, see E.-M. Meijers, *L'histoire des principes fondamentaux du droit international privé à partir du moyen age,* and Battifol and Lagarde, vol. 1, pp. 7–19.

2. Frederic W. Maitland, *The Constitutional History of England: A Course of Lectures Delivered by Frederic William Maitland* (Cambridge: Cambridge University Press, 1913), p. 67.

3. Simeon Guterman, *From Personal to Territorial Law: Aspects in the History and Structure of the Western Legal-Constitutional Tradition* (Metuchen, N.J.: Scarecrow Press, 1972), p. 37.

4. Arthur K. Kuhn, *Comparative Commentaries on Private International Law or Conflict of Laws* (New York: Macmillan, 1937), p. 16.

5. Kahn-Freund, *Growth of Internationalism,* p. 10.

6. J. A. C. Thomas, *Private International Law* (London: Hutchinson's University Library, 1955; repr. Westport, Conn.: Greenwood Press, 1975), p. 23.

7. Maitland, *Constitutional History,* p. 67.

8. Of course, the notion of "national" law in England, even after the unification of the early kingdoms, is problematic, as neither the English as a whole, nor the overlapping communities to which the English belong, can be said to comprise a "nation." Similarly, a distinction between conflicts among English customs and conflicts between English and other "national" law is somewhat contrived, as *extranei* could just as well come from neighboring boroughs as from nations across the sea. Whatever the conflict, however, the use of the mixed jury implicitly accorded at least some recognition to the law of the other. Such recognition was tied to the notion that every person belonged to a community—no matter how vague or indeterminate its boundaries and its definition of membership—which was identified in some way by its customs or laws.

9. George Rightmire, *The Law of England at the Norman Conquest* (Columbus, Ohio: The F. J. Heer Printing Co., 1932), pp. 62–63.

10. William Mitchell, *An Essay on the Early History of the Law Merchant* (Cambridge: Cambridge University Press, 1904), p. 23.

11. J. L. Bolton, *The Medieval English Economy* (London: J. M. Dent & Sons, 1980), p. 13.

12. J. H. Baker, *An Introduction to English Legal History,* 2d ed. (London: Butterworths, 1979), p. 6, citing H. G. Richardson and G. O. Sayles, *Governance of Medieval England* (1963), regarding the sixth century.

13. Historians generally divide non-royal and non-ecclesiastical courts into two types: the seignorial or feudal manor courts, and the local courts of the vill, the hundred, and the shire. But here general classifications end, as feudal and local courts operated and interacted in different ways in different parts of the country. Sometimes a manor consisted of several vills; sometimes a vill contained several manors. Sometimes the vill or the hundred fell into private hands and a manorial court leet replaced the sheriff's tourn in investigating the condition of frankpledges (the sureties required of every person). At times, no distinction was made among the jurisdictions of the court leet which was concerned with the manor, of the court baron which was concerned with matters of freeholders, and of the court customary which concerned itself with villeinage. See, generally, Baker, *English Legal History;* S. F. C. Milsom, *Historical Foundations of the Common Law* (London: Butterworths, 1981); Theodore F. T. Plucknett, *A Concise History of the Common Law,* 5th ed. (Boston: Little, Brown & Co., 1956); Pollock and Maitland, *History of English Law before Edward I;* R. C. Van Caenegem, *The History of the Common Law,* 2d ed. (Cambridge: Cambridge University Press, 1988).

14. The Crown made the hundred and the vill the administrative unit for collecting the taxes required by the Crusades. Thirteenth-century statutes systematized the police powers of the vill, requiring watchmen and the enforcement of the assize of arms. Statutes also made the hundred liable for undetected crimes committed within its boundaries. The Crown so distrusted the sheriff, or the "shire reeve," that the Exchequer audited his accounts annually. Judgments of county courts and seignorial courts could be examined in the (royal) court of common pleas by writs, and royal jurisdiction could even be invoked before the seigniorial or county court had declared judgment. The once extensive jurisdiction of the county over both civil and criminal cases was transferred to the royal Justices in Eyre, and eventually to other commissioners or travelling justices as the Eyre became obsolete. See Plucknett, *Concise History of the Common Law,* pp. 85, 86, 88, 104, 105.

15. Maitland, *Constitutional History,* p. 67.

16. Mary Bateson, ed., *Borough Customs,* 2 vols., Publications of the Selden Society, vols. 17 and 21 (London: B. Quaritch, 1904, 1906), vol. 1, p. xiii–xiv.

17. This claim does not foreclose the possibility that writing itself may be a way of knowing custom, as in the early French *coutumiers.* The possibility of nonpropositional writings of law that accompany custom (or nonpropositional knowledge of law) is discussed further in chapter 4.

18. Susan Reynolds, *Kingdoms and Communities in Western Europe, 900–1300*

(Oxford: Clarendon Press, 1984), p. 139, citing A. MacFarlane, *The Origins of English Individualism* (Oxford, 1978), p. 32.

19. Reynolds, *Kingdoms and Communities,* pp. 138–39, 147–49.

20. Frank Barlow, *The Norman Conquest and Beyond* (London: Hambledon Press, 1983), p. 38.

21. William Cunningham, *Alien Immigrants to England,* 2d ed. (London: Frank Cass & Co., 1969), pp. 19–24.

22. William I established Gherbord at Chester and Walcher of Lorraine at Durham; Rufus established a settlement at Carlisle. Henry I's colonies at Haverfordwest, Tenby, Gower, and Ross "may have been partly intended to keep the Welsh in check." Cunningham, *Alien Immigrants,* pp. 25–26.

23. Ibid., p. 5. (The Normans are "the most courteous of people and hold foreigners in equal honor with themselves," wrote William of Malmesbury.)

24. C. Warren Hollister, ed., *The Impact of the Norman Conquest* (New York: John Wiley and Sons, 1969), pp. 7, 9, 10, citing *Gesta Regum Anglorum, etc.*

25. Cunningham, *Alien Immigrants,* p. 19, citing Thorpe, *Ancient Laws,* Laws of William the Conqueror, III, iv. (I thank Nancy Triolo for pointing out to me that the cosmopolitan style of Edward's and William's courts appears similar to that of the Norman court in Palermo, Sicily, where the Normans were said to follow, at least for a while, Arab rule by allowing Romans, Greeks, and Muslims their own law.)

26. Ibid., p. 36.

27. Ibid., pp. 37–38.

28. Frederic W. Maitland and Francis C. Montague, *A Sketch of English Legal History* (New York: Putnam, 1915), pp. 27–28, citing Taswell-Langmead, *English Constitutional History,* p. 57.

29. Maitland and Montague, pp. 27–28, citing Stephen, *Hist. of Crim. Law of England,* vol. 3, pp. 31, 40 and referring to the statute of 14 Edw. III.

30. For examples, see Frederic W. Maitland and Mary Bateson, eds., *The Charters of the Borough of Cambridge* (Cambridge: Cambridge University Press, 1901). King John's 1201 Charter to the Borough is on p. 5.

31. Charles Gross, *The Gild Merchant,* 2 vols. (Oxford: Clarendon Press, 1890), vol. 1; see also Bateson, *Borough Customs,* vol. 1, p. xiii.

32. Reynolds, *Kingdoms and Communities,* p. 58.

33. Gross, *The Gild Merchant,* vol. 1, p. 66.

34. Bateson, *Borough Customs,* vol. 1, p. 10, citing *Cal. Pat. Rolls,* 1285, p. 182.

35. See Bateson, *Borough Customs,* vol. 1, for examples: Bristol, cap. 4 (1240), cited at p. 11; Dunstable (1227) *Ann. Dunst.,* cited at p. 105; and many royal charters. In some cases, such as Grimsby (1319), the exception is made, "nisi res ipsa tangat nos vel heredes nostros aut communitatem burgi illius."

36. *Borough Customs,* vol. 1, pp. 110ff.

37. Gross, *Gild Merchant,* vol. 1, p. 30.

38. Ibid., pp. 53–60.

39. See *Borough Customs,* vol. 1, pp. 115ff. for examples.

40. See Reynolds, *Kingdoms and Communities,* pp. 114ff.

41. Gross, vol. 1, p. 75.

42. Ibid., citing Ipswich as an example.

43. Ibid., p. 70.

44. *Borough Customs*, vol. 1, p. 115; other examples include: Thomastown (1210), John's charter to Dublin (1192), William the Lion's charter to Inverness (1165–1214), Moone charter (c. 1205), Dunwich charter (1210). An example of a charter with similar provisions, for those from overseas, is the charter to the merchants of Ypres (1261), cited in a case in Hubert Hall, ed., *Select Cases Concerning the Law Merchant*, vol. 2, Publications of the Selden Society, vol. 46 (London: B. Quaritch, 1929), p. 148, from *Coram Rege Roll* 64, m 33 d, *Calendar of Charter Rolls*, iii 78, 202.

45. Stat. West. I. c. 23; for discussion, see Maitland and Bateson, *Charters of the Borough of Cambridge*, p. xix.

46. See, for example, cases 35 (1309) and 39 (1321–25) in Hall, *Select Cases Concerning the Law Merchant*, vol. 2.

47. William Mitchell, *Early History of the Law Merchant*, p. 121. The provision and its qualification read: "that no merchant stranger be impeached for another's trespass or for another's debt whereof he is not debtor, pledge nor mainpernour, provided always that if our liege people, merchants or other, be indamaged by any lords of strange lands or their subjects, and the said lords duly required fail of right to our said subjects, we shall have the law of Marque and the taking of them again, as hath been used in times passed without fraud or deceit." 27 Edw. III st. 2, c. 17.

48. *Borough Customs*, vol. 2, pp. lii, liii, citing *Ad Fletam dissertatio*, c. 63 (hereafter, *Fleta*).

49. Ibid., p. liii.

50. Regarding tribal origin, see Baker, *English Legal History*, p. 7; regarding courts, see Bolton, *Medieval English Economy*, p. 23.

51. *Borough Customs*, vol. 2, p. liii.

52. James Bradley Thayer, *A Preliminary Treatise on Evidence at the Common Law* (Boston: Little, Brown and Co., 1898), p. 40.

53. *Borough Customs*, vol. 1, p. 32, referring to the Bristol Charter, cap. 3, (about 1188) and to Dunwich, cap. 2 (about 1210).

54. Ibid., pp. 32–33, referring to Fordwich, F. 46, cap. 14, sec. 5 (14th century).

55. Ibid., pp. 33–34, referring to London, Add. MS XXII, sec. 5 (about 1135).

56. *Borough Customs*, vol. 1, referring to records of the customs of many boroughs. The privilege against having to do battle appears to be one of the most commonly recorded customs.

57. Ibid., pp. 34–35, referring to Wearmouth, cap. 13 (1154–95); Newcastle-on-Tyne, cap. 12 (1100–1135); *Leges Quatuor Burgorum*, cap. 11 (about 1270).

58. Ibid., p. 33, referring to London, Add. MS XXII, sec. 5, (about 1135).

59. Ibid., p. 43, referring to Fordwich, cap. 85, sec. 1; Sandwich (Boys), p. 463 (15th century); Hastings, cap. 14 (1461–83); Rye, cap. 16 (15th century).

60. Ibid., p. 38, referring to London. Add. MS XVIII (1131–1155); see also *Liber Albus*, pp. 110–11, p. 92 (14 Hen. III) and p. 104 (25 Hen. III).

61. Owen Barfield, *History in English Words*, rev. ed. 1967 (Stockbridge, Mass.: Lindisfarne Press, 1988), p. 20.

62. Reynolds, *Kingdoms and Communities*, p. 152.

63. Thayer, *Preliminary Treatise on Evidence*, distinguishes the complaint-wit-

nesses or *secta* of the plaintiff, the witnesses who gave proof in ecclesiastical courts, and the oath-helpers or compurgators of the defendant.

64. Historians seem in general agreement about the description of trial that follows: this paragraph follows the formulation of Reynolds' description in her chapter on "Traditional Law," pp. 25ff.

65. The word "trial" is an anachronism, according to Thayer, *Preliminary Treatise on Evidence,* p. 16: "Even after the jury came in, *e.g.* in the early part of the thirteenth century, one is sometimes said to clear himself *(purgare se)* by a jury. . . . *Triare,* from the French *trier,* is, indeed, seen, although very seldom, in our early books, *e.g.* in Bracton, f. 105 (say 1259); *Fleta,* iv., c. 11, ss. 4 and 5 (say 1290); Britton, f. 12, and the 'Mirror,' iii., c. 34 (both near the same date as *Fleta*); but Pollock and Maitland (*Hist. Eng. Law,* ii., 596, n. 2) point out a more probable MSS. reading in Bracton, of *terminandae, instead of triandae,* and suspect the text of *Fleta.* In Y.B. 30 & 31 Ed. II, 528 (1302), it is said of challenges to several jurymen *triebantur per residuos de duodeccim.* In that century the word grew common. . . ."

66. "To 'prove' used to mean 'to test.' As in 'proof of the pudding.' [This is] why we say the exception 'proves' the rule." *San Francisco Chronicle,* July 9, 1988. (Confirmed by the *O.E.D.*)

67. See Baker, Maitland, Milsom, Plucknett, and Thayer, cited above, as well as Luis Hernan Castro-Leiva, "The Notion of Fact: Studies in the History of the English Jury as a Fact-Finding Institution," dissertation, Cambridge, Queen's College, 1975; J. S. Cockburn and Thomas A. Green, *Twelve Good Men and True: The Criminal Trial Jury in England, 1200–1800* (Princeton: Princeton University Press, 1988); William Forsyth, *The History of Trial by Jury* (London: J. W. Parker, 1852); Thomas A. Green, *Verdict According to Conscience: Perspectives on the English Criminal Trial Jury, 1200–1800* (Chicago: University of Chicago Press, 1985); W. S. Holdsworth, *History of English Law,* 16 vols. (1922–66), especially vol. 4, pp. 298–350; Robert von Mochzisker, *Trial by Jury,* 2d ed. (Philadelphia: Bisel Co., 1930); John Proffatt, *A Treatise on Trial by Jury* (San Francisco: Sumner Whitney and Company, 1877); and articles specifically mentioned below.

68. von Mochzisker, *Trial by Jury,* p. 54. But see later texts, cited above. Did the modern jury originate from the doomsmen of Saxon communities who found and declared the doom? Did it originate from the *secta* and compurgators or oath-swearers chosen by the parties—and sometimes by the court—to testify as to the parties' credibility? Or did it originate from the witnesses of deeds or contracts? Did the jury originate from the "recognitors" of Norman inquisitions who acted with a knowledge of the facts, or from the recognitors of the inquests introduced by Henry II, or from the addition, at the time of Edward III, of witnesses who communicated their knowledge to the recognitors but took no part in the decision? (Von Mochzisker, p. 54; citing, in part, Pomeroy, *Mun. L.,* sec. 124–31.) Was trial by jury to all intents and purposes "but trial by witness" until the time of Henry VI (1422–61), or until the nineteenth century when Lord Ellenborough wrote that a verdict based on a juror's own knowledge rather than on facts proved by evidence ought not be sustained? (Von Mochzisker, pp. 57–58, citing Macclachan, *Eng. Cyc.,* vol. 3, p. 26, and *Rex v. Hutton,* 4 Maule & S. 532 [1816].) Or is the origin of the petty jury to be found in the presentment jury of the

assizes, which served as community representative rather than witness? (Charles L. Wells, "The Origin of the Petty Jury," *Law Quarterly Rev.* 107 (1911): 347–61.)

69. Cf. William Forsyth, *History of Trial by Jury*, p. 162: ". . . and this explains the origin of the *venue* (vicinetum), which appears in all indictments and declarations at the present day." (In French, the *voisin* or "neighbor" lives in the *voisinage.*)

70. Thayer, *Preliminary Treatise on Evidence*, p. 300. Compare the *witan*, in Barfield, *History of English Words*, p. 20.

71. Compare such jurors' understanding of law, or knowledge of the embedded practice or action of the community, to that of William, in chapter 4, who "stands over" the law. Those who "under-stand" the law (and the community) form a support, a basis for such law. Their familiarity with the lived-in world of the community means that they know "how things are done" as well as "who we are." They know the characters and histories of their neighbors; when they don't know something, they know whom to ask about what, and when to believe the answer. See also Marianne Constable, "The Modern American Jury: Fact and Law in Law and Society," *Journal of American Culture* 15, no. 1 (Spring 1992): 37–44.

72. For a suggestive discussion of these points, see Castro-Leiva, "The Notion of Fact," pp. 198–202.

73. Some claim that "verdict" was derived from "say truly," which is a nice way of putting it. *Report on the Departmental Commission on Jury Service* (April 1965, G.B.), pp. 5–6.

74. For these general points, see Castro-Leiva; Margaret C. Klingelsmith, "New Readings of Old Law," *Univ. of Penn. Law Rev.* 66:107–22; S. F. C. Milson, "Reason in the Development of the Common Law," *Law Quarterly Rev.* 71 (1965): 496–517; S. F. C. Milsom, "Law and Fact in Legal Development," *Univ. of Toronto Law Jnl.* 17 (1967): 1–19; and S. F. C. Milsom, "Tenth Wilfred Fullagar Memorial Lecture: The Past and the Future of Judge-Made Law," *Monash Univ. Law Rev.* 8 (1981): 1–14.

75. Thayer, *Preliminary Treatise on Evidence*, p. 47.

76. Drawing on Tonnies and Homans, Castro-Leiva argues that although a fact-law distinction appears in the twelfth and thirteenth centuries, a different metaphysics and ontology informs it—that of custom—and its meaning is different. Facts (from *facere*) refer to deeds or actions.

77. Plucknett, *Concise History of the Common Law*, p. 88.

78. *Borough Customs*, vol. 1, p. 11; citing 1348 'Records of Carnarvon,' p. 130. (The Latin is "quod medietas inquisicionis seu jurate sit de communitate predicta et alia medietas sit de civitatibus vel burgis aliis vel villis propinquioribus nostre condicionis.")

79. *Borough Customs*, vol. 1, citing 'Chartae Hiberniae.' (The Latin reads: "et placitaverit ad patriam, medietas juratorum illius patrie erit de burgensibus ville predicte et alia medietas de forincecis ubi factum illud supponitur esse factum.")

80. Ibid., p. 165, referring to London, Add. MS. XXII, sec. 6.

81. Ibid., p. 166; citing *Leges Quatuor Burgorum*, cap. 29 (about 1270).

82. William Lambard, *Archainomia sive de priscis Anglorum legibus libri* (1568), p. 91; Sir Edward Coke, *The First Part of the Institutes of the Laws of England: or, A Commentary upon Littleton*, 15th ed. (London: E. and R. Brooke, 1794), L 2, C 12, sec.

234, fol. 159b, in original (1628) edition at 155b (hereafter, cited as Coke on Littleton); George Crabb, *A History of English Law* (London: Baldwin and Cradock, 1829), p. 270, writes "this mode of trial, per medietatem linguae, was not a novelty in our law for a similar practice existed among the Saxons, viris duodeni jure consulti, Angliae sex, Walliae totidem Anglis et Wallis jus diciento"—which he translates in a footnote as: "Let twelve men versed in the law, six English and an equal number of Welsh, dispense justice to the English and Welsh."

83. Reynolds, *Kingdoms and Communities*, p. 33, citing A. J. Robertson, ed., *Anglo-Saxon Charters* (Cambridge, 1956), no. 41.

84. Reynolds, citing R. C. van Caenegem, *Royal Writs in England from the Conquest to Glanville*, Publications of the Selden Society, vol. 77 (London, 1959), no. 138, and R. V. Turner, "The Origin of the Medieval English Jury," *Journal of British Studies* 7 (1967): 1–10, at p. 7. Charles L. Wells, "The Origin of the Petty Jury," lists at least fifteen instances of juries from two or more hundreds, from the Assise Rolls of Henry III. Wells's concern is with the development of the petty jury from the presentment jury, and his point is not to discuss as such the two-county juries that he mentions.

85. Frederic W. Maitland, ed., *Bracton's Note Book* (London, 1887), p. 779.

86. *Borough Customs*, vol. 1, p. 11, n. 2, citing *Rot. Cart.* p. 45.

87. Forsyth, *History of Trial by Jury*, p. 229.

88. Joseph Jacobs, ed., *The Jews of Angevin England: Documents and Records* (London: David Nutt, 1893; repr. 1969), p. 214.

89. Ibid., p. 215.

90. H. S. Q. Henriques, *Jewish Marriages and the English Law* (Oxford: Horace Hart, 1909), p. 3, citing pre-expulsion cases having to do with the conversion of Jews after marriage.

91. Jacobs, *Jews of Angevin England*, pp. 134–36.

92. Court of Exchequer, Exchequer of the Jews, *Select Pleas, Starrs and Records from the Rolls of The Exchequer of the Jews*, ed. by J. M. Rigg, Publications of the Selden Society, vol. 15 (London, 1901), p. 1; see also Jacobs, pp. 212–14 (*Rot. Cart.*, vol. 1., 93).

93. Jacobs, *Jews of Angevin England*, pp. 42–43.

94. Ibid., p. 192, citing *Pipe Roll Items* 20, 34, 50, 75, and 128.

95. Ibid., p. 55.

96. Ibid., pp. 48–49.

97. Pollock and Maitland, *History of English Law before Edward I*, vol. 1, p. 470.

98. See *Exchequer of the Jews*, pp, 103–4, 104, 105, 108–9, 112, 128.

99. Pollock and Maitland, *History of English Law before Edward I*, vol. 1, p. 470, n. 2.

100. Jacobs, *Jews of Angevin England*, pp. 216–17, citing *Placit. Abbrev.*, p. 36b, and Tovey, *Anglia Jud.*, p. 66, regarding The Hundred of Clipton (1202).

101. Jacobs, p. 306.

102. Ibid., p. 201, citing Roberts, ed., *Rotuli de Oblatis*, p. 92.

103. Ibid., pp. 219–20, citing *Pipe Rolls* and Madox, *Hist. of Exch.*.

104. *Jacob's Law Dictionary* (Tomlin's American edition from 2d London edition, 1811), vol. 4, p. 273.

105. Charles Viner, *A General Abridgement of Law and Equity, Alphabetically Digested under Proper Titles, with Notes and References to the Whole*, 2d ed. (London,

1791–95), vol. 21, p. 186, citing Sir James Dyer, *Les Reports des divers matters & reso-lutions des reverend judges & sages de ley*, vol. 2, 144, pl. 59 (1556–57). Citations to reported cases hereafter appear by volume, report, and page number, as, for instance, 2 Dyer 144.

106. Alice Beardwood, *Alien Merchants in England, 1350 to 1377: Their Legal and Economic Position* (Cambridge, Mass.: Medieval Academy of America, 1931).

107. William Evan Davies, *The English Law Relating to Aliens* (London: Stevens and Sons, 1931), pp. 15, 37–40; see also *Select Cases Concerning the Law Merchant*, vol. 2, p. xxxvi.

108. Davies, pp. 33, 39.

109. Beardwood, p. 33.

110. Ibid., pp. 59–60.

111. Ibid., pp. 59–62.

112. Information and quotations in this paragraph are from Beardwood, pp. 65–68; confirmed by other general histories of alien merchants.

113. Ibid., p. 75.

114. See Davies, p. 38, citing the following: Thomas Rymer, *Foedera, conventiones, liter,* 17 vols. (London: A. and J. Churchill, 1704–17), vol. 1, p. 398 (hereafter, *Foedera*); *Patent Roll* 9 Edw. I, m. 1 (1280); H. Zimmern, *Hansa Towns* (1989), p. 190–93; J. Stow,, *Survey of London* (1908), p. 32; *Rotuli parliamentorum*, 6 vols. (London: 1767–77), vol. 1, p. 315, no. 12 (hereafter, *Rot. Parl.*).

115. Beardwood, p. 77, citing N. S. B. Gras, *The Early English Customs System* (Cambridge, Mass.: Harvard University Press, 1918), p. 261, c. 10.

116. Pollock and Maitland, *History of English Law before Edward I*, p. 465, citing *Munimenta Gildhallae*, vol. 1, pt. 2, pp. 205–8.

117. The document, in Rymer's *Foedera*, 2d ed. (1727), vol. 4, p. 361, names "Al-emanniae, Franciae, Ispanniae, Portugaliae, Navarrae, Lambardiae, Tusciae, Provin-ciae, Tholosani, Caturcini, Flandriae, Brebantiae, & omnium aliorum Terrarum & Locorum Extraneorum."

118. Forsyth, *History of Trial by Jury*, p. 229, citing Rymer's *Foedera*, vol. 4, p. 362; the original reads: "Item, quod in omnibus generibus PLACITORUM (salvo Casu Crim-inis, pro quo infligenda fit Poena Mortis) ubi Mercator Implacitatus fuerit, vel alium implacitaverit, cujuscumque conditionis idem Implacitatus extiterit, Extraneus, vel Privatus in Nundinis, Civitatibus, five Burgis, ubi sufficiens copia fuerit Mercatorum praedictarum Terrarum, and Inquisitio fieri debeat, fit medietas Inquisitionis de eisdem Mercatoribus, & Medietus altera de aliis Probis & Legalibus Hominibus loci illius, ubi Placitum illud esse contigerit: & si de Mercatoribus, dictarum Terrarum, numerus non inveniatur sufficiens, ponantur in Inquisitione illi, qui idonei invenien-tur ibidem, & Residui sint de alliis Bonis Hominibus & Idoneis, de locis in quibus Placitum illud erit."

119. Beardwood, p. 78, citing Gras, p. 260.

120. Ibid., p. 75; Beardwood provides no explanation for the inconsistency and does not note that her claim about the mixed jury is an exception to the statement in the text accompanying the footnote immediately above.

121. *Select Cases Concerning the Law Merchant*, vol. 2, pp. 79–80; Case 34, 2 Edw. II (Exch. Plea, Roll 32).

122. Ibid., vol. 2, pp. 81–83; Case 35, from *Coram Rege Roll* 198. An English merchant had petitioned to recover debts owed by merchants of Groningen. When the Bishop of Utrecht had not responded, the sheriff arrested goods from Groningen at Ravenspur and Hull. The merchants who owned the goods claimed that the King of Almain was the lord of the town, and the Bishop could not do justice in the matter. On the appointed day, the parties "and likewise the jurors elected by consent of the parties, as well of the parts of Almain as of Brabant" came and said that the king of Almain was indeed lord of the town of Groningen, and the merchants who owned the goods were told to return to Chancery to have their mainprised goods delivered to them.

123. Forsyth, *History of Trial by Jury*, p. 230, n. 1, citing *Rot. Parl.*, vol. 1, p. 382.

124. *Select Cases Concerning the Law Merchant*, vol. 2, p. xxxvi, citing *Hansische Geschicte*, B6, p. 72, from *Close Roll*, 18 Oct. 11 Edw. III.

125. Ibid., vol. 2, p. xxxvi–xxxvii, citing *Coram Rege Roll* 331, m87d.

126. Ibid., vol. 2, 13 Edw. IV (1473), Pasc. f. 9, pl. 5.

127. Stephen Brodhurst, "The Merchants of the Staple," *Law Quarterly Rev.* 65 (1901): 56–74, at p. 64.

128. See Charles Gross, ed., *Select Cases Concerning the Law Merchant*, vol. 1, Publications of the Selden Society, vol. 23 (London: B. Quaritch, 1908). In a 1252 dispute between the abbott and the king about the extension of the stallage of merchants past the time of the fair onto the king's highway, the jury was of 12 knights from Huntingdonshire and Cambridgeshire and 12 merchants (p. xxviii). Examples from the year 1287 alone include: "jury of merchants and next neighbors," assault with vile words, p. 17; same, contempt, p. 18; "jury of neighbors and merchants," unjust detention of cowhide, p. 24; "merchants and neighbors," action regarding cloth, p. 25; "jury of merchants and next neighbors," defamation, trespass, contempt, pp. 29, 30; "merchants and next neighbors, who are sworn," assault on servant, pp. 29–30.

129. Ibid., p. 87, for a 1302 example.

130. Ibid., p. 90 (1311).

131. Mitchell, *Early History of the Law Merchant*, pp. 9–10.

132. Ibid., pp. 10–16.

133. Pollock and Maitland, *History of English Law before Edward I*, vol. 1, p. 466, citing a Year Book case from 1473, 13 Edw. IV, Pasc. f. 9, pl. 5.

134. Ibid., p. 467.

135. Ibid., p. 467.

136. Mitchell, p. 81.

Chapter Two

1. David Daube, "The Scales of Justice," *Juridical Rev.* 63 (1951): 109–29, at 129.

2. *Duncan v. Louisiana*, 391 U.S. 145 (1968).

3. *Batson v. Kentucky*, 106 S.Ct. 1712 (1986) at 1717, n. 6.

4. *Strauder v. West Virginia*, 10 Otto 303, 100 U.S. 303, 25 L.Ed. 664 (1880).

5. Indeed, a law professor commenting on an earlier draft of this chapter noted in the margin alongside the previous quote from *Strauder*, "This old stuff is of little modern significance."

6. *Batson*, 106 S.Ct. at 1716–17, citing: *Akins v. Texas* 325 U.S. 398, 403, 65 S.Ct. 1276, 1279, 89 L.Ed. 1692 (1945); *Strauder v. West Virginia*, 100 U.S., 303; and others.

7. *Lockhart v. McCree*, 476 U.S. 162 (1985), at 183–84.

8. For references to early use of the cross-sectional idea, in addition to those that appear below, see Comment, "Limiting the Peremptory Challenge," *Yale Law J.* 86 (1977): 1716, n. 44.

9. *Smith v. Texas*, 311 U.S. 128 (1940); see also *Strauder*, 100 U.S. 303.

10. *Glasser v. U.S.*, 315 U.S. 60 (1941).

11. *Taylor v. Louisiana*, 419 U.S. 522 (1975).

12. *Duncan*, 391 U.S. 145.

13. *Taylor*, 419 U.S. at 526.

14. *Duren v. Missouri*, 439 U.S. 357 (1979).

15. I intentionally use "tie" because *Duren* does not go so far as to "equate" the Sixth Amendment requirement for an impartial jury with cross-sectionality. According to the courts, the cross-section requirement is *one* of the elements of impartiality. I consider below how the statistical model, whose encroachment into law *Duren* epitomizes, can be extended conceptually (not necessarily legally) to the other elements related to the Sixth Amendment.

16. James H. Druff, "The Cross-Section Requirement and Jury Impartiality," *Cal. Law Rev.* 73, no. 5 (October 1985): 1553.

17. Daughtrey, "Cross-Sectionalism in Jury-Selection Procedures After *Taylor v. Louisiana*," *Tenn. L. Rev.* 43 (1975–76): 1.

18. *Duren*, 439 U.S. 357.

19. Comparative: comparing percentage of demographic group on the jury to percentage of the population. The difference between these two figures is divided by the group's percentage of the population to determine the level of underrepresentation or "rate of error." Absolute: looks only at the difference between the percentage of the group on the jury and the percentage of the group in the population (making it harder to find underrepresentation of small population groups).

20. *Holland v. Illinois*, 493 U.S. 474, 110 S.Ct 803, 58 Law Week 4162 (1990) at 4164–5.

21. The Jury Selection and Service Act, 28 U.S.C. ss. 1861–74 established a general duty to supplement source lists when a single source proves inadequate. Congress also required such supplementation when voter registration lists deviate substantially from the community's overall demographic patterns. S. Rep. no. 891, 90th Cong. 1st sess. 17 (1967). California's (Civil) Proc. Code requires the supplemental use of DMV lists when such inclusion can be effected practically and "without significant cost." Cited in Druff, "Cross-Section Requirement and Jury Impartiality," p. 1563. Also see *People v. Harris*, 36 Cal 3d 36, 679 P.2d 433, 201 Cal. Rptr. 782, cert. denied, 105 S. Ct. 365 (1984).

22. *People v. Harris*. See also "Casenote: Constitutional Law—Sixth Amendment—Jury Pools Drawn from Voter Registration List May Not Provide a Fair Cross-Section," *Cumberland Law Rev.* 15 (1984–85): 555.

23. See Jon Van Dyke, *Jury Selection Procedures* (Cambridge, Mass.: Ballinger, 1977).

24. *Williams v. Florida*, 399 U.S. 78 (1970), cited in *Ballew v. Georgia*, 435 U.S. 223 (1977).

25. *Ballew v. Georgia*, 435 U.S. 223 (1977). All of the "recent empirical data" that the Court cited in *Ballew* to hold five-member juries unconstitutional, could have been used just as well to overturn its earlier decision—that is, it could have been used just as well to say that six-member juries were also unconstitutional.

26. Numerous articles and comments address the issue of peremptory challenges in law journals. See, for example, Toni M. Massaro, "Peremptories or Peers?—Rethinking Sixth Amendment Doctrine, Images and Procedures," *N. Carolina Law Rev.* 64 (1986): 501–64; the articles listed in Massaro, pp. 502–3, n. 7; "Peremptory Challenges and the Meaning of Jury Representation," *Yale Law Jnl.* 89 (1980): 1177–98; "Affirmative Selection: Responses to Peremptory Challenge Abuse," *Stanford Law Rev.* 38 (1986): 781; Jonathan B. Mintz, "Note: *Batson v. Kentucky*: A Half Step in the Right Direction (Racial Discrimination and Peremptory Challenges under the Heavier Confines of Equal Protection)," *Cornell Law Rev.* 72 (1987): 1026; and many similar works cited in these notes or listed in the Index of Legal Periodicals each year.

27. *People v. Wheeler*, 22 Cal. 3d 288, 583 P.2 d 748, 148 Cal. Rptr. 890 (1978). See also "Limiting the Peremptory Challenge: Representation of Groups on Petit Juries," *Yale Law Jnl.* 86 (1977): 1715–41, suggesting distinguishing between peremptory challenges for "situation-specific" bias and those for group bias.

28. *McCray v. Abrams*, 750 F.2d 1113 (2d Cir. 1984), *reh'q denied*, 756 F.2d 277 (2d Cir. 1985) (en banc), *vacated*, 478 U.S. 1001 (1986). See also the Sixth Circuit decision in *Booker v. Jabe*, 775 F.2d 762 (6th Cir. 1985), *vacated and remanded*, 478 U.S. 1001, *aff'd on remand*, 801 F.2d 871 (6th Cir. 1986), *cert. denied*, 479 U.S. 1046 (1987).

29. See Massachusetts' *Commonwealth v. Soares*, 377 Mass. 461, 387 N.E. 2d 499, cert. denied, 444 U.S. 881 (1979); Florida's *State v. Neil*, 457 So. 2d 481 (Fla. 1984); New Jersey's *State v. Gilmore*, 103 N.J. 508, 511 A.2d 1150 (1986); and New Mexico's *State v. Crespin*, 94 N.M. 486, 612 P. 2d 716 (Ct. App. 1980).

30. *Swain v. Alabama*, 380 U.S. 202 at 223, 227; 85 S.Ct. 824; 13 L.Ed. 2d 759 (1965).

31. "Limiting the Peremptory Challenge," p. 1723, n. 36. In the twenty-one years after *Swain*, only two claimants succeeded in establishing a prima facie showing of discrimination. See Mintz, "Note: *Batson v. Kentucky*," 1031.

32. These sex discrimination cases, mentioned in *Batson*, 106 S.Ct. at 1720–21, notes 18 and 19, explain the operation of burden of proof rules in cases involving "purposeful discrimination."

33. *Batson*, 106 S.Ct. at 1723. The burden then shifts to the State to "explain the racial exclusion." The State must demonstrate, following the disparate treatment cases, that "permissible racially neutral selection criteria and procedures have produced the monochromatic result."

34. *Wainwright v. Witt*, 469 U.S. 412 (1985) at 423.

35. *Lockhart v. McCree*, 476 U.S. 162 (185) at 184.

36. Druff, "Cross-Section Requirement and Jury Impartiality," pp. 1558–59.

37. *Batson*, 106 S.Ct. at 1735 (Burger dissent), citing *Swain*, 380 U.S. at 219.

38. The Court in *Batson* does not suggest that a defendant could claim that mem-

bers of any cognizable group—whether of the defendant's race or not—had been unjustly excluded. It limits itself to "cognizable racial groups."

39. *Georgia v. McCollum*, 112 S.Ct. 2348, 60 Law Week 4574 (1992) and *Powers v. Ohio*, 111 S.Ct. 1364, 59 Law Week 4268 (1991).

40. *Batson*, 106 S. Ct. at 1736, (Burger dissent), citing Babcock, "Voir Dire: Preserving 'Its Wonderful Power,'" *Stan. Law Rev.* 27 (1975): 545, 553–54.

41. See *McCollum* and *Powers* as well as *Edmonson v. Leesville Concrete*, 111 S.Ct. 2077, 59 Law Week 4574 (1991) (extending *Batson* holding to civil cases).

42. See, for instance, Alfred Schaufelberger, *Blacks and the Trial by Jury: The Black Man's Experience in the Courts* (Frankfurt: Herbert Lang Bern, 1973).

43. Derrick A. Bell, Jr., *Race, Racism and American Law* (Boston: Little, Brown and Company, 1973), p. 992.

44. Druff, "Cross-Section Requirement and Jury Impartiality," p. 1561.

45. See Druff, p. 1562 and cites therein.

46. See "Beyond *Batson*: Eliminating Gender-Based Peremptory Challenges," *Harvard Law Rev.* 105 (June 1992): 1920–39 and cases cited in n. 14, p. 1921.

47. Diane Potash, "Mandatory Inclusion of Racial Minorities on Jury Panels," *Black Law Jnl.* 3 (1973): 80, n. 2: "Note that the all Black jury is one item of the Black power programme as discussed in S. Carmichael and C. Hamilton, *Black Power: The Politics of Liberation in America* (1967); H. Cruse *The Crisis of the Negro Intellectual and Rebellion or Revolution* (1967); B. Seale, *Seize the Time* (1970)." These three works discuss the Black power programme. I did not find explicit references to juries in them.

48. Compare Seale's slogan: "Black visibility is not Black power."

49. Druff, "Cross-Section Requirement and Jury Impartiality," p. 1561, referring to *Peters v. Kiff*, 407 U.S. 493, (1972).

50. But see Lewis H. La Rue, "Jury of One's Peers," *Washington and Lee Law Rev.* 33 (1976): 841–76, at 873–76.

51. Sheri Lynn Johnson, "Black Innocence and the White Jury," *Mich. Law Rev.* 83 (1985): 1611–1708, at 1699.

52. Ibid., p. 1696. As later chapters will show, however, avoiding prejudice was not the main rationale for the English mixed juries. Johnson, pp. 1705–6, writes: "That surmounting ordinary implementation difficulties is unlikely to be an enormous burden is suggested by the English and African experiences," citing her earlier text and footnotes. It is unclear what she has in mind about the English experience.

53. "Note: The Case for Black Juries," *Yale Law Jnl.* 79 (1970): 531–50.

54. Druff, p. 1553.

55. Van Dyke, *Jury Selection Procedures*, p. xiv. Excerpts from Van Dyke's 1977 book are cited in almost every law review article on jury selection.

56. *Ballew v. Georgia*, 435 U.S. 223 (1977). Many articles analyze and criticize jury size decisions. See, for instance, David Kaye, "And Then There Were Twelve: Statistical Reasoning, The Supreme Court, and the Size of the Jury," *Cal. Law Rev.* 68 (1980): 1004.

57. David W. Barnes, *Statistics as Proof* (Boston: Little, Brown and Company, 1983), p. 56.

Chapter Three

1. Max Weber, "Science as a Vocation," in H. H. Gerth and C. Wright Mills, eds., *From Max Weber: Essays in Sociology* (New York: Oxford University Press, 1946), p. 139.

2. Michael J. Saks and Charles H. Baron, eds., *The Use/Nonuse/Misuse of Applied Social Research in the Courts* (Cambridge, Mass.: Abt Books, 1980).

3. Bernard Grofman and Howard Scarrow, "Mathematics, Social Science and the Law," in Saks and Baron, eds., *From Max Weber,* pp. 117–27.

4. Judge Henry J. Friendly, as quoted in Harry Kalven, Jr., and Hans Zeisel, *The American Jury* (Chicago: University of Chicago Press, 1966; rev. [Phoenix] ed. 1970; printed 1971; Midway Reprint ed., 1986); in 1986 printing, back cover.

5. Rita J. Simon, *The Jury: Its Role in American Society* (Lexington, Mass: D.C. Heath and Co., 1980), p. 20.

6. Reid Hastie, Steven D. Penrod, and Nancy Pennington, *Inside the Jury* (Cambridge, Mass: Harvard University Press, 1983), p. 14.

7. Valerie Hans and Neil Vidmar, *Judging the Jury* (New York: Plenum Press, 1986), p. 19.

8. Saul M. Kassin and Lawrence S. Wrightsman, *The American Jury on Trial* (New York: Hemisphere Publishing, 1988), pp. 6, 215.

9. John Guinther, *The Jury in America* and *The Civil Juror: A Research Project Sponsored by the Roscoe Pound Foundation* (New York: Facts on File Publications, 1988).

10. The physical separation of the text of *The Civil Juror* (containing sections on method, subjects, questionnaires, data analysis, conclusions, appendices of survey questions, tables of analysis, and more) from that of *The Jury in America* also appears to be an effort to support this attempt.

11. See, for instance, Simon, pp. 41, 123, 146; Kassin and Wrightsman, ch. 2 and pp. 61–62, 108; Guinther, pp. 64, 105; Hans and Vidmar, p. 129: "the jury has not been shown, as a general matter, to be incompetent"; Hastie et al., p. 230: "Because jury performance of the fact-finding task is so remarkably competent, few innovations are needed to improve performance."

12. See, for instance, Max Weber, *Economy and Society,* edited by Guenther Roth and Claus Wittich (Berkeley: University of California Press, 1978), vol. 1, pp. 217–26 (on legal authority). See also Max Weber, "Politics as a Vocation," in Gerth and Mills, eds., *From Max Weber,* p. 79.

13. See H. L. A. Hart, *The Concept of Law,* esp. chs. 5 and 6.

14. Kalven and Zeisel themselves acknowledge some of the difficulties with their approach; see chs. 3, 4, and 38. Other writers have echoed them. See, for instance, Guinther, pp. xvii–xxi.

15. See also Hans and Vidmar, ch. 10, "The War with the Law."

16. Even far more sophisticated histories, such as that of Thomas Green, *Verdict According to Conscience: Perspectives on the English Criminal Trial,* in asking how it is that we allow juries to nullify law, confirm that "law" is what the officials say it is. My point, again, is not that such accounts are incorrect, but that in the construction of their questions, they make particular assumptions which, correct or incorrect, are worthy of thought.

17. See also Stanley Diamond, "The Rule of Law Versus the Order of Custom," in Robert P. Wolff, ed., *The Rule of Law* (New York: Simon and Schuster, 1971), pp. 115–41, for an argument that is, in some respects, similar to mine.

18. E. Allan Lind and Tom R. Tyler, *The Social Psychology of Procedural Justice* (New York: Plenum Press, 1988), pp. 91–92.

19. See Friedrich Nietzsche, *The Will to Power,* ed. Walter Kaufmann (New York: Vintage Books, 1967), sect. 80, "Toward a critique of the big words," p. 50. The "big words" include "Christianity, the revolution, the abolition of slavery, equal rights, philanthropy, love of peace, justice, truth." They "have value only in a fight, as flags: *not* as realities but as *showy words* for something quite different (indeed, opposite!)."

20. Simon attributes this view to attorneys (41).

21. See Hans and Vidmar: "The particulars of the case will determine whether social science methods can be effective" (92). Kassin and Wrightsman claim that the questionable step in the argument that personality determines verdict is that personality determines attitude, not that attitude determines verdict (62). They suggest that with greater knowledge of "specific predispositions" to some extent verdicts are predictable from general attitudes, although *really* a verdict depends on the idiosyncrasies of a particular case (35–36).

22. Hastie, Penrod, and Pennington, for instance, continue the passage cited in my preceding paragraph: "At a minimum, each jury's evaluations of witness credibility, reasonable inferences from the testimony, and reconstruction and interpretations of the judge's summary of the law must be considered in order thoroughly to assess verdict correctness. For example, in the stimulus case, if a jury decided that all testimony from defense witnesses was false, a verdict of first degree murder could be acceptable. Yet, such an interpretation of the evidence would be very unconventional. For the most part, the exceptional, nonsecond-degree murder verdicts were associated with jurors' errors of comprehension and memory for testimony or the judge's instructions" (62).

23. The resemblance of this ideal to the conditions under which John Rawls's "people in the original position" (POP's) come up with principles of "justice as fairness" bears further examination. (One might also mention, in this context, Habermas's "ideal speech forum.") Rawls has been criticized for assuming and/or arguing that principles of justice will result from the sort of agreement that risk-averse people ignorant of their own qualities and society would formulate; his approach is said to be formalistic in that it denies POP's knowledge of, and hence what makes them, who they are, which in turn is what gives meaning to discussions of justice. Although Kassin and Wrightsman avoid such a charge at one level, claiming that the jury is not a blank slate and that jurors' biases are to be overcome, excluded, or balanced out by others' biases, their understanding of what it is to be who one is (27–28) also appears somewhat empty of moral content.

24. For proposals to replace "common sense" with "social science," see, for instance, John Monahan and Laurens Walker, "Social Authority: Obtaining, Evaluating, and Establishing Social Science in Law," *Univ. Penn. Law Rev.* 134 (1986): 477; and Laurens Walker and John Monahan, "Social Frameworks: A New Use of Social Science in Law," *Va. Law Rev.* 73 (1987): 599.

25. Donald Black, *Sociological Justice* (New York: Oxford University Press, 1989).

26. Ibid., 69–71. Black himself is cagey as to whether he "favors" such reform. As an advocate of "pure science" he affirms the distinction between science and policy, appealing to "evolution" and "nature" as the direction in which to go. His reduction of "ought" (law and justice) to "is" (evolution and nature), in the name of a distinction between ought (value) and is (fact), is part of the story of Western metaphysics. See Friedrich Nietzsche's "History of an Error," *Twilight of the Idols,* pp. 40–41. See also Marianne Constable, "Sociological Justice and Jurisprudential Nihilism," *Oxford Journal of Legal Studies* 11, no. 1 (1991): 114–24.

27. In their second chapter, Kalven and Zeisel describe "the extent of the jury trial in the United States." Kalven and Zeisel move, in breathtaking fashion, in and out of a language of choice and decision, on the one hand, and of motivation, control, and determination on the other. They first present the three factors "that determine the universe of jury trials": law ("the availability of jury trial as a matter of right") and two "choices" left open to the defendant (the "decision" to plead guilty and the "choice" between judge and jury trial) (14). As the chapter continues, it becomes apparent that the defendant's "choices" are themselves determined (19) and motivated (26), "affected by the odds" (20) and by other factors including advice of counsel (30). By the end of the chapter, "the selection of jury cases" is presented as "the result of an interplay of custom, economics, strategy, and game theory played by the defendant and the prosecutor" (30). This interplay is in turn "in part informed by expectations of what the jury will do" so that ultimately "the jury is not controlling merely the immediate case before it, but the host of cases not before it which are destined to be disposed of by the pre-trial process" (31–32). Kalven and Zeisel recognize that the process does not stop here; to the extent that their study clarifies "the sources and occasions of [judge-jury] disagreement, it may through a feed-back process, modify the bar's expectations as to judge-jury disagreement and thus conceivably affect, in turn, the decisions on guilty pleas and jury waivers" (32, n. 34).

28. For analyses of (mock) jurors' speech, see, for instance, Kassin and Wrightsman, pp. 180–82, and Hastie, Penrod, and Pennington, pp. 151–62. For an analysis that looks at how things are said, rather than what is said, see William O'Barr, *Linguistic Evidence: Language, Power and Strategy in the Courtroom* (New York: Academic Press, 1982).

29. See *Williams v. Florida,* 399 U.S. 78 (1970); *Ballew v. Georgia,* 435 U.S. 223 (1977); and masses of law review articles concerning the court's use of social science research in these jury size cases.

Chapter Four

1. Nietzsche, *Twilight of the Idols,* pp. 25, 91.
2. William Blackstone, *Commentaries on the Laws of England,* 4 vols., 1765–69 (rpt., Chicago: University of Chicago Press, 1979), vol. 1 (1765), p. 73.
3. J. H. Baker, *An Introduction to English Legal History,* p. 1 (cf. ch. 1, n. 12).
4. Ibid.
5. Ibid., pp. 3–4, 6.
6. Theodore F. T. Plucknett, *A Concise History of the Common Law,* p. 13.

7. Dorothy Whitelock, "The Anglo-Saxon Achievement," in C. T. Chevallier, ed. *The Norman Conquest: Its Setting and Impact* (London: Eyre and Spottiswoode, 1966), p. 27.

8. R. H. C. Davis, "The Norman Conquest," *History* 51 (1966): 279–86; reprinted in C. Warren Hollister, ed., *The Impact of the Norman Conquest*, p. 128.

9. S. F. C. Milsom, *Historical Foundations of the Common Law*, p. 11.

10. Ibid., p. 16.

11. J. E. A. Jolliffe, *The Constitutional History of Medieval England from the English Settlement to 1485*, 4th ed. (New York: Norton and Co., 1961), p. 57.

12. Ibid., pp. 57–61.

13. Whitelock, "Anglo-Saxon Achievement," p. 29.

14. Baker, *English Legal History*, p. 3.

15. Milsom, *Foundations of Common Law*, p. 11, emphasis added.

16. J. H. Round, *Feudal England* (London, 1895), citing Freeman; in Hollister, *Impact of Norman Conquest*, p. 24.

17. Owen Barfield notes that "scarcely a word in our language expressing even remotely the notion of 'authority' . . . does not come to us from the Latin: *authority, chief, command, control, dictator, dominion, empire, government, master, officer, rule, subordinate*, are some of them. . . . Rome not only extended her jurisdiction over all Europe; she was responsible for the birth of a new idea in men's minds—the idea that 'authority', as such, based on an abstraction called 'law' and irrespective of real ties of blood or affection, of sympathy or antipathy, of religion or ownership, can exist as a relation between human beings." Barfield, *History of English Words*, p. 38.

18. Baker, *English Legal History*, p. 2.

19. See criticisms, for instance, by Julius Goebel, Jr., *Felony and Misdemeanor* (New York: Commonwealth Fund, 1937) and Wendy Davies and Paul Fouracre, eds. *The Settlement of Disputes in Early Medieval Europe* (Cambridge: Cambridge University Press, 1986). They criticize (p. 3) the *Recchtsschule*, in part, as founded on faith in a fundamental Germanic law and its 'spirit' *(geist)*, which reaches its apotheosis in H. Brunner's *Deutsche Rechtsgeschichte*. (Brunner, influenced by Grimm and Savigny, in turn influenced much nineteenth- and early twentieth-century English medieval legal history.)

20. John Austin often serves as the reference point of legal positivism. He is taken to have defined law as the command, backed by threats, of a sovereign whom subjects are in the habit of obeying. For the subtleties of Austin's position see John Austin, *The Province of Jurisprudence Determined* (New York: Noonday Press, 1954).

21. As Hart writes, "obeying a rule (or an order) *need* involve no thought on the part of the person obeying that what he does is the right thing both for himself and for others to do: he need have no view of what he does as a fulfilment of a standard of behavior for others of the social group. He need not think of his conforming behaviour as 'right', 'correct', or 'obligatory.' His attitude, in other words, need not have any of that critical character which is involved whenever social rules are accepted and types of conduct are treated as general standards. He need not, though he may, share the internal point of view accepting the rules as standards for all to whom they apply. Instead, he may think of the rule only as something demanding action from *him* under

threat of penalty; he may obey it out of fear of the consequences, or from inertia, without thinking of himself or others as having an obligation to do so and without being disposed to criticize either himself or others for deviations" (112).

22. Plucknett, *Concise History of the Common Law*, p. 11.

23. Ibid. See Davis, "The Norman Conquest," for another view of William's separation of church and state courts.

24. Ibid., pp. 11–12.

25. Jack Goody, *The Logic of Writing and the Organization of Society* (Cambridge: Cambridge University Press, 1986), p. 160.

26. Frederic W. Maitland, "Materials for the History of English Law," *Political Science Quarterly* 4 (1889): 496–518, 628–647; reprinted in Association of American Law Schools, ed., *Select Essays in Anglo-American Legal History* (Boston: Little, Brown and Company, 1908), vol. 2, pp. 53–95, at p. 77.

27. Charles Gross, *The Sources and Literature of English History* (London: Longmans, Green & Co., 1915), p. 407.

28. H. C. Darby, *Domesday England* (Cambridge: Cambridge University Press, 1976), p. 6.

29. Darby, citing A. Hughes et al., eds., *Dialogus de Scaccario* (Oxford, 1902), 107–8.

30. Darby, pp. 4–5, citing *Inquisitio Eliensis* from N.E.S.A. Hamilton, *Inquisitio comitatus Cantabrigiensis . . . subjicitur Inquisitio Eliensis* (London, 1876), p. 97.

31. Darby, p. 5, citing *Inquisitio* from V. H. Galbraith, *The Making of the Domesday Book* (Oxford, 1961), p. 161.

32. Darby, p. 5, citing J. H. Round, *Feudal England* (London, 1895), p. 120.

33. Darby, p. 5, citing Galbraith, p. 161.

34. Davis, "The Norman Conquest," pp. 127–28.

35. Ibid., p. 128.

36. Ibid.

37. Ibid., p. 129.

38. Ibid., p. 130.

39. Ibid., p. 132.

40. Ibid., p. 132.

41. Maitland, "Materials," p. 77.

42. Edward Freeman, "The History of the Norman Conquest," in Hollister, ed., *Impact of Norman Conquest*, pp. 54–55.

43. William apparently argued that while on a visit to England, Edward had promised to appoint him successor, but Edward had only done so privately, and the witan had never confirmed the promise. See J. R. Green, *A Short History of the English People* (New York: Harper & Brothers, 1886), p. 107.

44. Plucknett, *Concise History of the Common Law*, p. 13, citing William Stubbs, *Select Charters and other Illustrations of English Constitutional History.*

45. Frank Barlow, "The Effects of the Norman Conquest," in Hollister, ed., *Impact of Norman Conquest*, p. 34.

46. Heinrich Brunner, "The Sources of English Law" (1877), trans. Freund., rev. for Association of American Law Schools, ed., *Select Essays in Anglo-American Legal History* (Boston: Little, Brown and Company, 1908), vol. 2, pp. 8–52, at p. 22.

47. Ibid.

48. Ibid., p. 23.

49. Ibid., p. 17.

50. Ibid., p. 23.

51. Ibid., pp. 17–18.

52. Ibid., p. 18.

53. Goebel, *Felony and Misdemeanor,* pp. 412–13.

54. Whitelock, "Anglo-Saxon Achievement," p. 27.

55. Brunner, p. 12.

56. Dorothy Whitelock, "The Dealings of the Kings of England with Northumbria in the Tenth and Eleventh Centuries," in Peter Clemoes, ed., *The Anglo-Saxons: Studies in Some Aspects of Their History and Culture Presented to Bruce Dickins* (London: Bowes and Bowes, 1959), pp. 70–88, at p. 87, citing D. Whitelock, ed., *English Historical Documents,* vol. 1 (London, 1955), p. 511.

57. Brunner mentions "a statute concerning the law of the 'Dunsaete,' enacted about 935 at an Anglo-Saxon diet with the concurrence of Welsh notables, (Waliae consiliarii). It was intended for a border district, the country of the Dunsaetes, who are mentioned nowhere else, and should probably be located in Herefordshire; its purpose was to regulate the legal relations between the Dunsaetes of Kymric and English nationality separated from each other by a river (the Wye?), especially with reference to fresh pursuit, anefang, wergild, procedure, and international jurisdiction." Brunner, p. 13, referring to Liebermann, *Die angelsächsische Verordnung über die Dunsaete,* in the *Archiv für das Studium der neueren Sprachen und Literaturen,* vol. 102, pp. 267ff.

58. W. Lambard (or Lambarde), *Archaionomia sive de priscis Anglorum legibus libri,* p. 91; cited in Coke on Littleton, L 2, C 12, sec. 234, fol. 159b; translation by George Crabb, *A History of English Law,* p. 270. (Cf. ch. 1, n. 82.)

59. Respect, of course, does not mean an absence of what we call cruelty. The Dakota Indians, for instance, referred to their rivals as "our bravest enemies." Against them, however, their cruelties were no more than what they themselves voluntarily submitted to on ritual occasions. Dorothy Lee, "Responsibility Among the Dakota," *Freedom and Culture* (New York: Prentice-Hall, 1959).

60. Edward Jenks, *Law and Politics in the Middle Ages,* 2d ed. (London: John Murray, 1913), p. 11.

61. Hart, *Concept of Law,* p. 245, n. 1 to p. 97. See also Hart, pp. 107ff. for discussion of the rule of recognition as "law" and "fact."

62. What Hart suggests of the British common law courts is true of a conqueror: "The truth may be that, when courts settle previously unenvisaged questions concerning the most fundamental constitutional rules, they *get* their authority to decide them accepted after the questions have arisen and the decision has been given" (149). Hart continues: "The manipulation by English courts of the rules concerning the binding force of precedent is perhaps most honestly described in this last way as a successful bid to take powers and use them. Here power acquires authority *ex post facto* from success. Thus before the decision of the Court of Criminal Appeal in *Rex* v. *Taylor* the question whether that court had authority to rule that it was not bound by its own precedents on matters concerning the liberty of the subject might have appeared

entirely open. But the ruling was made and is now followed as law. The statement that the court always had an inherent power to rule in this way would surely only be a way of making the situation look more tidy than it really is" (150).

63. David Daube, Lecture on Ancient Law (Berkeley, Cal., Sept. 8, 1984); see also David Daube, *Studies in Biblical Law* (New York: Ktav, 1969), especially "Codes and Codas," pp. 74–101.

64. Pollock and Maitland, *History of English Law before Edward I*, p. 26; see also Maitland, *Constitutional History of England*, p. 3.

65. E. Young, "The Anglo-Saxon Family Law," in *Essays in Anglo-Saxon Law* (Boston: Little, Brown & Co., 1876), p. 121.

66. Charles Gross, *Sources and Literature of English History*, p. 257.

67. Bertram Colgrave and R. A. B. Mynors, eds., *Bede's Ecclesiastical History of the English People* (Oxford: Clarendon Press, 1969), p. 151.

68. Margaret Deanesly, *The Pre-Conquest Church in England* (London: Adam and Charles Black, 1961), p. 56.

69. Brunner, "The Sources of English Law," p. 10.

70. Pollock and Maitland, *History of English Law before Edward I*, pp. 11–12.

71. For an anthropologist's reflections on similar matters, see Paul Rabinow, *Reflections on Fieldwork in Morocco* (Berkeley: University of California Press, 1977), especially pp. 118–19.

72. Goody, *Logic of Writing*, p. 136.

73. M. T. Clanchy, *From Memory to Written Record: England 1066–1307* (London: Edward Arnold, 1979), p. 233; citing D. M. Stenton, *English Justice between the Norman Conquest and the Great Charter* (1965), p. 118.

74. Goody, *Logic of Writing*, p. 7.

75. Ibid., p. 6.

76. Daube, "Lecture on Ancient Law."

77. See Richard Abel, "Law Books and Books About Law," *Stanford Law Rev.* 26 (1973): 185–89, for examples of "gap" scholarship.

78. Fritz Kern, *Kingship and Law in the Middle Ages*, trans. S. B. Chimes (Oxford: Basil Blackwell, 1939), p. 233; cited in Goody, *Logic of Writing*, p. 164.

79. Bentham continues: "Questions the solutions of which depend upon skill in metaphysics." University College, London, Bentham Manuscripts, Box 69, Folio 181. I am indebted to David Lieberman for this reference.

80. Goody, *Logic of Writing*, pp. 147–51; in part citing Elizabeth Colson, "Possible Repercussions of the Right to Make Wills," *Journal of African Administration* 2:24–34.

81. Clanchy, *From Memory to Written Record*, p. 249.

82. Plucknett, *Concise History of the Common Law*, p. 267.

83. John Reeves, *A History of the English Law* (London: T. Wright: 1783), vol. 2, pp. 232–38; see also H. G. Reuschlein, "Who Wrote the Mirror of Justice?" *Law Quarterly Rev.* 58:265.

84. Although see Goebel, *Felony and Misdemeanor*, vol. 1, p. 339, n. 10: "By some occult process as yet undisclosed most scholars test and brand documents as forgeries and the lawyer has to accept the *ipse dixit*."

85. Clanchy, *From Memory to Written Record*, p. 233.

86. Heidegger draws a distinction between history as what is happening and his-

tory as historiology or the science of history. "What is happening means what sustains and compels history, what triggers chance events and *in advance* gives leeway to resolutions" (my emphasis). The history of events, what occurs, on the other hand, "goes on." It "passes before us in the foreground and background of the public stage of events and varying opinions. What happens can never be made historiologically cognizable." Martin Heidegger, *Nietzsche,* vol. 3, trans. Stambaugh (San Francisco: Harper & Row, 1987), p. 8. See also Heidegger, "The Age of the World Picture," *The Question Concerning Technology and Other Essays,* ed. and trans. William Lovitt (New York: Harper and Row, 1977), pp. 122–23.

Chapter Five

1. Stephen Brodhurst, "The Merchants of the Staple," 68. (Cf. ch. 1, n. 127.)

2. Ibid., p. 61.

3. Ibid., pp. 68–69; Alice Beardwood, *Alien Merchants in England, 1350 to 1377,* pp. 26ff. (Cf. ch. 1, n. 106.)

4. 27 Edw. III. c. 1.

5. 27 Edw. III. st. 2, c. 8, ss. 12–14.

6. 28 Edw. III. c. 13. The 28 Edw. III statute will also be referred to as the 1354 statute.

7. Brodhurst, "Merchants of the Staple," pp. 65–66.

8. Beardwood, *Alien Merchants,* p. 36, citing the Ordinance of the Staple, *Rot. Parl.,* vol. 2, 251.

9. 27 Edw. III. c. 8. The parenthetical "s. 1" in the text refers to the section number of chapter 8 of the 1353 statute.

10. 27 Edw. III. c. 5.

11. See the 1354 statute, and Beardwood, pp. 76–77. The provisions are described further in the next section.

12. 36 Edw. III. c. 7, s. 5 (1362).

13. 36 Edw. III. c. 7

14. Brodhurst, p. 65, n. 4.

15. See chapter 1 regarding the 1328 confirmation of the 1303 Carta Mercatoria.

16. Beardwood, Appendix G, p. 198, n. 7. Beardwood lists Bartholomew Myner, spicer from Lombard, as a freeman of London in 1361 (citing *C.P.R.* 1358–61, 550), who in 1369 counted as an alien for jury purposes (citing *Coram Rege Roll* 433, m. 19 Rex). See also p. 75, n. 3.

17. William Mitchell, *An Essay on the Early History of the Law Merchant,* p. 37 (cf. ch. 1, n. 10); Brodhurst, p. 67; 27 Edw. III. c. 21.

18. Beardwood, p. 78.

19. Ibid., p. 84.

20. Ibid., p. 77, n. 7.

21. Ibid., p. 77, n. 5.

22. Ibid., Appendix E, pp. 182–89, drawing on *Coram Rege Rolls.*

23. Ibid., p. 77, n. 9.

24. Charles Gross, ed., *Select Cases Concerning the Law Merchant,* vol. 1, p. xxv, citing a Year Book case of Edw. IV to make a different point.

25. R. M. Goode, *Commercial Law* (Harmondsworth, Middlesex: Penguin Books, 1982).

26. Mitchell, *Early History of the Law Merchant,* p. 82. "In 1613 the plea that an acceptor of a bill of exchange was not a merchant was held by the court to be a good defence to a claim on the bill, and it was not till 1692 that the English courts ventured to ignore the personal character of the Law Merchant by deciding that if gentlemen accepted bills they ought to pay them." Citing *Sarsfield v. Witherby,* Carthew 82.

27. For a general history of commercial law, see W. S. Holdsworth, *A History of English Law,* esp. vol. 1, pp. 562–73; vol. 5, pp. 60–154; and vol. 8, pp. 99–300 (cf. ch. 1, n. 1).

28. Insofar as such matters were thought of in terms of jurisdiction at all. The earliest reference to "jurisdiction" contained in the *O.E.D.* is in a royal statute dated the second half of the thirteenth century.

29. 36 Edw. III c. 7, s. 4.

30. Holdsworth, *History of English Law,* vol. 1, p. 333.

31. James Bradley Thayer, *Preliminary Treatise on Evidence at the Common Law,* p. 94 (cf. ch. 1, n. 52).

32. Recall the Latin text, from the endnote accompanying the citation to the charters, in chapter 1: "extraneus vel privatus."

33. Y.B. 7 Hen. IV, f. 40 (1428–29); Y.B. Mich. 3 Edw. IV, pl. 22 and Y.B. 3 Edw. IV, f. 11 b/12a, pl.3 in 1463–64; Y.B. 21 Hen. VIII, f. 32 b, pl. 23 (1505). These four cases each appear, and appear differently, in the Year Books, in three editions of Fitzherbert, and in two early editions of Brooke. Another Year Book reference to mixed juries occurs before the 1353 Statute and concerns a charter to German merchants: Y.B. 22 Edw. III, f. 14, (1348–49). Another reference, in Fitzherbert, to Lib. Intrat. f. 48 (or Y.B. Mich. 22 Edw. III, f. 14 and f. 20 [?]), could not be found. Citations are to the Year Book, the term (if available) and year of the reign of the monarch, the folio, and the plea. Plea numbers vary according to the numbering in the abridgements, and do not refer to the Year Book references themselves. The cases mentioned here are discussed further below.

34. 9 Hen. VI. c. 29.

35. 2 Hen. V st. 2, c. 3.

36. The law French version of the statute leaves out the comma. It says: "entre aliens & denzeins soient ils marchantz ou autres."

37. This appears to be the king's response to the concern raised by the Commons following the 1353 statute, and mentioned in the preceding section of this chapter, about the fairness of applying the law merchant to non-merchants under staple jurisdiction.

38. A recognizance "was a bond of record acknowledged before the mayor of the staple, in the presence of one or all the constables. To all obligations made on recognizances so acknowledged it was required that a seal should be affixed, and this seal of the staple was all that was necessary to attest the contract." Brodhurst, p. 67.

39. 36 Edw. III, c. 7, s. 6; emphasis added.

40. 23 Hen. VIII, c. 6.

41. Hubert Hall, ed., *Select Cases Concerning the Law Merchant,* vol. 3, Publications of the Selden Society, vol. 49 (London: B. Quaritch, 1932), p. xxii.

42. The "s." is perhaps an abbreviation for *scilicet,* or "one may know."

43. Fitzherbert's *Abridgement,* as cited in *Sherley's Case,* 2 Dyer 144, Pasch. 3 & 4 P. & M. (1556–57). "Pasch" refers to the Easter term, of the third and fourth year of the reign of Philip and Mary.

44. The view that English commercial power grew into its own in the fifteenth and sixteenth centuries is common in the literature. See, for instance, Holdsworth, *History of English Law,* vol. 4, pp. 315–19, and William Evan Davies, *The English Law Relating to Aliens,* chs. 2 and 3 (cf. ch. 1, n. 107).

45. *Barre's Case,* Moore (K.B.) Mich. 40 & 41 Eliz., pl. 758 (1598); reprinted in vol. 72 of *English Reports,* 178 vols. (Edinburgh: W. Green and Son, 1900–1932), hereafter, *Eng. Rep.*

46. The "venire facias" is defined by *Black's Law Dictionary,* 5th ed. (1979), p. 1395, as "a judicial writ, directed to the sheriff of the county in which a cause is to be tried, commanding him that he 'cause to come' before the court, on a certain day therein mentioned, twelve good and lawful men of the body of his county, qualified according to law, by whom the truth of the matter may be the better known, and who are in no wise of kin either to the plaintiff or to the defendant, to make a jury of the county between the parties in the action, because as well the plaintiff as the defendant, between whom the matter in variance is, have put themselves upon that jury, and that he return the names of the jurors, etc."

47. *Sherley's Case,* 2 Dyer 144.

48. *Heyward v. Lypson,* Cro. Eliz. 869, 44 Eliz., Case 3; 78 *Eng. Rep.* 1095.

49. *Sherley's Case* appears in the following reports: 2 Dyer 144; Jenck. 216, Case LVIII; Dal. 22, pl. 5.

50. 1 & 2 P. & M. c. 10.

51. *Sherley's Case,* 2 Dyer 145a.

52. *Sherley's Case,* Jenk. 206; 73 *Eng. Rep.* 145.

53. *Sherley's Case,* 2 Dyer 145a.

54. J. H. Baker, *An Introduction to English Legal History,* pp. 67–74.

55. Percy H. Winfield, *The Major Sources of English Legal History* (Cambridge, Mass.: Harvard University Press, 1925), p. 148.

56. David Mellinkoff, *The Language of the Law* (Boston: Little, Brown and Co., 1963), p. 139.

57. Baker, *English Legal History,* pp. 72–74.

58. Ibid., p. 75.

59. Mellinkoff, *Language of the Law,* p. 139, deriving his position from Plucknett, *Concise History of the Common Law,* p. 348 and the *O.E.D.*

60. I am indebted to David Lieberman for pointing this out to me.

61. Plucknett, *Concise History of the Common Law,* p. 348.

62. *Sherley's Case,* 2 Dyer 145 (1557 case, published 1585).

63. Winfield, *Major Sources of English Legal History,* p. 187.

64. Mellinkoff, *Language of the Law,* pp. 123, 130.

65. Several legal historians make this suggestion. In the preface to his reports, Edward Plowden writes in 1571 that his second purpose "was to commit to writing what I heard, which seemed to me to be much better than to rely upon treacherous memory, which often deceives its master." Cited in Van Vechten Veedder, "The En-

glish Reports, 1537–1865," *Harvard Law Rev.* 15 (1901): 1–24, 109–17; reprinted in Association of American Law Schools, ed., *Select Essays in Anglo-American Legal History*, 128.

66. Theodore F. T. Plucknett, "The Place of the Legal Profession in the History of English Law," *Law Quarterly Rev.* 48 (1932): 331; reprinted in *Studies in English Legal History* (London: The Hambledon Press, 1983).

67. Winfield, *Major Sources of English Legal History*, pp. 201, 211–12, 228, 233.

68. Baker, *English Legal History*, p. 163.

69. *Sherley's Case*, 2 Dyer 144b.

70. *Abbott of Westminster v. Leman Clarke*, 1 Dyer 27a, Hil. 28 Hen. VIII; 73 *Eng. Rep.* 59.

71. See Mellinkoff and others on this point. Modern rules of punctuation are different from older rules; at first, there were no grammars for English, and punctuation was used to suggest pauses and breaths for texts meant to be read orally.

72. Sir Anthony Fitzherbert, *La Graunde Abridgement* (1577 ed.), Triall. 32, Mic. 21 Hen. VI 4. The 1565 ed. is similar.

73. Sir Robert Brooke, *La Graunde Abridgement* (1573 ed.), Denizen and Alien 12, 21 Hen. VI 4.

74. Sir William Staunford, *Les Plees del Coron* (1557), fol. 160a, citing Y.B. Mich. 21 Hen. VI f.4.

75. *Vangangel v. Browning*, Trin. 15 Car. II B.R., Keb. 547 pl. 49; 83 *Eng. Rep.*

76. *Heyward v. Lypson*, Hil. 44 Eliz., Cro. Eliz. 869, Case 3; 78 *Eng. Rep.* 1095.

77. *Vangangel v. Browning*, Trin. 15 Car. II, Keb. 547, pl. 49.

78. *W.D.'s Case*, 3 Dyer 304a, pl. 51, 13 & 14 Eliz. 683; 73 *Eng. Rep.*

79. Y.B. Mich. 3 Edw. IV, f. 11b and f. 12a, (Fitzherbert, Inquest, pl. 3 and 22; Brooke, Octo Tales, pl. 18, Enquest, pl. 40, and Trials, pl. 125).

80. *Black's Law Dictionary*, p. 428: "In old English law, a writ commanding the sheriff to have the bodies of the jurors, or to *distrain* them by their lands and goods, that they may appear upon the day appointed. It issued at the same time with the *venire*, although in theory afterwards, founded on the supposed neglect of the juror to attend."

81. Charles Viner, *A General Abridgement of Law and Equity*, vol. 21, p. 188, marginal note citing Brooke. (Cf. ch. 1, n. 105.)

82. *W.D.'s Case*, 3 Dyer 304a.

83. *Symons v. Spinosa*, 3 Dyer 357, Easter 19 Eliz., pl. 45 (1577).

84. Mortimer Levine, "A More Than Ordinary Case of Rape: 13 & 14 Eliz. I" *Am. Jnl. of Legal History* 7 (1963): 159–164, at 161.

Chapter Six

1. Pierre Clastres, *Society Against the State* (New York: Zone Books, 1987), p. 127.

2. Y.B. Mich. 22 Edw. III., pl. 14. This is a 1348 or 1349 case regarding "marchantz Dalmaigne" who claimed a mixed jury by charter. It appears in Year Books printed in 1567 and 1619.

3. Y.B. Hil. 18 Hen. VII. Rot. 471, cited in Rastell, *A Collection of Entrees*, fol. 157 of 1566 edition and fol. 158–59 of 1596 edition.

4. Cited in Rastell, fol. 247–48 of 1566 edition and fol. 264–65 of 1596 edition; Rastell's source and the year of this case could not be determined.

5. See *Statutes* (1496). The statute of 11 Hen. VII. c. 21, s. 29 provides that grand juries in attaints in the City of London, where the trial was by half-tongue, shall be impanelled: "the one half of straungers of good fame and of the substance of goodes of C. li. and more, inhabytynge wythyn the same cyte at large. And the residue of the same graunde jury to be of lyke value and substaunce of goodes impannelled of cityzens as is aforsayd." See also Pickering's *Statutes* (1762), vol. 4, p. 72, and *Statutes at Large* (1763), vol. 2, p. 91, where the marginal comment "where the attaint shall be taken per medietatem linguae" has been added.

6. *The great abbrydgement of all ye statutes of Englande until the xxxiii yere of the reyge of our most soveraygne lord living Henry the eyght* (1542); statute of 22 Hen. VIII c. 12 (1530).

7. 22 Hen. VIII c. 10 (from 1542 *Abridgement*). For confirmation of the points in this paragraph, see also Rastell, *A Colleccion of all the Statutes (from Magna Carta to 1557) which were before that here imprinted* (1557). That collection contains: "every statute in the tongue that it was first written in. For those that were first written in latin or in frenche, dare I not presume to translate into English, for feare of misse interpretation. For many words and termes be there in divers statutes, both in latin and in frenche, which be very hard to translate into English." Rastell uses "half tong" in the 11 Hen. VII statute (1494) and "medietatem linguae" in the 22 Hen. VIII statute (1530). Rastell notes "medietate lingue" in the margins of both statutes.

8. The terminology employed in such records will be discussed further below (section 2).

9. James C. Oldham, "The Origins of the Special Jury," *Univ. Chicago Law Rev.* 50 (1983): 137–221, at 169; James Bradley Thayer, *Preliminary Treatise on Evidence at the Common Law*, p. 94, n. 4.

10. Oldham, pp. 169–170.

11. See Elizabeth Eisenstein, *The Printing Press as an Agent of Change: Communications and Cultural Transformations in Early-Modern Europe*, 2 vol. (New York: Cambridge University Press, 1979), and Walter J. Ong, *Orality and Literacy: The Technologizing of the Word* (London: Methuen, 1982).

12. See J. H. Baker, *English Legal History*, pp. 67–74; William Searle Holdsworth, "The Development of Oral and Written Pleading," first published in *Law Quarterly Rev.* 22:360–82; reprinted in Association of American Law Schools, ed., *Select Essays in Anglo-American Legal History*, pp. 614–642; David Mellinkoff, *Language of the Law;* Theodore F. T. Plucknett, *Concise History of the Common Law*, pp. 399–418; and others.

13. Glanville Price, *The Languages of Britain* (London: Edward Arnold, 1984), p. 175.

14. In 1536, the Act of Union incorporated Wales with England. In 1603 occured the union of Scottish and English Crowns.

15. See Price, *Languages of Britain*, and W. B. Lockwood, *Languages of the British Isles: Past and Present* (London: Andre Deutsch, 1975).

16. Mellinkoff, *Language of the Law*, p. 137.

17. Price, *Languages of Britain*, pp. 172–74, suggests that the different dialects of

Anglo-Saxon times may correspond to different groups who migrated to England. Certainly there is some correspondence between the four main pre-eleventh-century dialects and the ancient kingdoms: the dialects were Northumbrian, Mercian, Kentish, and West Saxon.

18. Such a claim is, of course, dependent on definition. Even today, standard written English is "more standard" than spoken English. The correspondence of "standard" law with "standard" English is interesting to consider: "at the beginning of the nineteenth century 'code' was still without standing in the vocabulary of our law, on either side of the Atlantic." Charles McGuffey Hepburn, "The Historical Development of Code Pleading in America and England," Association of American Law Schools, ed., *Select Essays*, p. 643.

19. *W.D.'s Case*, 3 Dyer 304a, 13 & 14 Eliz. I, pl. 683.

20. *Sherley's Case*, 2 Dyer 145.

21. *Sherley's Case*, 73 Eng. Rep. 316, n. 62.

22. Mortimer Levine, "A More Than Ordinary Case of Rape: 13 & 14 Eliz. I," p. 160.

23. Ibid., pp. 160–61.

24. Ibid., p. 161.

25. Ibid., n. 12.

26. Ibid., p. 159, n. 1.

27. Oldham, "Origins of the Special Jury," p. 169.

28. Thayer, *Preliminary Treatise on Evidence*, p. 94, n. 4.

29. Oldham, "Origins of the Special Jury," p. 169, citing Hall, ed., *Select Cases Concerning the Law Merchant*, vol. 2, p. xx.

30. Exchequer Plea Roll 17, m. 48 (1291), reprinted in *Select Cases Concerning the Law Merchant*, vol. 2, pp. 53–62.

31. Oldham, "Origins," p. 170.

32. Y.B. Pasch. 21 Hen. VI, 15 (1442–43), cited in Brooke, 1586, Ley Gager, fol. 62. The 1510 Year Book version of the same case notes that Brown read the record well to one who understood it and who knew how to speak Lombard, and he declared [the pleadings] in his language to the Lombard, who waged his law in his own language.

33. Lockwood, *Languages of the British Isles*, p. 243.

34. *Sherley's Case*, 2 Dyer 144b, referring to Y.B. Mich. 3 Edw. IV, 11b, 12a, (1463–64) as cited in Fitzherbert, Inquest.

35. Staunford, *Les Plees del Coron*, book 3, ch. 7, Challenge, fol. 159 of 1560 edition and 1607 editions. Both editions say the same thing although they use different abbreviations and punctuation. The quotation in the text spells out the abbreviations by combining both versions.

36. Y.B. 21 Hen. VII, fol. 32, 33; from 1555, 1567, 1640 editions of the Year Books.

37. Brooke (1573), Denizen and Alien, 4.

38. Brooke (1573), Triall, 56.

39. Brooke (1586), Panel and Array, 3.

40. Staunford, *Les Plees del Coron*, fol. 159.

41. John Cowell, *The Interpreter* (1607), alphabetical entry Medietas linguae.

42. Cowell (1672 edition), entry Medietas linguae.

43. Sir John Harington, *A Tract on the Succession of the Crown*, A.D. 1602, ed. by Sir C. R. Marcham (London: J. B. Nichols and Son, 1871), p. 24. A 1605 manuscript by Sir Thomas Craig, *De Unione Regnorum Britanniae Tractatus*, ed. by C. Sanford Terry (Edinburgh: Edinburgh University Press, 1909), also refers to W.D.'s *Case* in arguing that the Scots ought to be recognized as English citizens. He writes (p. 347) that "the accused demanded as a foreigner the customary privilege of *dimidietas linguae*, as it is called, in other words, that half the jury should be of his own tongue."

44. Similarly, Sir Thomas Gascoigne, a baronet accused of high treason, asked for "a jury of gentlemen, persons of my own quality, and of my own country, that may be able to know something of how I have lived hitherto." *Rex v. Gascoigne*, 7 St. Tr. 959, 963, King's Bench (1680), cited by Oldham, "Origins," pp. 157, 167.

45. *Wyngate v. Marke*, Cro. Eliz. 275, pl. 4, Easter 34 Eliz. (1592) in B.R. (78 *Eng. Rep.*); referring also to *Dr. Julio's Case*, 23 Eliz. (1580).

46. *Bland's Case*, Godbolt 448, pl. 516, Trin. 8 Car. I (1632–33) in K.B., at 449; 78 *Eng. Rep.*

47. *Wyngate v. Marke*, Cro. Eliz. 275.

48. Oldham, "Origins," p. 170.

49. Brooke (1573), Venire Fac., 37, citing Y.B. 22 Edw. III, 14 (1348–49).

50. Duncombe, *Tryals per Pais* (1685 ed.), p. 353.

51. Ibid., p. 355.

52. Ibid., p. 355.

53. A similar point could be made about law and community. To try to bring the two together, as this work does, points unfailingly to the distance that has come—or that is—between them.

54. *Nedham ag. S. Corsellis*, Cro. Eliz. 293, pl. 6, Hil. 35 Eliz. in B.R. (1593); 78 *Eng. Rep.* Since assumpsit was just developing in the mid-14th century (Baker, *English Legal History*, pp. 274–75), it is unlikely that separate investigations into damages were either "in" or "out" of the statute.

55. William Hawkins, *A Treatise of the Pleas of the Crown* (1716–21; 1795 ed.), book 2 (Of Challenges), ch. 43, sec. 42.

56. Matthew Bacon, *A New Abridgement of the Law*, 6th ed. (London, 1793), Juries 8, p. 263.

57. Viner, *General Abridgement of Law and Equity*, vol. 21, Trial N.b. 9., sec. 3, p. 189.

58. Hawkins, book 2, ch. 44, sec. 42.

Chapter Seven

1. Charles Dickens, *Hard Times*, in the Golden Library, *The Great Novels of Charles Dickens* (London: Magpie Books, 1992), p. 300.

2. William Hawkins, *A Treatise of the Pleas of the Crown*, book 2 (Of Challenges), ch. 43, sec. 42, p. 580. Section 42 reads: "Note, that some of the precedents for the award of a *venire* of a jury of half denizens and half aliens, in pursuance of 28 Edw.3. mention, that the aliens shall be of the same country whereof the party alleges himself; and others direct generally, that one half of the jury shall be aliens, without specifying

any country in particular. And this form seems most agreeable to the statute, which speaks of aliens in general; and it seems to be confirmed both by late practice, and the greater number of authorities" (citations omitted).

3. See chapter 6. Hawkins, bk. 2, ch. 43, sec. 38, p. 579. A. Fitzherbert, *La Graunde Abridgement* (1565), Trial 32; Sir Robert Brooke, *La Graunde Abridgement* (1573), Trial 42; Staunford, *Les Plees del Coron,* fol. 160a. They all cite Y.B. Mich. 21 Hen. VI, 4.

4. Year Books, 1510 and 1601 editions. The 1510 edition refers to the case as "21 H.6. 9" rather than "21 H.6. 4," but it is the same case.

5. Duncombe, *Tryals per Pais,* p. 356.

6. William Blackstone, *Commentaries on the Laws of England,* vol. 3 (1768), p. 360 (cf. ch. 4, n. 2). There is no such statute; Blackstone apparently means the Year Book case of this year referred to by other authors.

7. Charles Viner, *General Abridgement of Law and Equity,* N.b. 7, sec. 5.

8. 122 Comyn, Alien, c.8, p. 417.

9. Staunford, *Les Plees del Coron,* fol. 160a.

10. Duncombe, p. 356.

11. J. M. Beattie, *Crime and Courts in England, 1600–1800* (Princeton, N.J.: Princeton University Press, 1986), p. 340, n. 63.

12. Old Bailey Session Papers, 7th session, 1802, case no. 732 (Martin Henrick Peterson), and case no. 735 (Stephen Abrahams); I am indebted to Charles Lester for pointing out these references to me as I have not checked the Old Bailey Session Papers myself.

13. *R. v. Legava, Petrisi, and Barbaala,* mentioned in *The Solicitors' Journal & Weekly Reporter* 68 (Sept. 20, 1924): 950.

14. That one is *Guiseppe Sidoli's Case,* Newcastle, Sp. Assizes, 1832, 1 Lewin 243; 168 *Eng. Rep.* 1027. The relevant portion of *Sidoli's Case* states the provision of 6 Geo. IV, c. 50, s. 47, and says only that "the privilege which the above statute allows to foreigners was claimed by Guiseppe Sidoli, a native of Parma, in Italy, on an indictment for manslaughter, *cor.* Alderson, J., at the Assizes for the town of Newcastle, in the spring of 1833."

15. John Proffatt, *A Treatise on Trial by Jury,* p. 52 (cf. ch. 1, n. 67).

16. Ibid., p. 52; William Forsyth, *History of Trial by Jury* (London: J. W. Parker, 1852), p. 163, citing 7 St. Tr. 267.

17. Forsyth, pp. 163–64, discussing *Bushell's Case* (1670), Vaughan, Rep. 135.

18. Robert von Mochzisker, *Trial by Jury,* citing *Rex v. Hutton,* 4 Maule & S. 532 (cf. ch. 1, n. 67).

19. John H. Langbein, "Origins of Public Prosecution at Common Law," *American Jnl. of Legal History* 17 (1973): 313–35, at 314.

20. J. H. Baker, *English Legal History,* p. 190.

21. See discussion of Levine, Oldham, and Thayer in chapter 6.

22. 4 Geo. II, c. 26. The history of the struggle to make English the language of the law is worth noting and connecting to the points made in the text. See David Mellinkoff, *Language of the Law,* and others on the history of the English language and the sources of English law.

23. There are references to at least two cases where aliens refused mixed juries. One is that of Bernard, "indicted as an accessory before the fact to the murder of a

soldier in Paris, arising out of the 'attentat' against the life of the Emperor Napoleon III in the Rue Lepelletier, in 1858 (Ann. Reg. 1858, Law Cases, etc., p. 311)." The other involved "eight pirates who were tried at the Old Bailey before Baron Bramwell and a jury on the 4th February 1864 ("The Flowery Land" Case) . . . but they were sailors of the lowest type (coolies), little likely to be aware of their constitutional rights." *The Solicitors' Journal & Weekly Reporter* 68 (Sept. 20, 1924): 950.

24. 13 Geo. II, c. 2.

25. 22 Geo. II, c. 45.

26. *R. v. Manning and Manning*, 1 Den. 468; 169 *Eng. Rep.* 330 (1849).

27. Letters and articles in the *London Times* concerning the case of Manning and Manning, or "The Bermondsey Murder" as it was referred to, appeared August 24, October 27, October 29, November 5, November 6, and November 13, 1849. The case also received a passing reference in two of the first mystery novels of the nineteenth century. In Wilkie Collins's 1859 novel, *The Woman in White* (London: Dent, 1950), p. 193, one of the characters remarks, "I have invariably combated both these absurd assertions by quoting examples of fat people who were as mean, vicious, and cruel as the leanest and worst of their neighbors. I have asked whether Henry the Eighth was an amiable character? . . . Whether Mr. Murderer and Mrs. Murderess Manning were not both unusually stout people?" In Mary Elizabeth Braddon's *Lady Audley's Secret* (New York: Dover, 1862), p. 94, Robert Audley asks Lady Audley, "What do we know of the mysteries that may hang about the houses we enter? If I were to go tomorrow into that commonplace, plebeian, eight-roomed house in which Maria Manning and her husband murdered their guest, I should have no awful prescience of that bygone horror. Foul deeds have been done under the most hospitable roofs; terrible crimes have been committed amid the fairest scenes, and have left no trace upon the spot where they were done."

28. 7 & 8 Victoria c. 66, s. 16.

29. 6 Geo. IV, c. 50, s. 47.

30. James H. Kettner, *The Development of American Citizenship, 1608–1870* (Chapel Hill: University of North Carolina Press, 1978), p. 29.

31. 169 *Eng. Rep.* 340.

32. Ibid., 334.

33. Ibid.

34. Ibid., 335.

35. Coke on Littleton (1628), fol. 156b.

36. *R. v. Sutton and Others*, 8 B. & C. 417; 108 *Eng. Rep.* 1097 (1828).

37. Ibid.

38. *Black's Law Dictionary*, p. 1304: "When by means of challenges or any other cause, sufficient number of unexceptionable jurors does not appear at trial, either party may request a tales . . . a supply of such men as are summoned on the first panel in order to make up the deficiency."

39. *Caesar v. Cursiny*, Cro. Eliz. 305, Case 3, Mich. 35 & 36 Eliz. in B.R.; 78 *Eng. Rep.* 556 (1592). Another report of the same case appears in *Caesar v. Curtine*, Pop. 37 (1592).

40. 36 Hen. VIII c. 6.

41. *Caesar v. Curtine*, Pop. 37 (1592).

42. *Alfred Denbawd's Case,* 10 Co. Rep. 102a, Mich. 10 Jac. I, in B.R.

43. *Goodwin v. Montenaigh,* Cro. Eliz. 819, Easter 43 Eliz. in B.R.; 78 *Eng. Rep.* 1045 (1601).

44. *Regina v. Giorgetti,* (Oxford Circuit, Monmouth Crown Court, Summer Assizes, *coram* Channell B.), 4 F. & F. 546; 176 *Eng. Rep.* 684 (1865).

45. Ibid., 685. After the prisoner and the crown each challenged a portion of the original petit jury called by the clerk of arraigns before arraignment, the judge "directed the names on the panel to be called over in order, and upon intimation from either the prisoner or the Crown that the juror named was objected to, he was ordered to stand aside whilst those against whom no objection was offered went into the box. When the panel had been gone through in this manner, it appeared that ten jurymen only were in the box, of whom eight were Englishmen and two foreigners" (685). The object of having the whole panel called over was apparently "to give the prisoner an opportunity of knowing who appear and who do not, and thus be prepared to take his peremptory challenges" (p. 685, footnote).

46. 4 F. & F. at 550; 176 *Eng. Rep.* 686–87.

47. Ibid., 688.

48. *Levinger v. the Queen,* (Privy Council App.), 3 Law Rep. 282–92 (1870).

49. 3 Law. Rep. 285.

50. The statute reads: "On the prayer of any alien indicted against for any Felony, the Sheriff shall by command of the Court return for one-half of the jury a competent number of aliens, if so many there be in the town or place where the trial is had; and, if not, then so many aliens as shall be found in the same town or place, if any; and no such alien juror shall be liable to be challenged for want of freehold, or any other qualification required by this Act; but every such alien may be challenged for any other cause in like manner as if he were qualified by this Act." The act is apparently "identical" to the Imperial Statute, 6 Geo. IV, c. 50.

51. 3 Law Rep. 286.

52. Ibid., 287–88, citing *Mansell v. Reg.,* 8 E. & B. 71.

53. Ibid., 290.

54. Ibid.

55. See the discussion of the 1429 statute in chapter 5. The point had been reiterated in the 1591 case of *Tenancy v. Brown* and in the later jury statutes, and noted by several reporters and treatise writers.

56. *Report of the Royal Commissioners for inquiring into the Laws of Naturalization and Allegiance.* Presented to both Houses of Parliament by Command of Her Majesty (London: George Edward Eyre and William Spottiswoode, printers, for Her Majesty's Stationery Office, 1869), p. xi.

57. *Report of Royal Commissioners,* p. 90, citing Piggott.

58. Ibid., p. 91, citing Piggott.

59. Ibid., p. 90, citing Piggott, citing Storey.

60. Ibid., p. 49.

61. *Hansard Parliamentary Debates,* 3d ser., vol. 199 (1870), col. 1129.

62. Ibid., col. 1132.

63. *Hansard,* 3d. ser., vol. 200 (1870), col. 1738.

64. 33 Vict. c. 14.

65. 33 & 34 Vict. c. 77 (9 August 1870).

Conclusion

1. Martin Heidegger, " . . . Poetically Man Dwells . . ." in *Poetry, Language, Thought,* trans. Albert Hofstadter (New York: Harper Colophon Books, 1971), pp. 218–19.

2. Cases in several American states during the nineteenth century refer to former laws concerning mixed juries in England, but records on the matter of mixed juries in the United States are, if existent, not easily traceable. I am grateful to the State archivists of Alabama, California, Colorado, Illinois, Kentucky, Louisiana, Michigan, Missouri, Maryland, Nevada, New York, North Carolina, Pennsylvania, South Carolina, Washington D.C., and Virginia for their efforts. Most published cases are cited in Seymour Dwight Thompson and Edwin Garrold Merriam, *A Treatise on the Organization, Custom and Conduct of Juries* (St. Louis: Stevenson, 1882). See also references in Francis X. Busch, *Law and Tactics in Jury Trials, Encyclopedic Edition* (Indianapolis: Bobbs-Merrill, 1959), vol. 1, pp. 467–68. Although in a few cases, the jury *de medietate linguae* was made available, most state cases deny its availability and some state statutes expressly abolish it. Mixed juries in nineteenth-century Hawaii are described by Peter J. Nelligan and Harry V. Ball, "Social Change and the Development of Juries in the Hawaiian Islands During the Mid-Nineteenth Century," Paper Presented at 1985 Law and Society Association Annual Meeting, San Diego, California, and in Harry V. Ball and Peter J. Nelligan, "The Place of Ethnicity in the Courts of Hawaii in the Nineteenth Century," Paper Prepared for 1989 Law and Society Association Annual Meeting, Madison, Wisconsin. Plymouth Colony Records also refer to mixed (half-Indian) juries. See Yasuhide Kawashima, *Puritan Justice and the Indian: White Man's Law in Massachusetts, 1630–1763* (Middletown, Conn.: Wesleyan University Press, 1986), pp. 128–29, 142, 177, 191.

3. "Trial by Jury; and the Abolition of *de medietate linguae* by s. 5 of the Naturalization Act, 1870," *The Solicitors' Journal & Weekly Reporter* 68 (September 20, 1924): 949–50.

4. See Philippe Nonet, "What is Positive Law?" *Yale Law Jnl.* 100 (December 1990): 667–99.

5. Such priority is made necessary by the very terms of a positivism that posits a distinction between law and fact.

6. Foucault's famous description of power relations as "both intentional and non-subjective" is a most apt characterization of social policy as positive law. Michel Foucault, *The History of Sexuality: An Introduction,* trans. by Robert Hurley (New York: Vintage, 1990), p. 94. Although policy is intentional, the creation in some sense of human will, the identification of the determinate subject to whom to attribute "human" will in the case of policy is problematic. One can associate social policy with the particular power-knowledge relations corresponding to the "triangle: sovereignty-discipline-governmentality" of concerns in the "governmental State," described in Michel Foucault, "Governmentality," *Ideology and Consciousness* 6 (1979): 5–21, at 19, 21.

7. Laurens Walker and John Monahan, "Social Frameworks: A New Use of Social Science in Law"; see also John Monahan and Laurens Walker, "Social Authority: Obtaining, Evaluating, and Establishing Social Science in Law," p. 477. (Cf. ch. 3, n. 24.)

8. Walker and Monahan, "Social Frameworks," pp. 585–86.

9. H. L. A. Hart, *The Concept of Law,* p. 205.

INDEX